The Crisis
of Rome

The Crisis
of Rome

The Jugurthine and Northern Wars and the Rise of Marius

Gareth C. Sampson

Pen & Sword
MILITARY

First published in Great Britain in 2010 by
Pen & Sword Military
an imprint of
Pen & Sword Books Ltd
47 Church Street
Barnsley
South Yorkshire
S70 2AS

ISBN 978 1 84415 972 7

A CIP catalogue record for this book is available from the British Library.

Typeset in Ehrhardt, by Phoenix Typesetting, Auldgirth, Dumfriesshire.

Printed and bound in England by the MPG Books Group

Pen & Sword Books Ltd incorporates the Imprints of Pen & Sword Aviation,
Pen & Sword Maritime, Pen & Sword Military, Wharncliffe Local History,
Pen & Sword Select, Pen & Sword Military Classics and Leo Cooper.

For a complete list of Pen & Sword titles please contact
PEN & SWORD BOOKS LIMITED
47 Church Street, Barnsley, South Yorkshire, S70 2AS, England
E-mail: enquiries@pen-and-sword.co.uk
Website: www.pen-and-sword.co.uk

Contents

Rome in Crisis?

War on Two Fronts (111–105 BC)

The Age of Marius (104–100 BC)

To my wife, with love.

You're the rock upon which all my endeavours are built.

Acknowledgements

The first and most important acknowledgment must go to my wife, who as always is a bedrock of support and without whose assistance none of this would be possible.

A notable mention must also be made of my parents who have had to put up with this, some would say irrational, love of ancient history throughout my life.

There are a number of individuals who, through the years, have inspired the love of Roman history in me and mentored me along the way; Michael Gracey at William Hulme, David Shotter at Lancaster and Tim Cornell at Manchester. My heartfelt thanks go out to them all.

As always, greetings go to all the guys from or still at Manchester: Aaron, Gary, Greg, Old Ian, Young Ian, the Two Jameses (Moore & Thorne), Jamie, Jason, Jess, Peter and Sam. For those still there, best of luck. Also, a big hi to Pete and Nicki back in the US and Carsten in Denmark. Special thanks need to go out to Sam, for his additional help with bibliographical matters late on.

The John Rylands Library at Manchester receives a vote of thanks for use of their facilities and access to their first rate collection. Thanks also need to be extended to the University of Exeter Library for access to their collections and congenial atmosphere.

I would finally like to extend my thanks to Phil Sidnell, my editor at Pen and Sword, for his patience and perseverance; one of these days a book will be on time. Also to Rupert Harding for the initial vote of confidence.

Now on with the book.

List of Illustrations

[List of illustrations to follow once images are finalized.]

Maps

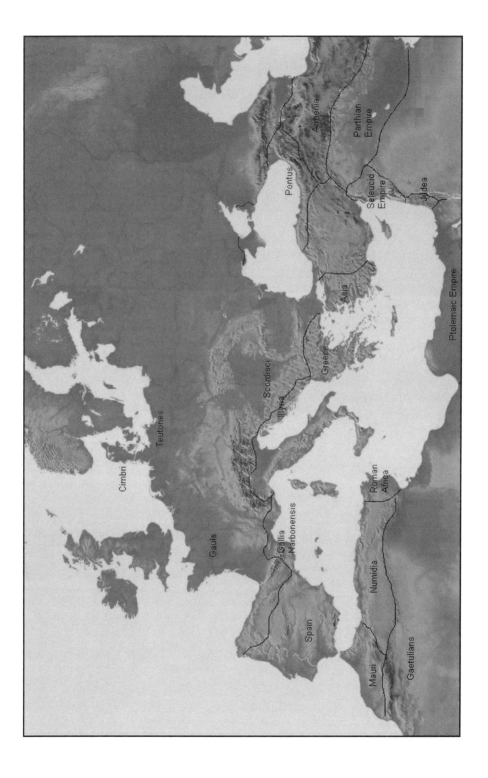

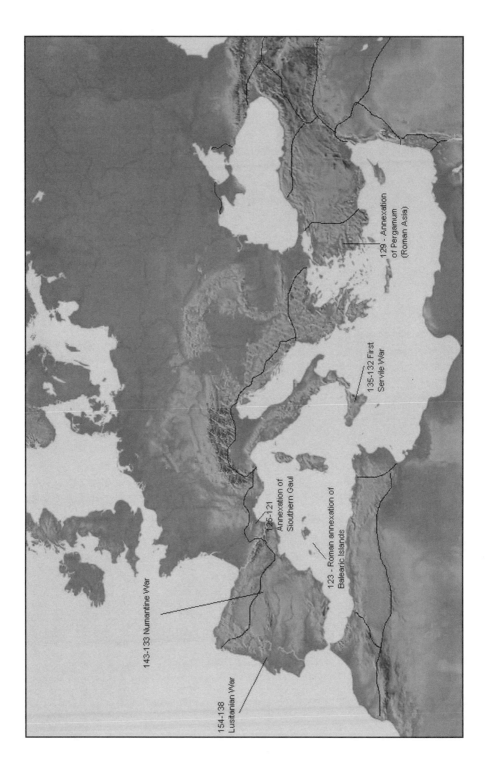

143-133 Numantine War

154-138 Lusitanian War

125-121 Annexation of Siouthern Gaul

123 - Roman annexation of Balearic Islands

135-132 First Servile War

129 - Annexation of Pergamum (Roman Asia)

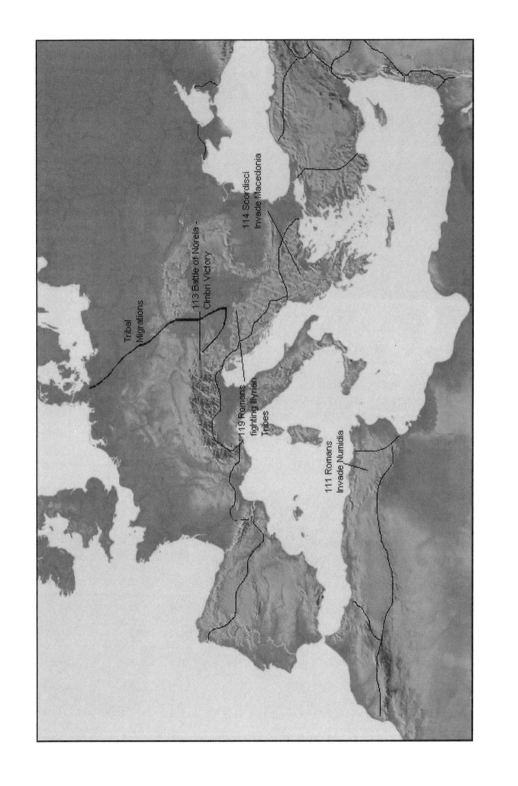

Tribal Migrations

113 Battle of Noreia - Cimbri Victory

114 Scordisci Invade Macedonia

119 Romans fighting Illyrian Tribes

111 Romans Invade Numidia

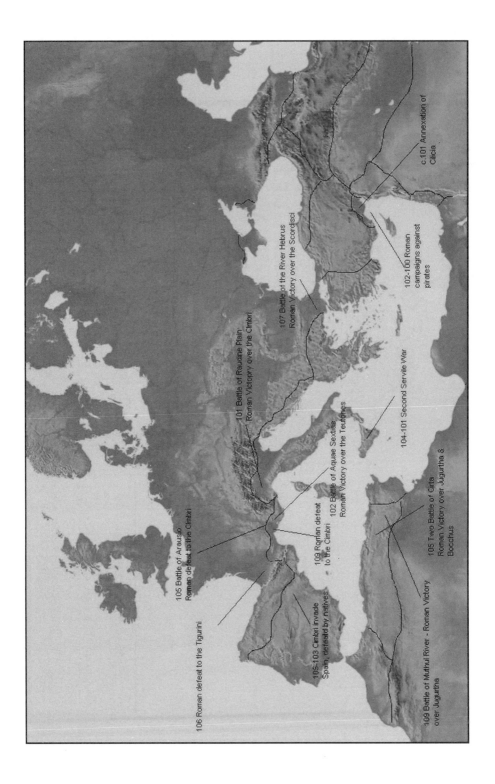

106 Roman defeat to the Tigurini

105 Battle of Arausio
Roman defeat to the Cimbri

105-103 Cimbri invade
Spain, defeated by natives

101 Battle of Raudine Plain:
Roman Victory over the Cimbri

109 Roman defeat
to the Cimbri

102 Battle of Aquae Sextiae
Roman Victory over the Teutones

107 Battle of the River Hebrus
Roman Victory over the Scordisci

c.101 Annexation of
Cilicia

102-100 Roman
campaigns against
pirates

104-101 Second Servile War

105 Two Battle of Cirta
Roman Victory over Jugurtha &
Bocchus

109 Battle of Muthul River - Roman Victory
over Jugurtha

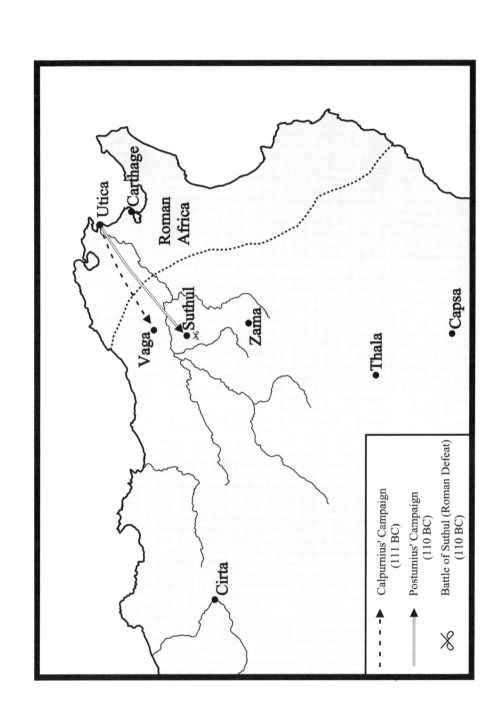

Carthage

Utica

Roman
Africa

Vaga

Suthul

Zama

Thala

Capsa

Cirta

Calpurnius' Campaign
(111 BC)

Postumius' Campaign
(110 BC)

Battle of Suthul (Roman Defeat)
(110 BC)

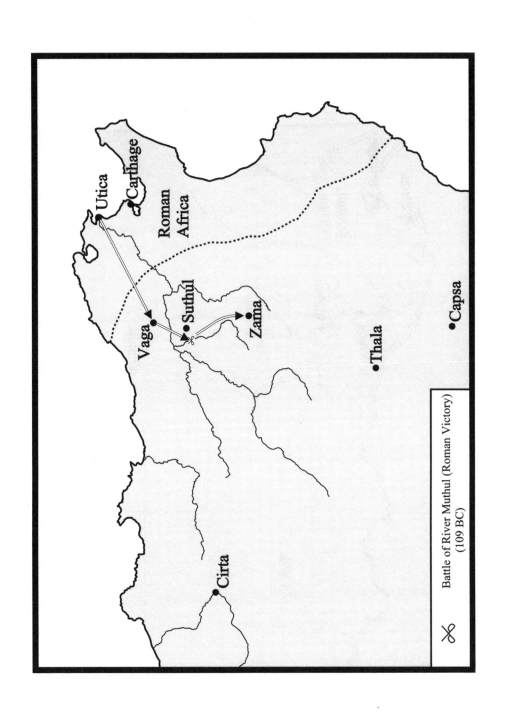

Battle of River Muthul (Roman Victory)
(109 BC)

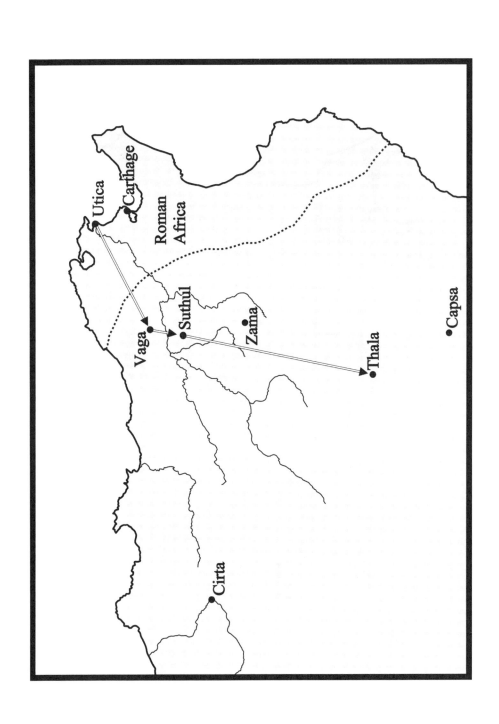

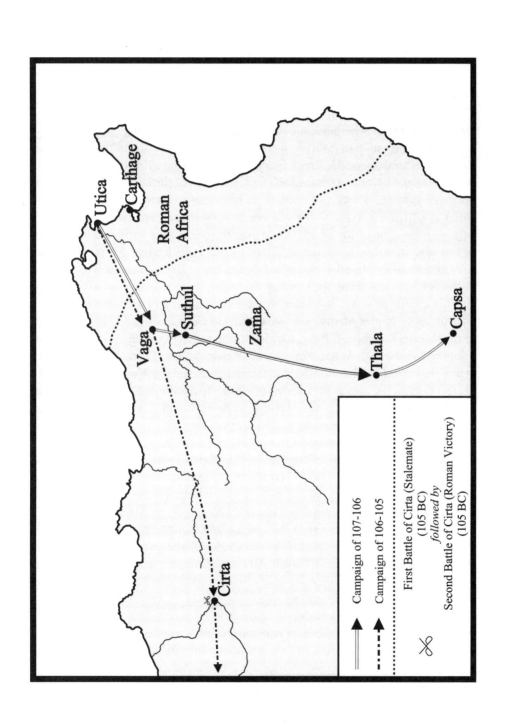

Carthage

Utica

Roman
Africa

Suthul

Vaga

Zama

Thala

Capsa

Cirta

Campaign of 107-106

Campaign of 106-105

First Battle of Cirta (Stalemate)
(105 BC)
followed by
Second Battle of Cirta (Roman Victory)
(105 BC)

Introduction

The last decade of what now equates to the second century BC saw the culmination of a generation of military overstretch and political turmoil in the Roman Republic. Simultaneously, Rome found herself fighting a difficult guerrilla war in the deserts of North Africa, whilst facing tribes of migrating barbarians from northern Europe. A series of reverses in both these theatres of war saw Rome suffer one of the heaviest defeats in her history at the Battle of Arausio and a barbarian invasion of Italy itself. Yet whilst the scenario of barbarian migration, defeat and invasion is all too familiar to the Late Roman Empire, all this occurred some five hundred years before the fall of Rome, at what is often seen as the height of the Republic's power.

This decade of crises is often noted for the rise of a perceived outsider (C. Marius) to an unprecedented six consulships in eight years and a radical reform of the Roman Republican army, which culminated in two of the greatest Roman military victories, at Aquae Sextiae and Raudian Plain (Vercellae). Yet many claim that these 'reforms' laid the foundations for the Republic's ultimate destruction at the hands of a series of oligarchs, such as Sulla, Pompey and Caesar (the latter of which was Marius' nephew). Upon examination, however, each of these assumptions can be challenged, but only through an in-depth study of the military situation of the period in question.

Anyone seeking an understanding of the period is faced with a number of difficulties which stem from our surviving ancient sources. Firstly, we lack a detailed narrative history of the period as a whole, giving undue weight to accounts that do survive, notably Plutarch's biography of Marius and Sallust's monograph on the Jugurthine War, which if not handled properly can provide a distorted picture of the period in question. Of the two wars which Rome faced, the Jugurthine War in North Africa is the lesser of the two in terms of severity, yet we have a fuller account of it and little detail for the wars in the north.

Furthermore, the Jugurthine War itself must be separated from Sallust's work on it, as he only represents one source and must be balanced, wherever possible, with other accounts to gain a better overall perspective of the war itself. No matter how detailed, relying on a sole account for any war should be avoided at all costs. Furthermore, given the loss of a wider narrative history, and the survival of works such as Appian's *Civil Wars* and Plutarch's biographies, it is all too easy to focus on the domestic political history of Rome in this period, as though it is somehow separate from the wars that were raging at the time.

Thus in many ways, a key part of this introduction is to establish just exactly what this work is not about; it is neither a commentary on Sallust's *Jugurthine Wars*, nor is it a biography of Caius Marius; there are a number of excellent works already in these fields (listed in the bibliography). This work seeks a broader perspective and attempts to analyse the period as a whole, taking in all the conflicts involved. This will allow us to analyse the origins, progression and ultimate solution to this decade of military crises. Only then can any political or military reforms be placed in their proper context.

Central to this process is the analysis of both wars, in Europe and Africa simultaneously. All too often the Jugurthine War is isolated from the rest of the period as though it exists in a vacuum, and this is down to the random survival of a historical monograph on the war, which itself isolates the events in Africa and Rome from the rest of the period. To study this war in isolation fundamentally undermines any conclusions we may draw from it. As the reader will soon notice, it is true that the balance of the surviving evidence relates to the war in Africa not the one in Europe, yet we must extract all that we can from what little remains.

The picture that emerges from our meagre evidence shows an empire on the brink of collapse, with conflicts being fought from Spain to the Balkans, engulfing southern Gaul, northern Italy and Sicily with Roman armies fighting across the deserts of North Africa, facing a range of native enemies. To this period belong some of Rome's greatest military disasters as well as some of their greatest victories. In Roman eyes the name Arausio stood alongside Cannae, Carrhae and Teutoburg Forest as a benchmark for military disasters, with some sources giving it as high a casualty rate as Cannae itself (see Chapter 8). Yet the battle is little known today, rendered obscure by the lack of a surviving account, an omission which hopefully will be corrected in this work.

There can be little doubt that the very future of the Roman Empire, as it came to be, was in peril at this point in its history. The culmination of these conflicts saw a barbarian army invade Italy itself, with the intent on settling there. Had the Romans failed at Aquae Sextiae and Vercellae, then Rome's presence in mainland Europe would have vastly diminished, undermining the basis of western civilization.

Two further points need to be made before our exploration of this period can begin.

The first relates to the nomenclature of these conflicts. The war in Africa has been known as the *bellum Iugurthinum* or Jugurthine War, after its principal protagonist, since it took place. Yet there is always a danger in these cases, as with references to the Pyrrhic, Hannibalic or Mithridatic Wars, that too much emphasis is given to the individual rather than the wider military or political issues. What started as a war against a sole king soon turned into a struggle against the combined races of North Africa with Roman domination of that region of the continent at stake. Yet whilst the Romano-Numidian or Romano-African Wars would perhaps be more appropriate, the weight of history makes the title of the 'Jugurthine War' an inevitable one.

There is no such clarity with the other conflicts however. Rome faced a multitude of different native enemies, from the Cimbri, Teutones and Ambrones from northern Europe to the Tigurini from Helvetia (Switzerland) and the Scordisci in the Balkans, with each conflict being assigned its own title. Yet, as argued in this work, these individual conflicts formed part of a wider process which saw the collapse of Rome's northern frontiers, in both western and eastern Europe. For that reason I have assigned this wider conflict the title of the Northern Wars, with reference to both Rome's northern frontier in this period, and the source of the threat to Rome in this period.

The second point is that whilst our surviving sources allow us to view the Jugurthine War from both perspectives – Roman and Jugurthan – we have no such ability for the Northern Wars. All we have to analyse are a number of fragmentary references by Roman and Greek sources many centuries after the events that they were describing. This regrettably renders any analysis of these conflicts so hopelessly one-sided that they can only be viewed from the Roman perspective. Added to this were the widespread Graeco-Roman fears and prejudices concerning Gauls, with Rome and Greece suffering Gallic invasions that scarred the collective memory. This left a tendency to view all native tribes as one-dimensional savages. Nonetheless this should not detract from the readers' understanding of these fundamental conflicts.

Timeline (148–100 BC)

Given that there are a number of events and conflicts taking place over a period of time, the following is a brief reference to the key events to aid the reader.

148   End of the Fourth Macedonian War.
          Creation of the Province of Macedonia.

          Death of Masinissa, king of Numidia.

146   End of the Third Punic War – Destruction of Carthage.
          Creation of the Province of Africa.

          Achaean War – defeat of the Achaean Federation.
          Greece added to the Province of Macedonia.

143   Revolt in Macedon.

141   Scordiscian invasion of Macedon – Roman defeat.

139   Murder of Viriathus in Spain.

138   End of the Lusitanian (Viriathic) War.

135   Scordisci defeated in Macedon.
          Slave Revolt in Sicily – Outbreak of First Servile War.

133   Tribunate and Murder of Ti. Sempronius Gracchus.
          Fall of Numantia, end of the Numantine War.
          Death of Attalus III of Pergamum; named the Roman People heirs.

132   Slave armies defeated in Sicily, end of the First Servile War.

129   End of the Asiatic War.
          Creation of the Province of Asia (Minor).

Death/murder of P. Cornelius Scipio Aemilianus
(Africanus/Numantinus).

125   Outbreak of Gallic War.
       Revolt and destruction of Italian town of Fregellae.

123   First Tribunate of C. Sempronius Gracchus.
       Balearic Islands annexed.

122   Second Tribunate of C. Sempronius Gracchus.

       Military Reforms of C. Gracchus.

121   Execution of Gracchus and his supporters.
       Roman armies defeat alliance of Allobroges and Arverni in
       southern Gaul.

119   Tribunate of C. Marius.
       Metellus 'Delmaticus' fights war in Illyria.

       Unnamed Battle – Pompeius, the Governor of Macedonia is defeated
       and killed fighting the Scordisci.

       Unnamed Battle. Annius defeats the Scordisci and their allies.

118   Death of Micipsa, king of Numidia - Outbreak of Numidian Civil
       War.

       Foundation of Narbo in southern Gaul.

117   Triumph of L. Caecilius Metellus Delmaticus for his campaign in
       Illyria.

114   Unnamed Battle – Roman army under Porcius Cato defeated by the
       Scordisci in Macedon/Thrace.
       Greece ravaged by the Scordisci. Temple of Delphi sacked.

113   Scordisci driven from Macedon.
       Cimbri arrive in Noricum.

       Battle of Noreia – Cimbri defeat the Roman army of Papirius Carbo.

112   Numidian Civil War restarts.
      Jugurtha takes Cirta, death of Adherbal, massacre of Italian traders.
      Rome declares war on Jugurtha – start of the Jugurthine War.

      Roman army in Thrace fighting Scordisci.

111   Consuls: P. Cornelius Scipio Nasica and L. Calpurnius Bestia.

      Triumph of M. Caecilius Metellus for Sardinian campaign.
      Triumph of C. Caecilius Metellus for Thracian campaign.

      Jugurtha summoned to Rome, organizes murder of Massiva.

110   Consuls: M. Minucius Rufus and Sp. Postumius Albinus.

      Triumph of M. Livius Drusus for victories against the Scordisci.

      Tribunician agitation in Rome, Consul recalled.

      Battle of Suthul – Roman army led by A. Postumius defeated by
      Jugurtha.

109   Consuls: Q. Caecilius Metellus and M. Iunius Silanus.

      Consuls remove a number of laws restricting military service.

      Praetor Servilius Caepio dispatched to Spain to fight the Lusitanians.

      Battle of Muthul River – Metellus defeats the forces of Jugurtha.
      Attempted coup to remove Jugurtha.

108   Consuls: Ser. Sulpicius Galba and Hortensius.

      Unnamed Battle – Roman army of Silanus defeated by Cimbri in
      Gaul.

      Unnamed Battle – Metellus defeats Jugurtha for a second time.

      Bocchus allies with Jugurtha, who also raises an army of Gaetulians.

107   Consuls: L. Cassius Longinus and C. Marius.

         Triumph of Q. Servilius Caepio for his campaign in Spain.

         Marius replaces Metellus as commander in Numidia by popular vote.

         Battle of River Hebrus – Roman victory over the Scordisci in Thrace
         End of the Scordiscian Wars.

         Unnamed Battle – Roman army led by Cassius defeated and massa-
         cred in Gaul by the Tigurini.

         Marius and Jugurtha clash near Cirta.

106   Consuls: Q. Servilius Caepio and C. Atilius Serranus.

         Triumph of Q. Caecilius Metellus Numidicus for victories over
         Jugurtha.
         Triumph of M. Minucius Rufus for his defeat of the Scordisci.

         Romans begin to subdue southern Gaul, recapturing Tolossa.

105   Consuls: P. Rutilius Rufus and Cn. Mallius Maximus.

         First Battle of Cirta – Stalemate.
         Second Battle of Cirta – Armies of Jugurtha and Bocchus defeated by
         Marius.

         Unnamed Battle – Roman army in Spain slaughtered by the
         Lusitanians.

         Battle of Arausio – Roman armies of Servilius Caepio and Mallius
         Maximus defeated and slaughtered by the Cimbri.

         Jugurtha captured by Bocchus and handed over to Sulla.
         End of the Jugurthine War.

104   Consuls: C. Marius (II) and C. Flavius Fimbria.

         Triumph of C. Marius for his defeat of Jugurtha.

Slave revolts in Italy and Sicily.
Start of the Second Servile War in Sicily.

103   Consuls: C. Marius (III) and L. Aurelius Orestes.

First tribunate of L. Appuleius Saturninus.

Battle of Triocala – Lucullus defeats the slave army in Sicily.

102   Consuls: C. Marius (IV) and Q. Lutatius Catulus.

Battle of Aquae Sextiae – Teutones and Ambrones defeated by
Marius.

101   Consuls: C. Marius (V) and M. Aquillius.

Battle of Raudian Plain (Vercellae) – Cimbri defeated by Marius and
Catulus.
End of the Northern Wars.

Unnamed Battle – Aquilius defeats the slave army in Sicily and ends
the Second Servile War.

100   Consuls: C. Marius (VI) and L. Valerius Flaccus.

Triumphs of Marius and Catulus for victories over the Cimbri.
Triumph of Antonius for victory over the pirates.

Second tribunate of L. Appuleius Saturninus.
Exile of Metellus Numidicus.
Insurrection and murder of Saturninus and Glaucia.

Note on Roman Names

All Roman names in the following text will be given in their traditional form, including the abbreviated first name. Below is a list of the Roman first names referred to in the text and their abbreviations.

A.	Aulus.
Ap.	Appius
C.	Gaius or Caius
L.	Lucius
M.	Marcus
P.	Publius
Q.	Quintus
Ser.	Servius
Sp.	Spurius
T.	Titus
Ti.	Tiberius

Rome in Crisis?

Chapter 1

Rome in Crisis? (146–120BC)

Before we assess the period in question, we need to understand the background to the crisis that faced Rome in what is now referred to as the late second century BC. Here we have a fundamental problem, namely the loss of a good narrative source for events after 167 BC (when our surviving books of Livy end[1]). Furthermore, the year 146 BC has tended to form a watershed in Roman Republican history, being the year that saw Rome defeat and destroy Carthage in the Third Punic War and annex Greece in the Achaean War. With the destruction of Carthage and the annexation of Macedon and Greece, our focus tends to shift towards domestic politics, aided by the survival of Appian's work on the Civil Wars (detailing events from 133 BC) and Plutarch's biographies of a number of prominent individuals from this period. However, this shift of focus to the domestic situation after 146 BC can also be found in a strand of Roman thought, best explained by Sallust:

"But when our country had grown great through toil and the practice of justice, when great kings had been vanquished in war, savage tribes and mighty peoples subdued by force of arms, when Carthage, Rome's rival for power had been destroyed, every land and sea lay open to her."[2]

Thus for Sallust, and many writers and historians who have followed him, after 146 Rome lay unchallenged and our attention should focus on domestic issues, along with narratives of decline (see Appendix V). Yet when we actually look at the period between 146 and the outbreak of the Jugurthine and Northern Wars, we see that this is not necessarily the case. In fact, the period was one of near constant warfare, albeit of a different manner, but one which saw Roman imperialism develop in many new and interesting ways.

Roman Warfare and Imperialism (c.146–120 BC)

i) Spain

The Viriathic or Lusitanian War (155–138 BC)
The Second Celtiberian War (153–151 BC)
The Numantine War (Third Celtiberian War) (143–133 BC)

Although the year 146 saw an end to Rome's conflicts in the east (Greece) and the south (Africa), in the west (Spain) it was a different matter. Roman imperialism and warfare in Spain had always been of a different nature to that in the south or east. The Romans fought not a united people or country, but a vast array of races and tribes in a region that was only unified by its unique geography (a vast isthmus jutting out into the seas and cut off from mainland Europe by the Pyrenees). Although Rome had taken possession of the Mediterranean coastline from Carthage, annexing the interior was a different matter, and turned into a two hundred year process of annexation and assimilation, which was not completed until the time of Augustus. The nature of this warfare famously led Polybius to state that whilst wars in Greece or Asia were decided decisively by one or two battles, in Spain the warfare was continuous, and by implication less suited to the Roman style of warfare.[3] Throughout the second century the Roman military effort in Spain was one of near-constant low-level warfare against the various native tribes and towns, punctuated by the occasional large-scale conflicts against a particular people, which we refer to as the wars, though the period between them could hardly be called peace, at least not in our understanding of the word.

As the Romans advanced northwards and westward from their coastal possessions, they encountered a number of hostile peoples; two of the most implacable of which were the Lusitanians and the Celtiberian peoples. Despite the fact that 184 BC saw two Roman commanders celebrate triumphs over both peoples, by the 150s BC, both once again rose to fight against the Roman occupation of their regions.[4] Both wars highlighted the problems that Roman military forces faced with barbarian armies, with Appian detailing a number of Roman reversals in battle.[5] The Lusitanian War saw the rise of Viriathus, who became one of Spain's great rebel leaders and a noted opponent of the Romans. Throughout the 140s Viriathus waged a successful war against the Romans, inflicting a number of defeats on them. It must be admitted that he was aided by the fact that Rome's most experienced commanders and seasoned troops were fighting in North Africa and Greece during this period, showing the dangers of Roman military overstretch; fighting no fewer than four major wars at the same time, two of which were in Spain.[6]

Following the success in Africa and Greece, Rome was able to devote more manpower and its finest commanders to the Spanish Wars. However, events soon soured when a fresh conflict arose with the Celtiberians, who, although initially pacified, rose up once more, stirred up by both Viriathus' success against the Romans and aid provided by him. Throughout the 140s Viriathus managed to inflict a series of defeat on the Romans. The war against Viriathus reached a peak in 141/140 under the Roman commander Q. Fabius Maximus Servilianus (the consul of 142).

As part of his preparations he even contacted the King of Numidia (Micipsa, see next chapter), which saw a number of African elephants deployed against the Lusitanians. In 141, Servilianus managed to defeat Viriathus and drive him back into Lusitania, bringing the region back under Roman control.[7] Unfortunately for Servilianus however, his pursuit of Viriathus was turned into an ambush and the Romans were soundly defeated.[8] Having pinned the Roman forces against a cliff, Viriathus then sought to bring the war to a conclusion by seeking a treaty with Rome.

With little option Servilianus agreed and Viriathus became a 'friend and ally of the Roman people', with his people's title to their lands confirmed, all of which capped a remarkable reversal in Rome's fortunes. However, the new commander of the war, Q. Servilius Caepio, the brother of Servilianus, saw the peace as a dishonourable one and immediately set about undermining it, apparently with senatorial backing.[9] War was soon re-declared and Viriathus, outnumbered and betrayed, embarked upon a guerrilla war against the Romans, proving impossible to either defeat or capture (much as Jugurtha himself would be some thirty years later). To end the war Caepio turned once again to underhand tactics and bribed two envoys sent by Viriathus to negotiate terms. Upon their return to Viriathus' camp, they murdered him during the night as he slept. Thus Rome achieved through treachery and murder what they could not on the battlefield (again a foretaste of the Jugurthine War). Without Viriathus, the Lusitanians were soon pacified.

The fragments of Diodorus preserve an excellent eulogy to the man:

> By common consent he was a most valiant fighter in battle and a most able and forward thinking general; most important of all, throughout his entire career as a general he commanded the devotion of his troops to a degree unequalled by anyone.
>
> The proofs of his abilities are manifest; for in the eleven years that he commanded the Lusitanians, his troops not only remained free of dissension but were all but invincible, whereas after his death the confederacy of the Lusitanians disintegrated once it was deprived of his leadership.[10]

The Third Celtiberian War, or Numantine War as it is also known, also proved to be an embarrassment to Rome, though for different reasons. Instead of throwing up a charismatic figurehead, it spawned an infamous siege centred on the town of Numantia in Spain. The town itself was high in the mountains surrounded by woodland and two rivers, with only one clear access road. Sieges in 142 by Q. Caecilius Metellus 'Macedonicus' (see Appendix IV) and Q. Pompeius in 141–140 BC, both failed.[11] The latter suffered such heavy casualties that he negotiated a secret peace treaty with the inhabitants for a cessation of hostilities.

Again such a treaty was greeted with contempt by the Senate and the war continued under a fresh commander, M. Popillius Laenas (the consul of 139), though he met with similar failure. He in turn was replaced by C. Hostilius Mancinus (the consul of 137), who not only continued his predecessors' records of failure but managed to get his entire army trapped and surrounded in their own camp. The army was only saved from annihilation by a treaty of surrender, partly negotiated by a young Ti. Sempronius Gracchus (see below). Naturally, upon his return to Rome, the Senate refused to ratify the treaty and actually had Mancinus sent back to the Numantines bound and naked.[12]

To date the siege of Numantia had being continuing intermittently for six years, longer than it had taken to besiege Carthage, and had done nothing but expose a series of incompetent Roman commanders and humiliate the reputation of the Roman army.

In 135 BC, sensing a chance for further glory, P. Cornelius Scipio Aemilianus (Africanus), the conqueror of Carthage, entered the fray. Offering himself to the people as the solution to the crisis, he had the tribunes suspend the laws regarding second consulships (his first being in 147 BC) and was not only elected as consul for 134 BC, but had the tribunes pass a law giving him command against the Numantines.[13] Such a process was to have resonance when we consider the career of C. Marius later on (see chapter seven).

The parallels continue as Scipio raised a fresh force of men to take with him to Spain. Appian states that this was due to the limited amount of manpower available at the time, though this is much debated (see below and Appendix III).[14] He recruited a number of his own clients into service as well as contingents from client kings and allies abroad, including a force of Numidians led by their prince Jugurtha.[15] He then joined up with the existing forces in Spain, amongst whom was a certain C. Marius. Appian details the exhaustive preparations made by Scipio for the siege and the detail of the siege itself, which included the creation of a wall around the city.[16] Under his clear leadership and with the Numantines suffering from exhaustion, the city fell to Scipio in 133 BC, bringing him more plaudits and glory. The surrender of the inhabitants was followed by the destruction of the city, taking his personal tally of destroyed cities to two: Carthage and Numantia. The fall of Numantia brought an end to a turbulent period of Roman warfare in Spain, which had resulted in a number of reversals and humiliations. It also saw the rise of a charismatic rebel leader who continued to elude Rome and a Roman general who used the situation for his own advantage, overturning established practice.

ii) Macedon and Illyria

Macedonian Revolt (143 BC)
Scordiscian War (c.141–130s BC)

For the campaigns in the east in this period we have little more than fragmentary notices, yet the annexation of Macedon proved to be problematic for several reasons. Firstly, although the pretender Andriscus had been defeated and Macedon annexed in 148 BC, another rebellion soon broke out, this time in 143 BC, led by a man claiming to be Philip VI, a son of Perseus. This pretender soon gathered an army of slaves, numbering 16,000, but was defeated by the quaestor L. Tremellius Scrofa.[17]

Nevertheless, it does show how tenuous a grasp Rome had on the newly conquered Macedon. As well as internal threats from Macedon there were numerous fresh external threats. By annexing Macedon, Rome now had a massive exposure to the tribes of Central Europe, and a responsibility to defend Macedon's borders (such as they were).

One of the key threats to Rome's new province came from the tribe of the Scordisci, who will be detailed more later on (see Chapter 3). Rome's first contact with the Scordisci apparently came in a war in Dalmatia in 156 BC, when Rome defeated an invasion of Illyria, though the details of the Scordiscian involvement are obscure.[18] However, by 141 we find references to a Scordiscian invasion of Macedon and Rome being defeated in battle by them; the *Periochae* of Livy called it a disaster.[19] Interestingly, there is a note in Appian stating that an unknown Roman commander name Cornelius met with a disaster against some unidentified Pannonians at roughly the same period. He goes on to say that the disaster was so great that the peoples of Italy feared for their safety (expecting a resulting invasion), however fanciful that may sound.[20] The two events have been linked by a historian who argues that the 'Pannonians' were the Scordisci and that they invaded Macedon from the 140s through to the 130s.[21] Again we have few details of these wars, but in 135, a praetor M. Cosconius is recorded to have defeated the Scordisci over the border in Thrace itself. We still find him in Macedon in 133 indicating the length and severity of the campaign.

The history of Roman involvement in Illyria was much like that of Spain, a near-constant series of small-scale wars with the tribes of the region to establish Roman authority. In 135 BC, we find one of the consuls of 135, Ser. Fulvius Flaccus, defeating the Vardaei tribe, who had raided the region under Roman suzerainty.[22] Roman armies can again be found being deployed in Illyria, when in 129 BC, one of the consuls, C. Sempronius Tuditanus, fought against a tribe known as the Iapudes. Though we only have two references to the campaign, it is clear that Sempronius was defeated by the Illyrian tribe, though the situation was rescued by one of his legates, D. Iunius Brutus, and the Iapudes were ultimately defeated. Sempronius then returned to Rome to celebrate an (ill-deserved) triumph.[23]

iii) Sicily

The First Servile War (135–132 BC)

A new and unusual threat arose in this period, in what had been one of the oldest provinces of Rome's empire, namely Sicily. The threat was a full-scale slave uprising on a scale that had never been seen before, so much so that it is often refered to as the First Servile War. Slave revolts had been a common enough occurrence, but had always been sporadic and localized and never posed a serious military threat. We will never perhaps understand what sparked off such an uprising, but factors such as charismatic leadership, geography and an unusual harshness of treatment have all been raised as factors.[24]

Whilst we have no full narrative account of the conflict, there is a lengthy fragment of Diodorus which preserves a number of details. The rebellion began around the town of Enna, in central Sicily and was led by a Syrian slave named Eunus, who apparently had something of a mystical air to him:

> he was an Apamean by birth and had an aptitude for magic and the working of wonders. He claimed to foretell the future, by divine command, through dreams and because of his talents deceived many.[25]

Eunus belonged to a Sicilian named Damophilus, who was especially cruel to his slaves, which was the initial spark. The original rebellion centred on just 400 slaves, but they successfully managed to attack the town of Enna, slaughtering the freeborn inhabitants, an action which soon brought fresh recruits and spawned a number of other revolts on the island. Soon Eunus had an army of 6,000. A second revolt led by a slave named Cleon was equally successful, raising a force of 5,000 slaves, all of whom fell under the overall command of Eunus, who proclaimed himself a king in the Seleucid Syrian manner, taking the title of 'Antiochus, king of the slaves' and even minting his own coins.[26]

What further marks this revolt out, and what turned it into a war, was its being the first (recorded) conscious attempt by a slave force to fashion and conduct itself in military style and attempt to take and hold territory of their own.

Given the importance of Sicily to Rome, it being the main domestic provider of grain, the staple food product of the populace, a Roman army was soon dispatched to deal with this threat under the command of L. (Plautius) Hypsaeus. However, given that he had only a force of 8,000 Sicilian troops at his command, it is not that surprising that he was soon defeated.[27] He was followed by the consul of 134, C. Fulvius Flaccus, who met with no greater success, though the details are unclear.[28]

Given that the war was taking place at the same time as that in Numantia, and that Scipio decided/was forced to raise his own additional forces, it begs the question how able Rome was to contend with an additional war in its own core territories.

The first notable Roman progress came under a consul of 133 BC, L. Calpurnius Piso Frugi, who captured the town of Murgantia and attacked Enna itself.[29] He was succeeded by a consul of 132 BC, P. Rupilius, who stormed and retook the towns of Tauromenium and Enna, the key slave strongholds, killing over 20,000 of the slave army, finally bringing the war to an end.[30] Of the ring-leaders, Cleon had been killed in combat and Eunus fled but was eventually captured by the Romans, dying in captivity.[31]

The war is notable for a number of reasons. Firstly, it was the first time that a slave rebellion had taken on all the trappings of a full-blown military campaign. It came at a time when Roman forces were already overstretched, with wars in Spain and Asia ongoing. Furthermore, it appeared to spark off widespread, though short-lived, slave rebellions across Rome's empire. Orosius mentions outbreaks in Italy itself, at Minturnae and Sinuesa, while both he and Diodorus mention rebellions in Attica, all of which required military action.[32] A further rebellion was crushed by the inhabitants of Delos.[33] The vital importance of the grain from Sicily would also have had an important domestic effect in Rome, especially for the urban populace, and it is not a coincidence that this war formed the backdrop for the tribunate of Ti. Sempronius Gracchus.

iv) Asia Minor

The Asiatic War (132–129 BC)

It is all too easy to fall into a narrative of imperial decline, but the next two theatres of war actually reversed this trend and saw Rome expand into new regions, both of which were to have crucial consequences in the future. The first one concerns Asia Minor and the famous so called 'inheritance' of the

Kingdom of Pergamum. Pergamum had been one of Rome's closest allies in Asia Minor, initially borne out of a desire to counterbalance Seleucid power in the region. This alliance took an unusual twist in 133 BC when the King of Pergamum, Attalus III, died without a clear successor. A will was found, now supported by epigraphic evidence, which named the Roman People as his inheritors.[34] The whole incident is more known for its involvement with Ti. Sempronius Gracchus, who attempted to lay claim to the kingdom's wealth to fund his land distribution policy (see below) than the details of its annexation and wider foreign policy issues.

Initially, we have the issue of just what Attalus had in mind when he made such a bequest or what the Senate's initial thoughts were towards this unique situation. It is clear that Attalus wished his old allies to protect his people from what was certain to be the avaricious desire of Pergamum's Asiatic neighbours, including Pontus and Bithynia. We can perhaps also detect a certain maliciousness from the grave towards his kingdom's enemies, by permanently shackling them with Rome's presence in the region. The scope of his intentions are another problem though, as the remaining fragments of the will appear to relate only to the city of Pergamum itself, not the rest of the kingdom.[35]

An equally interesting question is whether Rome initially intended to annex the region and establish a permanent foothold in Asia Minor, bringing them into close contact with the near-permanently feuding kingdoms of the region or merely take an income from the king's property and leave the region autonomous. As was usual in such cases, the Senate established a five-man commission to go to Pergamum, assess the situation and report their findings.[36] The only member of the commission we know of was P. Cornelius Scipio Nasica, the man so closely involved in the murder of Tiberius Gracchus, in a clear attempt to get him out of the city and calm tensions. This policy worked only too well when Scipio died whilst at Pergamum of what were reported to be unknown causes, though foul play cannot be ruled out.[37]

What was initially a benign situation erupted into a full-scale armed insurrection, when a royal pretender to the vacant throne, by the name of Aristonicus, rose up to claim the throne aided by the lower strata of Pergamum's social order, thus mixing up internal class struggle and external intervention.[38] The commission, without an army, initially had to rely upon the armies of Pergamum's neighbours, all Roman allies to one degree or another. These included Nicomedes II of Bithynia, Ariarathes V of Cappodocia, who died during the rebellion, and Mithridates V of Pontus. Although Aristonicus was driven back into the interior of the kingdom, consular armies had to be sent out in 131 and 130. The commander of the 130 campaign, P. Licinius Crassus Dives Mucianus (consul of 131 BC) made some initial headway but was attacked as he was leaving the province, defeated and executed by Aristonicus near Leucae.[39] However, Mucianus was succeeded by M. Perperna (consul of 130) who defeated Aristonicus in battle and forced his surrender.[40] He died, a prisoner in Rome, soon afterwards.

One of the consuls of 129 (M. Aquilius) now had the job of organizing a settlement in the region, aided by a new ten-man commission. The fertile plains formed the new Roman province of Asia, whilst the mountainous inland regions were divided up between Pergamum's neighbours, as both an expedient method of getting rid of areas that would be hard to administer and rewarding their earlier assistance, though the process did stir up jealousies amongst the claimants, notably Bithynia and Pontus. Rome, however, took the prize, the coastal cities of Asia Minor, which soon proved to be one of Rome's richest provinces. Whatever their original intentions, the rebellion of Aristonicus and the hard fought campaigns of 132–130 turned the Senate's policy towards annexation, at least of the richer parts of the region. Thus Asia became the first province Rome had taken since 146 BC and added greatly to the wealth flowing into Rome's coffers. It did, however, tie Rome more closely with the feuding kingdoms of Asia Minor, which would ultimately lead to the Mithridatic Wars.[41] Nevertheless, in the short term it was a military and imperial success.

v) Gaul

The Gallic War (125–120 BC)

Whilst the phrase 'Gallic War' has become synonymous with the campaigns of C. Iulius Caesar in the first century, it was in the 120s BC that Rome made its first concerted effort to control Gaul, at least its southern region. Until this point, Rome had no formal control of the region between her provinces in Spain and Italy itself, relying on allies such as the city of Massilia (Marseille) to keep the route free. However, strategic necessity dictated that sooner or later the Romans would need to secure that vital route for themselves. The danger lay in becoming too entangled with the seemingly borderless region of Gaul and the vast network of tribes that lay within it.

As is usual with this period, we have no narrative history for the campaigns, merely a few fragmentary references to it. Nevertheless it represented a major Roman campaign in itself and set Rome towards the acquisition of new territories. The war began when Rome's old ally of Massilia sent an appeal for assistance against the Gallic tribe of the Salluvii, whose territory surrounded their city. One of the consuls of 125, M. Fulvius Flaccus was dispatched[42] and not only defeated the Salluvii, but also the Ligurians and the Vocontii as well, though we do not know how they became involved in the conflict.[43] For this Fulvius celebrated a triumph on his return in 123 BC.

The celebrations proved to be premature as one of the consuls of 124 BC (C. Sextius Calvinus) can be found fighting the same enemies during the next few years as well.[44] During the course of another victorious campaign, Calvinus founded the town of Aquae Sextiae (see Chapter 9). Once again a triumph was celebrated over the Ligurians, Salluvii and Vocontii, this time in 122 BC. Such campaigns were a standard part of Rome' northern defensive system, and had been conducted against the same enemies in 154 BC.[45]

However, on this occasion the war escalated, when the Salluvian king (Toutomotulus) fled to the neighbouring tribe, the Allobroges, probably the leading tribal power in the region.[46] Again, Rome dispatched a consul, Cn. Domitius Ahenobarbus, who defeated the Allobroges near the town of Vindalium. Yet it appears that the anti-Roman feeling merely spread and we find one of the consuls of 121, Q. Fabius Maximus 'Allobrogicus', fighting an alliance of the Allobroges and the Arverni. The battle (at an unnamed location) took place on what now equates to the 8th August 121 BC, and saw 30,000 Romans facing an army in excess of 125,000 (which is the total number given for the Gallic dead, if we are to believe Livy's compiler[47]). This victory brought the war to an end, with both tribes surrendering and Bituitus, the Arvernian king, going to Rome to make peace and surrender in person (where he and his son were held as hostages). Both Domitius and Fabius returned to Rome in 120 and both celebrated triumphs for their victories.

Clearly these campaigns were major ones, four consuls taking the field and the war ending with a massive battle against an alliance of two of the most powerful Gallic tribes. The war has an incredibly-low profile today, due to the few surviving sources that mention it and the fact that it took place at the same time as the tribunate of Caius Gracchus in Rome.[48] Nevertheless, this should not obscure its significance. In total, the Romans defeated some five Gallic tribes, including two of the regional powers, the Allobroges and the Arverni.[49] Furthermore, the Romans then established a permanent presence in the region, founding the town of Narbo in 118 BC, and carving out the embryonic province of Transalpine Gaul, formally connecting Spain to Italy for the first time.[50] This connection was cemented by the construction of the Via Domitia.[51] From a logistical point of view, securing a land connection between Spain and Italy, rather than relying on the declining power of Massilia, makes good sense. From a military point of view, defeating the leading powers of southern Gaul and ensuring their loyalty to Rome would not only secure this route, but also eased any pressure on Rome's Alpine borders. However, as soon became clear, it did link Roman interests and holdings more openly to the varying balances of power in the Gallic region, a danger that they would not resolve until the time of Caesar.

vi) Other Campaigns of the Period

Two other campaigns in this period are worth mentioning, though we only have scant references to them. Firstly, in 123 BC, one of the consuls, Q. Caecilius Metellus 'Baliaricus' (see Appendix IV), having been given command against the pirates inhabiting the Balearic Islands, invaded and annexed the islands for Rome, establishing two citizen colonies on Majorca (Palma and Pollentia), formed from Roman colonists in Spain. Florus preserves a brief account of the campaign.[52] This annexation merely cemented Rome's dominance of the western Mediterranean, securing vital sea routes to Spain, but also continued the trend of an increasing Roman empire.

A second and less glorious campaign took place within Italy itself when in 125 BC the Italian town of Fregellae rose up in revolt against Roman control, stirred up over the issue of acquiring Roman citizenship. On its own, the revolt stood little or no chance of success and a praetor (L. Opimius) soon took the town by storm and destroyed it.[53] Nevertheless, it was a sign that, even in Italy, Roman supremacy could be challenged.

Summary

Thus the events of the period 146–120 BC do not appear to meet the impression which we find in Sallust, namely that after Carthage had been defeated Rome lay unchallenged. With the more clear-cut wars against Macedon and Carthage won, we can see that Rome became entangled in a number of conflicts with tribes who bordered Roman territory. Although on a map both Spain and Illyria were Roman territories, the tribes of the regions had other ideas. In both the Viriathic and Numantine Wars, Rome tasted defeat and setback, with repercussions at Rome. Policing Illyria and Macedon brought Rome in contact with the numerous central European tribes, none of whom respected Rome's territorial borders, such as they were. Furthermore, the period saw the first full-scale slave war break out in Sicily, as well as the revolt of an Italian city.

Nevertheless, the period also saw Rome make some major steps forward in expanding her empire, in both Asia Minor and Gaul, both of which would lead Rome into future conflicts. Of the two, it is clear that the Gallic War of 125–120 was a major war, where Rome faced and defeated an alliance of the leading Gallic tribes of the region and took the strategic view that it was necessary to annex the coastal region of southern Gaul. If anything, in both this annexation of the coast of Asia Minor and, to a lesser degree, the Balearic Islands, we can see the development of a more strategic view to Rome's actions. Both Transalpine Gaul and the Balearics secured vital routes to Spain, whilst Asia gave them vastly-increased revenue and established a firm Roman presence on the far side of the Aegean, securing the route to Greece.

Thus, we have evidence for Roman successes and failures in this period, all of which are essential background for covering the main period in question (120–100 BC) as well as when looking at the more well known domestic situation.

Roman Domestic Politics (146–111 BC)

At the same time as the events detailed above, Roman domestic politics entered an unprecedented upheaval, spilling over into bloodshed on the streets of Rome itself. Although this topic has been the subject of perhaps more scholarly effort than any other in Roman Republican history, and falls outside the remit of this work, several key themes do need highlighting, notably around the issue of military recruitment and the highly-vexatious manpower question.

Just as the year 146 BC acts as an unwanted cut off point in Roman foreign affairs, the year 133 BC has the same effect in Roman domestic politics. However, the tribunate of Ti. Sempronius Gracchus was not the first time that issues of land and military recruitment had been raised on the domestic stage.

Pre-Gracchan Tensions & Scipio Aemilianus

As Taylor showed so well in her groundbreaking article,[54] tensions in Rome over military issues were common throughout this period, with repeated clashes between the tribunate and the rest of the Senatorial oligarchy.[55] The two most obvious examples of this came in 151 and 138 BC, when on both occasions tribunes had the consuls actually imprisoned during disputes over the military levy for the wars in Spain.[56] Had we books of Livy which covered the period 167–133 BC then we would no doubt uncover a number of other such clashes between the two offices. Thus the issue of continued military service appeared to be weighing heavily on the citizen population, who got the tribunes to vent their frustrations at the increasing burden.

It is during this period that we also hear of a proposed a law by a C. Laelius[57] concerning the ownership of the *ager publicus* (public land), an issue at the heart of Ti. Gracchus' measures in 133 BC and which plays a central role in the debate over manpower issues (see Appendix III). This unknown measure was dropped by Laelius after encountering strong Senatorial opposition, for which he received the cognomen of *sapiens* (the wise). It is also note-worthy that

Plutarch makes a point of introducing Laelius as being an ally of Scipio Aemilianus, who plays an important role in these proceedings.[58]

At the same time as these events, a number of tribunes also passed measures which affected Rome's electoral and judicial systems. The initial and main measure came in 139 with the *lex Gabinia*, introducing secret ballot for elections, which went some way to reducing the nobility's control over their clients' voting.[59] This was followed in 137 BC by a *lex Cassia* which extended the principle of secret ballots to all judicial trials, except treason.[60]

As well as these tribunician measures, we also have the figure of P. Cornelius Scipio Aemilianus, twice consul and destroyer of Carthage and Numantia. As well as his noted military accomplishments it is instructive to review the methods he used in domestic politics. It is interesting to note that for both of his consulships (147 and 134 BC) he utilised tribunes to clear any constitutional objections raised to his election. In 148 unnamed or 'anonymous' tribunes threatened to remove the Senate's supervision of the consular elections unless they allowed Scipio to stand (being below the minimum age). When this tactic did not meet with success, these tribunes then repealed the law on age restrictions, restoring them after Scipio had been elected.[61] In 135 BC, Scipio again faced a bar on being elected consul, as a law prevented repeated consulships within a decade. Once again Scipio turned to the tried and trusted use of tribunes and had the law repealed for his election and then reinstated.[62]

On this occasion though, Scipio went far further than anyone had gone before, and had 'anonymous' tribunes pass a law granting him command in Spain against the Numantines. Such an act was unprecedented (though it would be repeated often in later times), utilizing the tribunes to have the assembly grant him an overseas command, which lay, by the power of custom and practice, in the hands of the Senate. Given that such practices are more normally associated with the various key figures of the late Republic, notably C. Marius himself, it is fascinating to find their origins in this period, especially given the connections between Scipio and Marius.

The Tribunate of Ti. Sempronius Gracchus (133 BC)

This period of tribunician activity hit a peak in 133 BC, with the election of Ti. Sempronius Gracchus. His tribunate remains one of the most contentious and written about periods of Roman history and whilst there is neither the space, nor the scope to do more than highlight some key themes, there exist a number of good works on the subject (see bibliography).

Ti. Sempronius Gracchus hailed from one of Rome's most distinguished plebeian aristocratic families. His father had been twice consul and censor,[63] his mother was the daughter of Scipio Africanus and his father in law was Ap. Claudius Pulcher, the Princeps Senatus.[64] His tribunate and subsequent murder at the end of his term of office marked the first death as a result of a domestic political struggle and many say ushered in a new era of violence in Roman domestic politics.[65]

The root cause of his death and the controversy was a law he passed which set a limit on the amount of public land (*ager publicus*) a man could hold, with a confiscation of any of this type of land over the limit and its distribution to the poorer landless citizens.[66] It is said to have been similar in type to the law proposed (and subsequently dropped) by C. Laelius a few years earlier and allegedly harked back to ancient statues in the limits of *ager publicus* a man could hold.[67]

Gracchus' stated motives, which have been the focus of scholarly argument for over 2,000 years, were that he was motivated by his awareness of the growing problem of Roman citizens losing their farms due to extended military service, leading to the twin problems of there being less available manpower and an increase in slaves. It is alleged that the citizens who lost their farms were selling them to rich landowners who amalgamated them into super-estates run by slaves, whilst the landless citizens were moving into the city. By virtue of their being landless then they were not eligible for military recruitment, as the law stated that a man must possess a certain amount of land to be eligible to fight for Rome. The argument being that Roman tradition believed that a man with land fought harder for his country than a man without, being little better than a mercenary (see Appendix III).

Thus, it was argued that Gracchus' law was aimed at getting the citizens out of the city and a life of dependency, back onto the land, thus making them eligible for military recruitment (which, it must be pointed out, would only start the cycle of extended service, neglect of farm, sale and city dwelling all over again). Furthermore, it would reduce Rome's dependence on vast slave estates, which brought with it the threat of slave rebellions. Given that his tribunate in 133 coincided with the First Servile War in Sicily (see above), we can understand that this was a palpable fear.

This *ager publicus* itself was a special category of Roman land, whose ultimate ownership rested with the state. During the earlier centuries when Rome extended her rule throughout Italy, a portion of land was usually confiscated by Rome from the defeated Italian states. The land was owned by the Roman state itself and rented out to various interested parties to farm it, with the title remaining in public hands. Naturally, over the decades and centuries, many of the families which owned this land came to view it as a hereditary possession, despite the state being the ultimate owner.

Under Gracchus' law all ancient *ager publicus* would be assessed by a three-man commission and each owner limited to 500 *iugera* (slightly higher than an acre), plus an extra 250 *iugera* for any sons (up to a limit of two). The commission was composed of himself, his younger brother and his father in law.[68]

Naturally enough, there were going to be a number of prominent landowners who would lose land which they considered to be theirs by right of inheritance, even though they had no legal title to it. Furthermore, the three-man board and the whole issue did carry the trace of political factionalism and Tiberius himself would certainly have benefited from it in terms of public popularity.[69] For these reasons it was not surprising that the law was opposed in both the Senate and the assemblies by some of his fellow tribunes.

If the law itself was controversial then Tiberius' methods only inflamed the situation. Facing opposition in the Senate, he did not present the law to them, but took it straight to the assemblies, which, although constitutionally legal, was against the accepted tradition and a clear snub to the Senate. When faced with the veto of a fellow tribune, rather than see if it could be argued out[70], he had his fellow tribune, M. Octavius, deposed from office by popular vote, claiming that he was betraying his office by preventing a measure which clearly benefited the people.[71] This was perhaps the most outrageous step Tiberius took, claiming a theory of popular sovereignty, which had no precedent. Although in theory the assemblies could vote out a tribune, it had never been done and undermined centuries of Roman constitutional practice.

Tiberius followed this by going yet further. When the Senate voted his commission insufficient funds to carry out its task, he then sequestered monies from the recent bequest of Pergamum in the will of Attalus III, thus completely encroaching on the Senate's prerogative to decide on foreign affairs. Given these actions, it is easy to see why so many in the Senate were opposed to Gracchus, including many who, given more reasonable actions, would have supported his proposals. For many the final straw came when Tiberius stood for re-election to the tribunate for 132 BC. Such a move was highly contentious and had not been done in 200 years, since the (in)famous tribunates of Licinius & Sextius in the fourth century.[72] This would allow Tiberius to be elected for a second year in succession and prevent him from prosecution for any of his acts (for that additional year).

To many in the Senate, this represented a dangerous situation and, fearful of his intentions, a mob of Senators attacked Gracchus and his supporters at the elections and lynched them. It is said that Tiberius was killed by P. Cornelius Scipio Nasica, the chief pontiff of Rome (the Pontifex Maximus).[73] The years that followed saw a continuation of this factionalism, with a number of Tiberius' supporters being put on trial for their support of the dead man, combined with a popular backlash against his murderers.

As noted above, Scipio Nasica was sent to Pergamum to deal with the bequest, but died soon after. Scipio Aemilianus, who had been in Numantia throughout this year when he heard of the news, famously quoted Homer, 'So perish all who commit such wickedness', even though he was married to Tiberius' sister.[74] By 129 BC, the rift caused by Tiberius' murder continued, with a number of tribunes voicing their support for his actions.[75] The year was notable for the mysterious death of Scipio Aemilianus himself, who was found dead in his bed the morning he was due to advocate measures limiting the powers of the Gracchan land commissioners.[76] At the time everything from murder to suicide was advanced as theory behind his death and certainly murder was widely suspected.

The Tribunates of C. Sempronius Gracchus (123–122 BC)

Thus we can see the atmosphere that formed the backdrop of the Roman political scene throughout the years that followed 133 BC. Another shadow hung over Roman politics in this period, namely Tiberius' younger brother Caius, widely expected to take up his brother's cause. Caius did not disappoint, being elected as tribune in both 123 and again in 122 BC. Throughout the two years he produced a raft of legislation with far wider aims than his brother. Again the chronology of these measures is confused, as are some of the measures themselves.

In terms of the land issue, he re-issued his brother's law of 133, which was probably more symbolic than meaningful, but went further by proposing a programme of founding new colonies, including one on the site of Carthage itself (Iunonia).[77] More direct military issues were tackled with laws that provided clothing and equipment for legionaries at public expense rather than the soldier's own (though again this may have been more a case of formalizing existing practice, and will be discussed later, in Appendix II). A further law barred the recruitment of young men under the age of seventeen.[78] Caius also passed a law stating that all consular provinces must be named in advance of the election, to stop the Senate manipulating consular commands to favour certain individuals. He also introduced the right to collect the taxes in the province of Asia being auctioned off to the business community, favouring the equestrian order of businessmen. Another notable measure was the issuing of corn, the staple diet of an average Roman citizen, to the inhabitants of Rome, at a subsidized rate.[79]

Following his re-election for 122, which passed remarkably smoothly considering the issues it had raised when his brother attempted it, he widened his scope and attempted a more lasting alteration of the balance of Roman politics.

He passed a law allowing all juries in corruption trials to be drawn from the equestrian order, reducing senatorial influence over the outcomes and ensuring equestrian corruption was dealt with sympathetically. He then proposed extending the franchise of Roman citizenship throughout Italy, in stages.[80] Both measures would have extended Caius' powerbase and raised issues that were not to be solved until decades later, perhaps not until the Principate itself. He clearly favoured the equestrian businessmen, themselves not an altogether separate class from the senatorial elite, by his measures on the Asian taxes and juries.[81] Perhaps his most fundamental issue was his raising the prospect of extending the Roman citizenship franchise throughout Italy (albeit in a controlled manner), which was a Pandora's Box not dealt with until the Social War and the censorship of 70 BC.

Thus Caius went far beyond his brother's scope in terms of legislation. Again scholars have spent two millennia arguing over his motives, but the scope of these laws and proposals shows a desire to alter the shape of the Roman political landscape in a remarkably short period of time. It is equally clear that many of those who stood to benefit from these proposals would back him personally as well. In response, the Senate initially adopted a more measured approach and set about undermining his support, certainly within Rome itself.

One of Caius' fellow tribunes of 122, M. Livius Drusus, proposed his own programme of colony foundation, on a reduced scale and vetoed the measures on extending the citizenship throughout Italy.[82] On this occasion there was no resultant deposition of Drusus, perhaps as the urban populace of Rome were not enamoured with the prospects of sharing citizenship rights with the inhabitants of Italy. Thus Drusus presented a more subtle opposition to Caius and not one that could easily be dismissed. Furthermore, Caius spent a period time out of Rome, organizing the foundation of Iunonia on the site of Carthage and clearly suffered in popularity on his return.[83] The obvious sign of this decline was his failure to be elected for a third consecutive tribunate, for 121 BC.

With Caius no longer a tribune, the Senate made a move in 121, via a compliant tribune (Minucius Rufus), to annul some of his previous legislation.[84] When the day came for the measure to be passed Caius and his supporters protested at the assembly, during which a servant of the Consul L. Opimius was killed. Opimius was a noted opponent of Gracchus and used this death to argue that Caius was attempting an armed sedition, a charge levelled against his brother. On this occasion, rather than resort to a religiously-sanctioned lynching, the Senate, at Opimius' behest, passed a unique piece of legislation known as the *senatus consultum ultimum* (the ultimate/final decree of the Senate), equivalent to the Riot Act in Great Britain, or Martial Law; a suspension of the usual laws and the rights of the individual. Caius and his supporters were then hunted down and murdered, legally, though that can have been of little comfort to those involved.[85]

Thus the 120s saw another round of state-sanctioned murder, this time veiled in a legal framework. These murders form the backdrop to the period in question and highlight the divisive nature that reform, political, agrarian or military, had taken. The decade that followed Caius Gracchus' death repeated the pattern of the early 120s, with individual tribunes taking up the Gracchan cause (as it had become). Further agrarian laws were seen, the latest being in 111 BC, all of which amended Tiberius' original proposals in some way. A notable tribune of this period was a certain C. Marius who was tribune in 119 and tapped into this atmosphere (see Chapter 7). It was in such a febrile atmosphere as this that key decisions were taken with regard to the Jugurthine Wars.

Chapter 2 (206–112BC)

The Rise of Numidia

In 112 BC the Senate and People of Rome found themselves having to declare war on an allied African prince. The war that followed dragged on for seven years, confounded all expectations of an easy victory and exposed crucial military and political failings within the Roman Republican system. Yet, as always there is a danger of viewing the war from a one-sided (Roman) perspective. Even the most common name assigned to this conflict, the *Bellum Iugurthinum*,[86] or Jugurthine War can obscure important longer-term factors. From ancient times onwards, many historians have viewed this war as unforeseen and a result of an accidental set of circumstances. Indeed, this is probably how many in the Senate at the time saw it, especially as its immediate causes were to be found in a succession dispute between the princes of an African kingdom. It is perhaps Florus who, writing some 200 years after the event, summed this attitude up best with the phrase 'Who, after the fall of Carthage could expect another war in Africa?'[87]

This view sums up many commentators' attitudes, both ancient and modern, namely, that after the Third Punic War and the Roman annexation of Carthage, Africa itself could be left alone and attention shifted to other theatres of conflict. Yet in many ways the Third Punic War itself obscures the issue. Aside from the fact that it was little more than an extended siege of one city, it overlooks the fact that by 149 BC the chief power in North Africa was the kingdom of Numidia, not the frail state of Carthage. By the time the Romans annexed Carthage in 146 BC it was little more than a coastal strip dwarfed by the entity that was Numidia.

Thus in order to avoid falling into the same mindset that would have us see the war of 112– 105 BC as coming out of the blue, and having no wider issues, we need to analyse the preceding century of North African history to gain a clearer understanding of the events that brought Rome and Numidia to war.

North Africa during the Punic Wars

When dealing with North Africa in the third and second centuries BC the image of Carthage looms large. What we must never forget is that Carthage was always more of a Mediterranean power than an African one. As a Phoenician maritime colony Carthage's focus was always going to be the Mediterranean, in terms of economic and imperial activity, and this is reflected in our surviving sources. It is only during the Second Punic War that we gain our first real glimpse of the peoples and politics of the North African interior.

Carthage itself had only a small portion of the North African continent under its direct control and had little in the way of native population. What it could call upon was the manpower of the African interior, either through a system of hegemony, or via the use of mercenaries. Greg Daly has produced the finest analysis of the Carthaginian army during the Second Punic War, which was mostly made up of allied or mercenary contingents from Spain and North Africa, under Carthaginian command.[88]

Throughout the Second Punic War, Carthaginian armies fielded contingents of Numidians, as well as a number of other races covered by the terms Libyans, Mauri, Gaetulians and Liby-Phoenicians. This reveals the patchwork nature of North Africa at this time. However, we must remember that we are looking at them through the eyes of the Romans and Greeks, who had little familiarity with these peoples at that time.

This leaves us with the initial question of just who the Numidians were. The name was that given to the region immediately to the west of the coastal region of Carthage. By the time of the Second Punic War, there appears to have been two main tribes of Numidians: the Masaesulii in the west and the Massyli in the east, both of which appeared to be tied to Carthage by alliance. We have no clear details on Carthaginian-Numidian hostilities prior to this period, but we can assume that at some previous date, Carthage had managed to assert their dominance over the tribes of the region, without annexing them. This would have been made all the easier given the hostility between the main Numidian tribes at the time.

The Numidians first come to our attention in 213, when the Masaesulian chieftain, named Syphax, began a revolt against Carthaginian overlordship. In response to this revolt the Carthaginians withdrew their commander in Spain, Hasdrubal, and a portion of their army, to deal with Syphax.[89] To the Romans fighting in Spain, under the command of the Scipio brothers (Publius and Cnaeus), the benefits of opening a second front against the Carthaginians in North Africa were immediately obvious. According to Livy the Scipios dispatched three centurions to Syphax to assess his needs and offer Roman friendship. Of the three, one of them, Q. Statorius remained with Syphax in order to raise and train his army in the art of Roman infantry tactics. This Roman-trained Masaesulian army then went on to defeat a Carthaginian force, whose size is not reported, in a set-piece battle.[90]

Carthage's response to this Roman-led army was to fall back upon the Masaesulian's traditional enemy, the Massyli. At the time the Massyli were ruled by a chief named Gala, who sent an army to join forces with the Carthaginian forces, led by his young son Masinissa, who was to figure prominently in later events. In the battle that followed Syphax and his Roman-trained army were comprehensively defeated by the Carthaginians and their Massylian allies. Livy lists Syphax's casualties at 30,000 dead, a figure which must be treated with the usual caution.[91] Appian reports that the Carthaginians were now able to send Hasdrubal back to Spain, along with a larger force than the one which had been withdrawn, along with Masinissa and his Massylians.[92] As Polybius reports, this result actually placed the Scipios in a worse position than they originally were before the revolt.[93]

However, in the longer term the Romans had been introduced to the concept of a strong African counterbalance to the Carthaginians. This concept, however, would not have been lost on the Numidian tribes either, who could now look outside of Africa for allies against Carthage.

Our knowledge of events in Africa following these events is obscured, due to our few surviving sources, but in 210 BC Syphax sent an embassy to Rome reminding them of his enmity to the Carthaginians.[94] What he was hoping to gain from this embassy Livy does not relate, but the most logical conclusion is that he was expecting some form of Roman help to regain his chiefdom. All he got in return was a Senatorial embassy which presented him with gifts of a purple toga and tunic, an ivory chair and an amount of gold. Given this turn of events, it is hardly surprising that when we next encounter Syphax, in 206 BC, we find him back in command of the Masaesulians and a firm Carthaginian ally. With Syphax defeated and cowed, the Carthaginians were able to secure their control of North Africa, aided by Roman indifference to the region.

However, following his victories in Spain, P. Cornelius Scipio turned his attention to North Africa. Naturally, any Roman invasion would have been greatly aided by having allies in the region. Thus once again, the Romans turned their attentions to the Numidians and in particular Syphax. After sending his legate C. Laelius to meet with Syphax, Scipio then apparently sailed to Africa himself. This bold move is given a dramatic twist in the sources, as he apparently arrived to meet Syphax at the same time as the Carthaginian commander, Hasdrubal. Livy puts this down to Hasdrubal retreating from Spain whilst Appian has him there seeking to secure Syphax's allegiance to Carthage. In both sources, this scenario ends with Scipio and Hasdrubal dining together at the same couch in the presence of Syphax, who then secretly pledges his allegiance to Rome.[95] Needless to say, we must take this story with a large pinch of salt. Nevertheless, it does demonstrate the importance that the Numidian tribes had taken on in the oncoming battle for Africa.

Given that the balance of the war had shifted considerably in Rome's favour by 206 BC, it was not surprising that Syphax had apparently agreed to side with Rome. However, with Scipio out of the way, Syphax soon reversed his allegiances and agreed an alliance with the Carthaginians, sealed by his marriage to the daughter of Hasdrubal. Why Syphax chose to ally with the Carthaginians over the Romans in the face of an impending Roman invasion of Africa is an interesting question, and one that was to have far reaching implications for the history of North Africa. It certainly proved to be a fatal miscalculation on the part of Syphax, as into this breach stepped the figure of Masinissa. According to Appian, Masinissa, who had been a loyal Carthaginian ally fighting for their cause in Spain, had been promised Hasdrubal's daughter in marriage and when he discovered that his enemy Syphax had been granted her, he then defected to the Romans.[96]

However, Appian's account of the Punic War is inferior to that of Livy, who presents us with a large digression on Numidian affairs.[97] Though he does not give us an exact dating of the events, the detail gives us a clear idea of the clouded world of Numidian affairs at this time. Central to this process was a succession crisis and civil war amongst Masinissa's tribe the Massyli, sparked off by the death of Masinissa's father Gala, and his own absence fighting in Spain. During the struggle Masinissa' main rival, Mazaetullus, sought refuge first with Carthage and then with Syphax, both of which naturally antagonized Masinissa.

Encouraged by Hasdrubal, Syphax declared war on Masinissa and it was probably now that the two agreed a marriage alliance. For Syphax, this war made perfect sense, given Carthaginian backing and a weakened enemy. For the Carthaginians, though, we must question whether African security was best guaranteed by an ongoing war between the tribes. We can only assume that they believed that the security of North Africa would best be served by one strong Numidian kingdom, securely allied to them, rather than the usual near constant state of war between the tribes. Ironically, it was the same policy that Rome was to use so effectively against them.

Syphax and Masinissa met in battle, with Masinissa being defeated and forced to flee to the mountains. Carthage's policy had appeared to pay off rich dividends, with Syphax easily gaining control of the Massyli and uniting all of Numidia under his rule. Masinissa was reduced to the status of a bandit, being chased by Syphax or the Carthaginians. As is usual in these cases, Livy reports a romanticized narrative involving dramatic chases, escapes and hiding in caves.[98] Following an undetermined period of time, Masinissa made a fresh attempt to reclaim his tribe, raised a new Massylian army and began attacking both Syphax and Carthaginian targets. Once again Masinissa and Syphax met in battle and once again Masinissa was defeated and forced to flee. This time, however, he fled to the Romans and offered Scipio his allegiance.

Upon the eve of the Roman invasion of Africa, the internal situation very much favoured the Carthaginians. The two main Numidian tribes had been united by Syphax who was now attached to the Carthaginians. How firm this attachment was is a matter of debate, considering that approaches had been made by both sides for Syphax to become a Roman ally once more. In the end though, they came to nought, and the Romans had to content themselves with having only Masinissa, an exiled prince with a small force of cavalry as African allies. Nevertheless, the Romans would have been hoping that he could be used as a figurehead to stir up revolt in the Massylians and undermine Syphax. The wider implications were that the balance of power in North Africa had been irrevocably disrupted. Constantly warring tribes had been replaced by a strong monarch uniting all of Numidia under his rule. In the short term this was ideal for the Carthaginians, in order to present a united force to resist the Roman invasion. In the longer term, it had the potential to backfire on them, over-turning a long-standing policy of keeping their North African enemies disunited and thus weakened.

As events turned out, it was Scipio and the Romans who determined the future of North Africa. The Roman invasion of Africa and their subsequent victories fall outside the scope of this work, having been covered in great detail in a number of other works, both on the Punic Wars and Scipio 'Africanus'.[99] For this study, it was the consequences that are far more important. Syphax having attached himself so firmly to the Carthaginian side, his defeat became one of Scipio's priorities, which was accomplished by a combined Romano-Massylian force led by Masinissa and C. Laelius. By the end of 203 BC Syphax had been defeated and Masinissa had not only retaken command of the Massyli, but also conquered Syphax's own tribe of the Maesuli, including the capital city of Cirta (modern Constantine). Syphax himself was wounded and taken prisoner and transported to Rome as a trophy, where he soon died, most probably of his injuries.[100]

It may seem strange to state that the Romans were not the true victors of the Second Punic War in Africa; after all, Scipio had defeated Hannibal at Zama and taken the title of 'Africanus'. Yet when the dust cleared the new power in North Africa was Masinissa and his newly-united kingdom of Numidia. Just fifteen years earlier, Masinissa's family had been the rulers of the Massyli tribe, sandwiched between the might of Carthage to the east and their traditional enemies the Masaesulians in the west. Yet the peace treaty that ended the

Second Punic War gave Masinissa an unparalleled position. Firstly, Carthage was forced to recognize his annexation of Syphax's kingdom and the de-facto creation of the kingdom of Numidia. Secondly, and more importantly, the Carthaginians were prevented from making war in Africa without express Roman consent and authorization. Thus for Carthage, not only had a new power been created on their borders, but they were prevented from defending themselves, and Masinissa knew it.

For Rome, the situation seemed ideal. Not only had Masinissa been a loyal ally in the African War, overlooking his earlier fighting against Rome in Spain (above), but a strong Numidia would be the perfect way of keeping Carthage in check in Africa. Following two Punic Wars the Romans had annexed Sicily, Sardinia, Corsica and coastal Spain, but had clearly no wish to annex Africa at this point. In truth Spain was probably considered to be a step too far for the Romans at this point, but could clearly not be allowed to fall back into Carthaginian hands. Thus, using the client kingdom of Numidia to keep Carthage in check seemed ideal.

The problem was whether the jailer was more dangerous than the prisoner. The Second Punic War had radically altered the situation in North Africa. Through the interventions of both main protagonists, instead of a patchwork of warring tribes, there was now a united Numidian kingdom, first under Syphax and then Masinissa. On the Carthaginian side, this was a matter of expediency, needing a united front in the face of a Roman invasion. The Romans, however, through their peace treaty, not only confirmed this change as permanent, but altered the balance in favour of Numidia. Blinded by the dangers of Carthage, they had laid the foundations for a potentially stronger North African power, something that they were slow to see.

The Rise of a New Power (Numidia 201–150 BC)

When examining the history of this period, there are few greater figures than that of Masinissa.[101] In just a few years he had gone from being a prince in a lesser Numidian tribe, and a Carthaginian vassal, to being the king of a united Numidia. Yet his story did not end there. He ruled Numidia for the next fifty years until his death in c.148 BC (aged over ninety), and spent his reign forging the disparate Numidian tribes into a powerful and united kingdom. By his death Numidia was the strongest kingdom in North Africa by far. We have no clear narrative of the next fifty years, but the fragments we do possess allow us to clearly follow his policies. For the rest of his reign it is clear what Masinissa's most cherished principal was total loyalty, or apparent total loyalty, to Rome and her interests. His success in following this policy can be seen by the high regard he is always held in when mentioned by the ancient (Roman) sources (see below).

The policies of his reign can be broken down into the duel principles of consolidation and expansion. In terms of consolidation, he was faced with unifying the various tribes which formed Numidia into one people under one king. The two biggest tribes, the Masaesuli and the Massyli had been traditional rivals and enemies. Furthermore, there were a number of smaller tribes and princedoms in the region that had to be brought under his control. Under his leadership, the Numidian economy grew, the few cities, such as his capital Cirta, developed, and trade flourished.

The clearest evidence we do have for Masinissa's activities stem from his foreign policy and his activities concerning Carthage. Rome clearly had in mind the creation of a strong Numidia to keep Carthage in check. Masinissa clearly had in mind the conquest and elimination of Carthage. From 201 to 151 BC, he pursued a consistently antagonistic policy towards the Carthaginians, yet did so in such a way that he would never incur Rome's wrath. His policy was one of steady encroachment, as Carthaginian territory was raided, their costal towns harassed and settlers placed upon their territories. In response all Carthage could do was appeal to Rome, as they could take no direct action against Masinissa without being considered in breach of the peace treaty with Rome, all of which Masinissa knew only too well.[102] Furthermore, he could be assured that his standing with the Romans, and the Scipios in particular, was high.

From time to time, the Senate was forced to answer Carthage's appeals and send a commission to investigate. Appian claims that the commissioners were told explicitly to favour Masinissa, but it is unlikely that this would have needed to be stated.[103] The first commission arrived as quickly as 193 BC and was headed by P. Cornelius Scipio 'Africanus' himself. Needless to say, the commission ruled in favour of the Numidians. Thus the tone was set for the next fifty years. Major border disputes flared up in 182, 174 and 162 BC. Each time a Roman commission ruled in Masinissa's favour. Slowly and surely therefore, Numidian territory advanced and Carthaginian territory shrunk.

Masinissa further proved his use as a Roman ally by providing them with both military assistance (elephants and cavalry) and grain from Numidia, to support their various wars of this period, both in Spain and Macedon.[104] He used his largesse to enter onto the wider Mediterranean stage with donations of grain to the island of Delos in the 160s, for which statues were raised in his honour.[105] He further established diplomatic links with Egypt, Bithynia and Rhodes and his son Mastanabal was admitted to the Panathenaean games in Greece.[106]

By the 150s, it appears that the Numidian raids into Carthaginian territory had increased in frequency, perhaps motivated by Masinissa's advancing age.

Though we cannot know for certain what his ultimate ambitions were, it would be surprising if they did not include the annexation of Carthage itself. This last step would require very careful planning if he was to avoid a breach with Rome. Nevertheless, one clear sign of this ambition was the development amongst the Carthaginian elite of a pro-Numidian faction, alongside pro-Roman and nationalist factions.

Although the chronology of events is confused in our surviving sources, it appears that by the late 150s the Numidians made a push into the Great Plains around Carthage, temporarily occupying a considerable part of them. As usual Roman Senatorial commissions were dispatched to arbitrate, in c.153 and again in 152. Both were particularly noteworthy. The commission of 153 BC included an aged M. Porcius Cato (the Elder) who, holding a traditional Roman prejudice, saw the situation as proof of a dangerous rise of Carthaginian power, rather than a Numidian one. This apparently led to Cato's now infamous statements whenever he was in the Senate that 'Carthage must be destroyed', though the surviving sources do not support the often (mis)quoted '*cathago delenda est*'.[107]

Obviously, the border raids and disputes continued, as in 152 BC another Senatorial commission arrived, this time including P. Cornelius Scipio Nasica. In a break from both Roman and Scipionic tradition he ruled in favour of Carthage. Furthermore, back in Rome, he attempted to counter Cato's influence by arguing for Carthage's preservation. We can only assume that unlike Cato, he saw through the stereotypes of noble ally and Punic villain and saw the real rising power in the region. This was followed in 151 by the final war reparation payment made by Carthage to Rome, which had two possible effects.

Firstly, it may have created the feeling amongst the Carthaginian elite that their obligation to Rome was now clear and that they were free of all ties (which included those of not going to war without Rome's authorization). Secondly, it may have created a similar feeling in Masinissa' mind that Carthage was no longer under Rome's protection, now the debt had been cleared. In any event it is indicative that within a year from the end of Carthage's war reparations, open warfare broke out between Numidia and Carthage.

The Numidian-Carthaginian War (151–150 BC)

When war did break out, the immediate cause was the pro-Numidian faction amongst the Carthaginian elite. Perhaps buoyed by clearing their obligations to Rome, the nationalist faction expelled the pro-Numidians amongst them from the city, which occurred c.152/151 BC. These men naturally went straight to Masinissa, who saw his chance to exploit the situation and demanded their reinstatement. What happens next is best described by Appian: Masinissa sent two of his sons, Gulassa and Micipsa to Carthage as envoys, who, after being turned away, were attacked by anti-Numidian elements in Carthage.[108] Though they survived, it gave Masinissa the perfect excuse for war and he laid siege to the town of Oroscopa. In response, the Carthaginians, having been harassed for decades by Masinissa and being denied the chance to retaliate, and now perhaps thinking themselves free of Rome, raised an army of 25,000 infantry and 400 cavalry and declared war on Masinissa. They were led by another Hasdrubal, who marched towards the Numidian positions, hoping to engage Masinissa in battle. Along the way they received a boost by the addition of 6,000 Numidian cavalry led by two Numidian chiefs, Asasis and Suba, who had fallen out with Masinissa' sons.

What followed was a battle between the Numidians, led by the aged Masinissa and the Carthaginians led by Hasdrubal. According to Appian, this battle had a special observer, as P. Cornelius Scipio Aemilianus (grandson of Africanus) had come to Numidia to procure elephants for the war in Spain. Appian states that the forces totalled 110,000 men, which places the Numidian forces at 80,000 men (which is clearly too high). The battle apparently ended with no clear winner and both sides entrenching.[109]

However, what could not be accomplished on the battlefield was accomplished during the stalemate as hunger and pestilence swept through the Carthaginian camp, destroying their army. Having no other option, Hasdrubal apparently agreed to peace terms. Interestingly, Masinissa's terms were another fifty years of war reparations (totalling 5,000 talents of silver), this time payable to him, as well as the return of the deserters and most probably the territories around the town of Emporium. With the deal apparently agreed, Hasdrubal then marched his survivors back to Carthage, when Gulassa, one of Masinissa's sons, attacked them with his cavalry. A massacre ensued, leading to the deaths of Hasdrubal and the survivors of the Carthaginian army. Appian puts the total Carthaginian losses at 58,000, which is surprising given the fact that they left Carthage with 25,400 and gained an additional 6,000.[110] Where the additional 27,000 men came from is never explained.

For Masinissa, despite the way it was obtained, his victory was total. Carthage's army had been destroyed, additional territory had been gained and Carthage was now beholden to him in terms of war reparations. Clearly, Carthage was now firmly in his sphere, not the Romans'. Carthaginian territory was now restricted to a coastal strip (which later became the Roman province of Africa) with Numidia dominating the plains of Libya. However, his victory was short-lived as events at Rome soon overtook him. As was usual in these cases, the majority of the Senate saw this war as proof of Carthage's renewed threat, not a Numidian one, and despite Scipio Nasica, the clamour to finish Carthage once and for all was too great. Whether the Carthaginian's had actually broken the 201 peace treaty now that they had paid off the war reparations is an interesting, but ultimately (especially for the Romans) irrelevant point. The Roman declaration of war and the destruction that followed must have been a blow to Masinissa and his plans.[111] As it happens he did not live to see the destruction of Carthage in 146 BC, by P. Cornelius Scipio Aemilianus, who took his grandfather's title of Africanus as reward for the slaughter that ensued. The city was destroyed with the survivors sold into slavery, though no salt was sown amongst the ruins, despite modern reports.[112]

Whilst the war has frequently been viewed from the Roman perspective, little thought has been given to that of Numidia. For Masinissa, the outcome of the war undid decades of work. The remaining Carthaginian territory was turned into a Roman province, establishing a permanent Roman presence in North Africa, controlling the Mediterranean trade routes. Although he did not live to see this, dying in c.148 BC, we can assume that he foresaw the outcome. In the end, the Romans did block his ultimate aims, but not through deliberate actions, but by the paranoia he had helped to stoke amongst the Roman elite.

Of the surviving obituaries, the following seem to encapsulate the man:

> Masinissa, the king of the Numidians in Africa, one of the best and most fortunate men of our time, reigned for over sixty years, enjoying excellent health and attaining great age, for he lived until ninety. He also excelled all his contemporaries in bodily strength, for when it was necessary to stand, he could stand in the same place for a whole day without shifting, and again, if he were seated, he never used to get up. And he could also continue to ride hard by night and day without feeling any the worse.
>
> At the age of ninety, the age at which he died, he left a son of four years old called Sthembanus, subsequently adopted by Micipses, besides nine other sons. Owing to the affectionate terms they were all on he kept his kingdom during his whole life free from all plots and from any taint of domestic discord.
>
> But his greatest and most godlike achievement was this. While Numidia had previously been a barren country thought to be naturally incapable of producing crops, he first and he alone proved that it was as capable as any other country of bearing all kinds of crops, by making for each of his sons a separate property of 10,000 plethra which produced all the crops.[113]

As Walsh points out this is somewhat of an exaggeration given the longstanding agricultural production that took place in this region.[114]

Masinissa achieved many brilliant military successes, for which, after the defeat of Carthage and the capture of Syphax, the possessor of a vast and powerful empire in Africa, he was rewarded by the Romans with a gift of all the cities and territories that he had taken in war. Consequently, Masinissa remained a loyal and true friend to Rome until his rule ended with his death.[115]

He had been a fortunate man in all respects. By divine favour he regained his ancestral kingdom that had been snatched from him by Syphax and the Carthaginian, and extended it greatly from Mauretania on the ocean as far inland as Cyrene. He brought a good deal of land under cultivation where Numidian tribes had lived on herbs for want of agricultural knowledge. He left a great sum of money in his treasury and a large and well disciplined army. Of his enemies he took Syphax prisoner with his own hand, and was a cause of the destruction of Carthage, having left it prey to the Romans, completely deprived of strength.[116]

The Roman Settlement of North Africa

Although the reasons for the Romans declaring war on Carthage and its subsequent destruction have been much commented on, less thought has been given to the decision to annex the remnants of the Carthaginian territory. Certainly the decision to annex Macedonia in 148 BC gives the action some consistency, but the two cases are different. Macedonia was a highly populated kingdom, with natural resources, which when utilized under an aggressive monarch was a power to be reckoned with. With the destruction of the city, the Carthaginian territory was a small coastal strip centred on the few remaining coastal towns and cities, the greatest of which was now Utica.

However, having reviewed Numidian history to date, we may see another reason in the Roman minds. If the Romans pulled out, the rest of North Africa would be annexed by Numidia, which had proven itself to be a powerful force in the region. Furthermore, Masinissa's death had removed Rome's staunchest ally in the region. At the back of Roman minds must have been the first inklings of the monster that they had created. His death had also given them a great opportunity to stop Numidia in its tracks. Upon his death Masinissa had made Scipio the executor of his will. This in itself is not surprising given the strong ties of friendship and clientage that existed between the Scipiones and Masinissa. It seems that there were to be three principal heirs: his sons Micipsa,

Gulassa and Mastanabal. Appian states that they were the only legitimate sons, but this is probably working back from the result rather than any notions of what constituted legitimate heirs in Numidian society

What Masinissa' exact instructions were and how far Scipio followed them is not clear. The *Periochae of Livy* states that Masinissa left his kingdom un-divided upon his death,[117] obviously fearing a return to the pre-Second Punic War situation. Both Appian and Zonaras detail Scipio's division of Numidia.[118] What emerges is a tripartite division of power over an apparently-united kingdom. According to Appian, Micipsa, as the eldest received the capital Cirta and the royal palace, Gulussa was placed in charge of Numidia's armies and Mastanabal was placed in charge of the judiciary.[119] Thus Scipio left Numidia with three joint rulers, each with their own sphere of influence: political, mili-tary and judicial. Again it is unfortunate that we do not have Polybius' views on this unusual inheritance.

How accurately Appian reported this division is open to question and we must wonder whether there was any territorial division to accompany it, especially given the events of 118 BC when Numidia was divided equally between three sons. In any event, it is clear that Numidian power was weakened under this tripartite agreement, a situation which suited Rome perfectly. With the creation of the Roman province of North Africa, Numidian power was reduced further.

The Monarch in the Shadows – The Reign of Micipsa (148–118 BC)

The only evidence we have for the triumvirate that ruled Numidia comes from Appian, who states that during the Third Punic War, the brothers were eager to offer material assistance to Rome's efforts but slow to come through on these promises, waiting to see what would happen.[120] It is at this point that Numidia disappears from our sources almost completely. Given the general paucity of our sources for Roman history in general in this period, especially those not centred on events in Rome, this is not surprising. Yet this period proved to be a highly important one for Numidia.

Central to this process is the shadowy figure of Micipsa, the eldest son of Masinissa. Upon his father's death he received either sole political power in Numidia as a whole, or a region of Numidia centred on Cirta.

What is clear is that either by 142 or 134 BC he was the sole ruler (political military and judicial) of all Numidia. On both occasions we have Roman appeals for military aid for wars in Spain. In 142 it is Appian who reports that the Roman commander, Q. Fabius Maximus Servilianus, requested Numidian elephants for his war in Spain (see Chapter 1) from Micipsa, though whether he did this because Micipsa was sole king or still the brother in charge of Numidian politics is unclear.[121] In 134 BC it was Scipio Aemilianus appealing for Numidian military aid, which was again duly dispatched, this time under the command of the Numidian prince Jugurtha, the son of Mastanabal who was dead by this point.[122] Thus we can date the deaths of Micipsa's brothers, who both died supposedly of natural causes, to between 148 and 134 (if not 142 BC).

Given the fratricidal nature of the Numidian royal family in the following period, we must ask ourselves how much of a coincidence it is that Micipsa' two brothers both conveniently died of disease, leaving him as sole ruler of a united Numidia. Reading between the lines, can we see the hand of fratricide here? In any event, whether by accident or design, the Roman plan of dividing power in Numidia, or dividing Numidia itself, had come to nought and for the next twenty years Micipsa ruled Numidia as its sole monarch. We know next to nothing about his reign, save that he again proved to be a staunch ally of Rome and the Scipiones in particular, sending a contingent of Numidian cavalry to fight for Rome at Numantia. We can assume that trade flourished under his rule, given the number of Italian merchants in Numidia during later events. He will also have benefited from the removal of the city of Carthage and perhaps from the resettlement of refugees from their territories.

The fragments of Diodorus preserve the only detailed character assessment of the man:

> Now Micipsa was the most civilised of all the Numidian kings, and lived much in the company of cultivated Greeks whom he had summoned to his court. He took a great interest in culture, especially philosophy, and waxed old both in the exercise of power and in the pursuit of wisdom.[123]

Towards the end of his life Micipsa was faced with the same problem that had faced his father, namely the succession. In addition to his own two sons, Adherbal and Hiempsal, he had also adopted the illegitimate son of his brother Mastanabal, named Jugurtha. Returning to the earlier Polybius obituary of Masinissa, if the Micipses mentioned is to be identified with Micipsa himself, then we do not know the fate of Sthembanus, as he certainly is not mentioned again. Furthermore, if this is the case, then it provides a precedent for Micipsa adopting other royal princes into his own immediate family (as was to happen with the Julio-Claudian Emperors of Rome). In any event, seeing little alternative, Micipsa made all three of his sons his joint heirs and apparently, as reported by Sallust, made Jugurtha swear to abide by his division and seek no conflict with his step brothers.

Whether he knew if this division would stand is an interesting question, especially given his own accession to the throne. Sallust's report of Micipsa's warning to Jugurtha does not necessarily have to be a purely dramatic device, given Jugurtha's age, undoubted military abilities and Roman contacts. Thus at his deathbed, it is entirely possible that Micipsa knew what lay ahead for his family and his kingdom.

Jugurtha

That Numidia was a formidable power in North Africa has now been established. Given Rome's belligerent attitude towards strong regional powers, a Numidian war has the air of inevitability about it. Yet, the timing and its nature centres upon the figure of Jugurtha and his actions during the Numidian Civil War (118–112 BC), which must be analysed. For these events we have an excellent source in the form of Sallust, writing some seventy years after the events he detailed (see Appendix V).

For later writers such as Florus, Jugurtha represents a new Hannibal, a stereotypical African prince who launched into a war against the Romans.[124] For Sallust, Jugurtha is far from the stereotypical oriental villain, but is entirely a Roman creation. In fact, Sallust wrote the whole Jugurthine War pamphlet to illustrate his point about Roman moral degeneration, and in Jugurtha he found the perfect Roman creation. Jugurtha was the son of Mastanabal, the third eldest son of Masinissa. He was not born a Numidian prince as his mother was a concubine, and as such we are told that he was excluded from Masinissa's will. We do not have a year of his birth, but given his age, he would have been born in the 150s. In 148 his father was made joint ruler of Numidia, with special responsibility for justice, if we are to believe Appian. However, within the decade, his father was dead, in mysterious circumstances, leaving his uncle Micipsa as sole king.

Nevertheless, Jugurtha remained a part of the extended Numidian royal family and was brought up in the royal court at Cirta along with the other young princes. An interesting anomaly is that Jugurtha appears to have been the eldest of the royal children, which given the fact that his father had two elder brothers seems somewhat odd. King Micipsa's own children were relatively young by the time of his death, meaning that they were probably not born until Micipsa acceded to the throne. Therefore despite his illegitimate birth and commoner status, he was the eldest royal son of the next generation (that we know of). This accident of birth was backed up by his personal qualities, as described by Sallust:

As soon as Jugurtha grew up, endowed as he was with physical strength, a handsome person, but above all with a vigorous intellect, he did not allow himself to be spoiled by luxury or idleness, but followed the custom of that nation, he rode, he threw the javelin, he contended with his kinsmen in foot-races; and although he surpassed them all in renown, he nevertheless won the love of them all. Besides this, he devoted much time to the chase, he was the first to strike down a lion and other wild beasts, and he distinguished himself greatly, but spoke little of his exploits.[125]

Thus we can see why Micipsa was so worried, as Jugurtha may not have been a prince by title, but acted like one and was held in high esteem by the Numidians. Although Jugurtha had made no overt moves on his crown, Micipsa was clearly worried about the succession, and acted upon events to remove a potential threat to his crown. As detailed in chapter one, in 135 BC Scipio Aemilianus was elected consul for the second time and placed in charge of Rome's war against Numantia (see Chapter 1). Given his close ties with Numidia, and his need to raise fresh forces, he naturally requested that the Numidians dispatch a military force to Spain. Micipsa readily agreed to this and chose to send Jugurtha as their commander. On the one hand it was a great honour for the young man, whilst on the other it not only removed him from Numidia, but placed him in what until now had been a hard-fought and at times disastrous war in Spain. Sallust explicitly states that this was Micipsa's reason for sending him.[126] However, as events tuned out, it was to be the making of Jugurtha, not the opposite:

In fact, he was both valiant in war and wise in counsel, a thing most difficult to achieve, for most often wisdom through caution leads to timorousness, and valour through boldness to rashness. Therefore Scipio relied upon Jugurtha for almost all difficult undertakings, treated him as a friend, and grew more and more attached to him every day, since the young Numidian failed neither in judgement nor in any enterprise. He had besides, a generous nature and ready wit, qualities by which he had bound many Romans to him in intimate friendship.[127]

Thus, it is safe to say that Micipsa's plan backfired spectacularly. He left Numidia as popular young prince, but returned as a battle-hardened commander, well trained in the Roman art of war and with a significant number of Roman contacts, from Scipio downwards. Upon Jugurtha's return to Numidia, Scipio apparently sent the following letter to Micipsa:

The valour of your Jugurtha in the Numantine war was most conspic-
uous; as I am sure you will be glad to learn. To us he is dear because of
his services, and we shall use our best efforts to make him beloved also
by the Senate and People of Rome. As your friend I congratulate you;
in him you have a hero worthy of yourself and his grandfather
Masinissa.[128]

If the letter is to be believed, certainly in tone, if not the actual words, then we
have some very interesting evidence. Certainly it is evident that Scipio had
befriended the young man, repeating their grandfathers. Nevertheless, it is also
clear that the Romans had found someone with whom, to use the casual expression, 'they could do business'. This is in contrast to the role of Micipsa himself,
who had few apparent direct dealings with the Romans and certainly never
appeared to have fought with them as Masinissa and Jugurtha had done. If the
Romans were worried about Numidia without Masinissa, as it appears they
were beginning to, then Jugurtha appeared to be the solution to their problem,
a thoroughly Romanized prince, who they knew and trusted.

To Micipsa, the implication was clear. Sallust states that Micipsa soon
adopted Jugurtha as a son, though later he contradicts himself and states that
this was only done between 121 and 118 BC.[129] One way out of this is the possibility that upon his return Micipsa made him a Numidian prince, reversing his
commoner status, without formally adopting him as a son. We know little of
events between Jugurtha's return and Micipsa's death, but Jugurtha's position
can only have increased with Micipsa's frailty. Sallust reports that for the last
five years of his life Micipsa was hardly of sound body or mind.[130]

By 121 BC, whatever his state of mind, Micipsa was faced with a dilemma.
His own sons were of age, but the clear figure to succeed him, both at home,
and more importantly in Rome, was Jugurtha. Rome had indicated some twenty
years before that Jugurtha was their preferred candidate and although we have
no explicit testimony, we must assume that this view was expressed in the intervening years. Faced with no other option, Micipsa formally adopted Jugurtha
as a son and made all three his joint heirs. Sallust reports that he held talks with
all three sons in an attempt to foster reconciliation and future harmony. In all
reality he probably knew that it was a lost cause, given the disparity between
birth and standing between Jugurtha and the other two.

The Numidian Civil War (118–112 BC)

Micipsa finally died in 118 BC, with three named heirs: Jugurtha, Adherbal and
Hiempsal. It is clear that Hiempsal and Jugurtha clearly did not get along well,

with Adherbal playing the peacemaker. Added to this potent mix was the absence of Rome. In 148, Scipio was on hand to act as executor and ensure that the three sons named as heirs cooperated in their inheritance. By 118 BC, Scipio was dead and it appears that the Romans left the Numidian princes to their own devices. Given the recent disturbances at Rome this was understandable, but in hindsight it was an error.

Coming to no comparable understanding, as apparently occurred in 148 BC, the three brothers agreed to physically divide the kingdom between them. Given the nature of the three men and the kingdom they inherited, a breach between them was not unexpected, nor long in coming. Prior to partitioning the kingdom the three agreed to partition the treasury first. En-route to the partition, the youngest brother Hiempsal stopped off in the town of Thirmida. Unfortunately for him, the governor of the town was a follower of Jugurtha. Notified of his arrival, Jugurtha arrived at night along with an armed retinue, gained entry into the house where Hiempsal was staying and murdered him.

This act plunged the country into a full-scale civil war, with cities and nobles lining up behind either Adherbal or Jugurtha, and with both sides raising armies. The two princes met in battle, and despite Adherbal having the larger army, he was defeated by the Roman-trained Jugurtha. Surviving the battle, Adherbal fled to the Roman province of Africa and then to Rome, to plead his case. Even without the close ties between Rome and Numidia it was natural that the Senate would render a judgement on this matter, as throughout the second century BC they had arbitrated on such issues across the Mediterranean, acting as an international court of arbitration and peacekeeper, rolled into one.

The escape of Adherbal placed Jugurtha in a dangerous position, as he must have hoped to have presented the Senate with a fait accompli, with him as the sole surviving ruler. Yet Adherbal was an unknown quantity to the Romans, whilst Jugurtha had many friends amongst the Roman aristocracy. Furthermore, he now had the whole resources of Numidia backing him. Given his contacts, knowledge of the Romans and financial resources, Jugurtha immediately sent envoys to Rome, to ensure that his ambassadors would have a favourable response amongst the Roman Senate, through a mixture of friendship and overt payment. On the day of the hearing in the Senate, Sallust reports that Adherbal gave a long emotional speech appealing to his father and grandfather's service to Rome. Jugurtha's envoys pointed out that Jugurtha had acted in the interests of Numidia, and that he himself had proved his loyalty to Rome on the battlefield of Numantia.[131]

In the end the Senate was split on the matter, but took the logical course, a division of Numidia between the two parties, without pursuing Jugurtha for his step brother's murder. Such a course suited Rome's interests in the region and once more divided Numidia, thus reducing her power and threat to Rome. For

Jugurtha, this was a setback, but one that he could live with for now. A Senatorial commission was dispatched to divide Numidia, with the western region going to Jugurtha and the eastern to Adherbal. Jugurtha received the bulk of the population and fertile regions, Adherbal the coastal cities. Despite Sallust's preoccupation with Jugurtha bribing every Roman senator he could, the commission came up with an even-handed division.[132] In fact, this division superficially returned Numidia to the situation it had been before Masinissa's time, with two, potentially antagonistic, regions (east and west). The obvious problem would be how long this settlement would hold. Both kings had met once on the battlefield and both had good cause to continue the war.

On the Roman side, the obvious question was whether they actually expected the settlement to hold. Given the circumstances, it appears to have been a forlorn hope. Yet, throughout the preceding century the Roman Senate had made such settlements before and they had always been honoured, with the threat of Roman armed force always being enough to ensure that whatever person or peoples involved adhered to them. Although Sallust attributed the breakdown of this settlement to Roman decline (moral and imperial), in reality Numidia represented something of a different case to the norm. For a start, Numidia had been a staunch Roman ally for over eighty years and had never been to war with Rome, let alone defeated. Secondly, Jugurtha knew the Roman elites well and this gave him greater confidence, some would say arrogance, when dealing with the Romans.

Once the Roman commission had left, Jugurtha drew up fresh plans for the annexation of Adherbal's kingdom. To deter Rome's wrath for breaching the agreement, he apparently planned to provoke Adherbal into declaring war on him, thus making him the victim of aggression. To these ends he sent raiding parties into eastern Numidia, destroying towns and seizing cattle. Adherbal, however, refused to be provoked, well remembering his previous military failure. Thus the situation continued for a number of years, until in 112 BC, the situation was so desperate for Adherbal that he had no option but to raise an army and meet Jugurtha in battle once more.

The two armies met near the city of Cirta, the old capital of a unified Numidia. Given the lateness of the day when the two armies met, battle was postponed until the following morning and both armies retired for the night. Once again Jugurtha proved his military superiority when he attacked Adherbal's army as they slept. The attack soon ended in the rout and destruction of Adherbal's army, with Adherbal himself fleeing once more, this time taking refuge in Cirta.[133] Jugurtha immediately laid siege to the city, which, as the one of the strongest in Numidia, resisted all his attempts to take it by storm. For Jugurtha, it was a question of time, as it soon became clear that Adherbal had once again been able to send envoys to Rome, apparently before the armies met. Thus Jugurtha could soon expect the arrival of another Senatorial commission and it would be better for him if they were presented with a fait accompli of Adherbal's death and Jugurtha as the ruler of Numidia. A further complication arose for him, however, in the presence of a sizeable population of Italian merchants in Cirta, who aided in the defence of the city. This would give the Romans a more tangible stake in the events.

When the envoys arrived, however, Jugurtha gave them no opportunity to speak to Adherbal, but assured them the fault lay with the other party and that he would soon send envoys to Rome to explain the matter. Apparently, he also promised to end the siege of Cirta. Amazingly the three-man commission accepted his word and left Africa to report the matter to the Senate, without waiting for the siege to be lifted. It is hard to credit their actions without the shadow of bribery being raised. With the commission returning to Rome to make their report, Jugurtha continued his siege of Cirta. Unfortunately for him, Adherbal had two of his men slip through the siege and take a letter to the Senate, which laid out the situation in full, revealing Jugurtha's duplicity.

Although some advocated sending a military force to aid Adherbal, the Senate could only agree to the sending of a further Senatorial commission to Jugurtha, this time led by M. Aemilius Scaurus, the Princeps Senatus.[134] Sallust explains this action by returning to the theme of Jugurtha' bribery of the Senate, though in reality there can have been little appetite for involving themselves in a Numidian civil war, especially given the situation in Illyria and Macedon (see Chapter 3).

Nevertheless, the urgency with which the Senate viewed the matter can be seen by the fact that the commission left Rome for Africa in just three days and once there immediately summoned Jugurtha to Utica, the de-facto capital city of Rome's African province.[135] Despite Sallust, we do not know exactly what the Commission said, but Sallust states that 'terrible threats were made in the name of the Senate.'[136] From this it must be the case that the commission ordered Jugurtha to end the siege of Cirta, return to his own kingdom and abide by the earlier Roman settlement.

For Jugurtha, this was the moment of truth. Agreeing to the Roman demand would overturn the last year's successes and leave him with just Western Numidia. To continue the siege would be to directly disobey a command from the Senate. For Jugurtha the crucial calculation must have been whether Rome would go to war with him. With Adherbal dead there was no other clear rival to the Numidian throne, so would Rome replace him? It was at this point that events took an unusual turn. Despite holding off the siege for a number of months (at least four), the inhabitants of Cirta, including Adherbal himself, surrendered to Jugurtha. Sallust attributes this to the Italian community living in Cirta who believed that Jugurtha would adhere to the orders of the Senate.[137]

Whether this was a spontaneous action or whether Jugurtha made overtures to
Adherbal and the Italians is not reported. What followed next sealed the issue.
Jugurtha took Adherbal captive and had him tortured to death. Furthermore,
an apparent massacre took place in Cirta, with the primary victims being the
Italian trading community.[138]

At first such a provocative act seems difficult to understand. Not only did
Jugurtha disobey a direct Senatorial command, but apparently slaughtered the
Italians living in Cirta. Yet although Sallust states that this was done on
Jugurtha's command, we have to question this.[139] Killing Adherbal made
perfect strategic sense. The Senate had never fully supported him anyway and
his death created the fait accompli of there being only one Numidian heir of
Micipsa left, and one who had himself fought in Rome's cause. Yet the
massacre of the traders seems to be a blatant act of provocation or a very casual
attitude to Roman sensibilities.

Here a parallel is useful. In 88 BC when the Pontic King Mithridates VI
invaded the Roman province of Asia, he ordered a massacre of the Italian
traders, which was enthusiastically undertaken by the locals, despite their
inhabiting a Roman province for the past fifty years. Was the massacre undertaken on Jugurtha's orders or a spontaneous act by the locals? Given that the
Italians had been the most belligerent group, thus ensuring a long siege, with all
the suffering that must have engendered, added to the natural dislike that such
a group of privileged traders must have stirred up in any case, it would not be
surprising that they were unpopular. Furthermore, we must question just how
popular a group they would have been without the Senators themselves.

In any event, the massacre took place and Jugurtha, now sole king of a
unified Numidia had to wait upon Rome's reaction, which surprisingly was
mixed. Sallust reports that despite this massacre, the Senate was still reticent
about declaring war on Numidia, which he again assigns to Jugurtha's
bribery.[140] In all fairness, the Senate's options were limited. Jugurtha had been
a staunch Roman ally of old and the massacre had taken place during a civil war
siege, and frankly Adherbal was less known and had fewer contacts amongst the
elites of Rome. Furthermore, Numidia was a vast and wild country about which
the Romans knew little and had never operated in militarily since the days of
Scipio Africanus. Such a war was not especially attractive and would have
required a fresh levy of men for fighting overseas, with all the problems that
came with that. Furthermore, it was clear that a barbarian migration was
underway in Europe and having an army across the Mediterranean operating in
the North African interior was not the best form of defence.

In any event, once again, the crucial decision was taken away from the
Senate, and here we must look to the other two constituent elements in Roman
politics in this period: the equestrian order and the people. For the equestrian

order, recently brought into Roman politics by C. Gracchus, the massacre at Cirta was of men from their own order and struck at their business interests in Africa. Thus they had the two motives of revenge and the opportunity offered by a successful settlement of any war. As for the people, we are told that one of the tribunes, C. Memmius, ran a successful anti-senatorial campaign, demanding revenge on Jugurtha for the massacre and stating that the 'greedy' aristocracy were all in the pocket of a corrupt African prince. For an urban populace still smarting from the murder of C. Gracchus and his followers by the Senate, such a view hit home.

Thus the Senate found themselves, ironically like Jugurtha, pushed towards a war they did not want.[141] In the end the Senate came to a compromise and allocated the two consular provinces for 111 BC as Italy and Africa.[142] From such an inauspicious start came the war which was to determine the dominant power in North Africa.

Summary

What are we to make of the outbreak of the Jugurthine War? Taken from a long-term perspective, a clash between Rome and Numidia for dominance of North Africa seems inevitable. Although a unified Numidia had been created by Syphax and the Carthaginians, it was the Romans and Masinissa who ensured its survival and prosperity. As seen above, Numidia had been created to keep Carthage in check and had done such a good job of it that within Masinissa's lifetime, Numidia had become the dominant power of the North African region. It is clear to us that Rome had created a monster, which after the fall of Carthage had now outlived its original purpose. Furthermore, Numidia now became a powerful kingdom bordering Roman territory. Although this is clear to us, it is unclear how the Romans at the time saw this, though Scipio Aemilianus' division of Numidia coming so soon after the Roman attack on Carthage perhaps indicates that the Romans realized that they no longer needed a unified and powerful Numidia. Yet on two occasions a divided Numidia inevitably fell into the hands of a single ruler. Thus, taken from this perspective, war between the two powers does seem inevitable at some stage.

On the other had though, this inevitability is contrasted by the strenuous efforts made by both parties (Jugurtha and the Senate) to avoid a war on this occasion. Furthermore, Rome declared war on Jugurtha on a very flimsy set of circumstances, the defiance of their order to settle the civil war by negotiation and the massacre of a number of traders who had gotten themselves entangled in a siege. Many have argued that this was nothing more than a pretext and that the Senate saw their chance to reign in the new sole king of a unified Numidia, others that Jugurtha's actions were a direct challenge to Roman authority and implied supremacy in the Mediterranean. In point of fact, though, given the other events taking place, both at Rome and in their empire, both of the above points of view seem to flounder on the fact that Rome really had more pressing issues on their mind at the time and could ill afford a war in North Africa against their oldest ally in the region and it's strongest power.

In many ways the only satisfactory explanation is to discard theories of inevitability or vague challenges to Roman authority and see the war as resulting from events and pressures outside of the main players' control. It is unlikely that Jugurtha wanted a massacre of the Italian traders or that the Senate would view it as an unforgivable act.

As we have seen, in Rome, the Senate's once-unassailable grip on issues of foreign policy had been undermined by the tribunes (either on their own initiative or working for others). In this case, whilst the Senate probably did not wish for war with Jugurtha, the matter was taken out of their hands and public outrage (real or whipped-up) ultimately had to be appeased.

However, just because the Senate declared war on Jugurtha did not mean that they intended it to be a war of conquest or even one which would involve large-scale fighting, nor resemble in any form the war that actually took place. In the public eye Jugurtha had challenged Rome's authority and murdered (however unintentionally) its citizens (though whether they actually had Roman citizenship is another question). Thus the Senate had to act, or at least be seen to act, and be seen to bring Jugurtha back in line. From such an innocuous start came a war that was to determine the future of the North African continent and one that was to have dramatic effects on the shape of Roman politics.

Chapter 3

The Northern Wars:
The Threat from the North (120–111BC)

However, before we can analyse the early phase of the Jugurthine War, we must first take a step back, in order to see how this war interconnects with the other events occurring in the Roman and non-Roman worlds (something that Sallust fails to do). In fact the survival of Sallust's monograph on the war and the loss of a continuous narrative history such as Livy's, can, if we are not careful, give us a dangerously one-sided approach to the period. In order to understand Rome's reticence about engaging in a war in North Africa and their seemingly lacklustre early efforts, we must investigate the other concerns that were facing the Senate at the time.

The Lack of Sources

As mentioned earlier, the period of history we are covering suffers from a lack of surviving sources, especially in matters of foreign affairs. This is doubly the case when dealing with Rome's Northern Wars in this period where, for great periods, we are reduced to scraps of information from the annalists, with barely more than names of generals and the peoples they fought, and sometimes not even that. For the last phase of the war, we are better informed, thanks to Plutarch's biography of Marius, though this brings it own problems (see appendix five for a full analysis of the sources available).

This dearth of information is contrasted with the survival of Sallust's monograph on the Jugurthine Wars, which, from a historian's point of view, can create a one-sided view of the period. Thus we have wars in at least three major theatres of operation in this period – the North East (Macedon and Illyria), the North West (Gaul and Spain) and the South (Africa) – yet we only have a detailed narrative of one of them. However, any analysis of the importance of these areas of conflict should not be dependant on which one has sources available and which do not.

For the Northern Wars, we have an additional problem. As well as a lack of

detailed campaign or battle narratives, we lack an understanding of the enemy
that Rome faced. Although we have no Numidian sources, we can still try to
construct an analysis for the war from the Jugurthine and Numidian perspectives, balancing out that of Rome's. However, for the enemies that Rome faced
in this period, there are almost no details which allow such a reconstruction.
Thus the easiest course of action is to reduce them to the status of a faceless and
anonymous enemy, and merely judge the war from Rome's point of view, a
course of action that we must try to avoid at all costs. Even using the term
'barbarian' is a dangerous one as it homogenizes a number of different peoples
and races, and thus tactics and motives. This will be seen most clearly in the
wars of the northwest when Rome faced a multitude of different races, most
notably the Cimbri, Teutones, Ambrones and Tigurini. Nevertheless, these
limitations and problems should not act as a deterrent for what is a crucial
period of Roman military history.

Rome's Northern Borders

When examining the detail of Rome's territories in this period, there is marked
difference between how neat and clinical they appear on a map and the reality
of the situation on the ground. During the period of the Roman Empire,
Rome's northern borders had a far greater rigidity to them, with geographical
boundaries such as the Channel (and eventually Hadrian's Wall), the Rhine and
the Danube. In this period of the Republic, however, there were no such fixed
barriers; even the Alps and Pyrenees, although natural barriers, did not neatly
correspond with areas of Roman control, as we shall see below. For the
purposes of clarity we can split Rome's 'northern borders' into two distinct
regions, the northeast and northwest, as they represent two different situations
and two different theatres of war.

Rome's empire at this time was a disjointed affair, and in particular had no
firm borders. As such, provincial boundaries were flexible, especially where it
came to the Roman/non-Roman border. Furthermore, aside from Rome's
newly-acquired Gallic sphere of influence, all that lay to the north of Spain,
Italy, Illyria and Macedonia was open barbarian territory. Here lay the vastness
of the European continent, populated by a large and ever-changing array of
native tribes, most of whom are only names to us now.

Furthermore, there was never an easy or clear-cut differentiation between
Roman and non-Roman regions, on either a political or cultural scale. An area
under Roman control contained peoples who had strong links with those
not under Roman control.

In addition, there is the issue of alliances between Rome and those tribes not under their control. In most case these were nothing more than statements of friendship between the two, but as was seen in the case of the Cimbric migration below, these alliances allowed Rome to create buffer zones around their areas of formal imperium. This could have benefits as well as drawbacks. On the positive side, Rome would be alerted to any impending threat, long before it actually reached Roman territory, as happened in the case of the Cimbri. The only potential drawback with this system was that if they were not careful, Rome could get drawn into affairs that did not directly need its intervention, though these appear to have been few in number.

The Northern Wars – The Northeast

In annexing Illyria and then Macedon and Epirus, Rome acquired a huge exposure to 'barbarian' or tribal Europe, with few natural barriers between what was Roman and non-Roman and a large number of peoples within the Roman sphere but by no means Romanized. The Kingdom of Macedon itself had always had an ill-defined northern border and was prone to periodic raids and the occasional full-scale barbarian invasion (as seen by the Gallic invasions of the 280/279). In turning the kingdom into a province the Senate now had the problem of not only governing Macedon itself, but defending it from the barbarian tribes who did not respect Roman territorial boundaries. In effect this led to an almost constant period of warfare (whether on large or small scale) until Augustus took the north-eastern border up to the Danube, which in itself created new problems. The two decades in question (120–100 BC) were a period of intense military activity in this region.

The Illyrian Wars of 119–117 BC

As mentioned in Chapter 1, the Romans had already experienced their fair share of victories and defeats in Illyria in the 130s and early 120s. Yet in 119 BC it appears that once again Rome had to send forces to the region to quell rebellious native tribes. Our sources for these campaigns are few and unclear. Nevertheless, one clear campaign that we can identify was that of L. Caecilius Metellus, one of the consuls of 119 BC, who hailed from one of Rome's leading families (see Appendix IV).

Our sources report that Metellus fought a Dalmatian tribe in Illyria, and came back to Rome in 117 BC to celebrate a triumph, after which he earned the name 'Delmaticus' to celebrate his victory. He also restored the Temple of Castor and Pollux in the Forum, part of which can still be seen today. As for the war itself we have only four references, two of which are simple single-line entries in the surviving annals. The first of these comes from an abridgement of Livy stating that he subdued the Dalmatians.[143] The second comes from Eutropius who states that both the consuls of 119 campaigned in Illyria against the Dalmatians.[144] The third source is Appian, from the surviving fragments of his work on the Illyrian Wars, who is less than complementary about Metellus' campaign:

> in the consulship of Caecilius Metellus, war was declared against the Dalmatians, although they had been guilty of no offence, because he desired a triumph. They received him as a friend and he wintered among them at the town of Salona, after which he returned to Rome and was awarded a triumph.[145]

It is possible that Appian, writing several hundred years after the event, was using a source hostile to Metellus, though such actions can never be entirely ruled out. The scale of the war in Illyria is given greater scope by Appian, who slightly earlier in his narrative, stated that both Metellus 'Delmaticus' and his consular colleague, L. Aurelius Cotta, campaigned together against the Illyrian tribe of the Segestani. Morgan has an excellent analysis of the campaign and the sources.[146]

Thus, from these scattered fragments, it appears that both the consuls of 119 BC were sent to subdue rebellious tribes in Illyria, with Cotta returning (most probably to hold the consular elections for 118 BC) and Metellus staying to fight the Dalmatians as well. The potential scale of the war can be seen from the need to have both consuls fighting there and the fact that there were two major tribes involved in the fighting. Though we are denied any details about the war itself, it does seem to have been a serious affair and a threat to Rome's interests, albeit one that they successfully dealt with.

The Scordiscian Wars I (c.120–111 BC)

As we have already seen, one of the greatest threats the Romans faced on their northeastern borders came from the Balkan tribes of the Scordisci. From the initial encounter in the 140s BC they were to be one of Rome's most persistent enemies in the Balkan region, not being finally defeated until the reign of the Emperor Augustus (c.15 BC).[147] Much of the information we have on them is both fragmentary and contradictory. There was no clear Romano-Greek concept of what ethnic group the Scordisci were. Strabo, Justin, the *Periochae of Livy* and Athenaeus all labelled them as Gauls; Appian named them as Illyrians and Florus as Thracians.[148]

Those who labelled them as Gauls had them originating as the survivors of the great Gallic invasion of Greece in 279 BC, which sacked the Temple of Delphi.[149] Again we see the Romano-Greek obsession with Gauls, fostered in Rome by the Gallic sack of c390–386 BC and in Greece of the invasions of 280–279 BC, as well as their lack of understanding of the tribal regions of Europe.[150] The best modem analysis of them is by Papazoglu, in his work on the early Balkan tribes (see bibliography).

Whatever their origins they were a powerful collection of tribes based on the Ister (Danube) in modern Serbia. Strabo divided them up into two main tribes, the Greater and the Lesser Scordisci, but again we have no way of telling how accurate a picture this was.[151] What is clear is that they were clearly an expansionist tribe dominating the lower Danubian region. Again we have no clear idea of the process this took, but it is argued that they expanded both north and south from the Danube, dominating the tribes around them. This inevitably brought their sphere of influence to the borders of Macedon, which in 148 BC became Roman. It is interesting to note how quickly they clashed with the Romans following their annexation of Macedon, with our earliest reference being to a Roman defeat at their hands in 141 BC, which was possibly a catastrophic one, though we have no clear details.[152] By 135, we find the Romans with the upper hand, operating outside the borders of Macedon and inflicting a defeat on them, with the sources then going silent on the matter.

However, this peace was broken in the period around 120 BC when we find traces of a massive Scordiscian invasion of Macedon. The primary piece if evidence we have for this lies in an inscription which details the defeat and death of the governor of Macedon, Sex. Pompeius, at the hands of 'Gauls'. This is backed up somewhat uncertainly by a fragment of Diodorus.[153] The inscription comes from a commemorative stele set up in the town of Lete (in Macedonia) thanks to the victorious Roman commander M. Annius and contains details of the campaign. The stele is dated in the twenty-ninth year of the Romano-Macedonian era, which is most commonly agreed amongst scholars to equate to 120/119 BC.[154]

The inscription gives us the basic details of the campaign, with a large tribal army invading the province of Macedonia. Naturally the governor, a Roman praetor named Sex. Pompeius met them in battle, but was killed and his men routed. They were rallied by the presence or arrival (this is not made clear) of Pompeius' quaestor, M. Annius, who then led the Roman forces to victory, routing the invading tribe. Annius then moved forward towards the boundary of the province, where after several days he met another tribal force, re-enforced by a Thracian tribe, named as the Maedi, led by their chieftain Tipas, and was again victorious. It is difficult to estimate the size of the force opposing him, but given his ability to defeat two tribal forces with relatively few men, we must be careful not to overestimate the strength of the enemy forces. Despite the stele of admiration for Annius, it is possible that these were no larger than raiding parties, rather than a full-scale tribal invasion.

Unfortunately, there is a gap in our sources for events in Macedon between these battles in 119 and those of 114 BC. One view to take is that these Roman victories saw the Scordisci withdraw back to their own territory only to invade once more in 114 BC. However, it is has been argued that one of the consuls of 116, Q. Fabius Maximus Eburnus, fought a series of campaigns in Macedon in 115–114 BC and that the most likely opponents were the Scordisci.[155] This puts an entirely different complexion on matters and argues for a long-running war or series of clashes from 120 onwards, with little respite for Rome. Once again, we see that in this period Rome's military attention was in the northeast, not elsewhere.

By 114 we hear of the dispatch of another consul, C. Porcius Cato, to battle the Scordisci. Once again our sources for the campaign are meagre, but what emerges is that an unnamed battle, either in Macedonia or Thrace, took place between Cato and the Scordisci which ended with the utter defeat and destruction of the Roman army.[156] Cato survived and returned to Rome, where he was prosecuted and disgraced. We have no details of the size of the forces involved or the Roman casualties. For Rome, the consequences were grave, as with no force to oppose them, the Scordisci rampaged throughout Greece, apparently reaching as far as the Adriatic and sacking the temple at Delphi.[157] The fear at Rome was such that they engaged in a traditional human sacrifice and had two Greeks and two Celts buried alive in the Forum Boarum.[158] Though the sources are confused, it does appear that a Roman commander, M. Didius managed to defeat the Scordisci and drive them, at least temporarily from Macedon.[159]

The situation became graver for Rome when they received the news from their new allies in the northeastern Alps, the Taurisci (see below), that a large northern tribe, the Cimbri, was migrating towards them. For the consuls of 113 BC, civil war in Numidia was of little importance. On two fronts now Rome's northern borders were under threat. Macedon and Greece had been invaded and ravaged by the Scordisci, whilst to the west, the Cimbri were approaching Roman-allied territory. The two consuls of the year were C. Caecilius Metellus and Cn. Papirius Carbo; Metellus received the command against the Scordisci and Carbo was sent to investigate the arrival of the Cimbri.

For Metellus' campaign we have no details other than a brief note that in 111 BC he was awarded a triumph for his activities in Thrace.[160] His triumph was held on the same day as that of his brother (see Appendix IV) and it is again possible that this triumph was awarded more for political than military reasons.

Other than his triumph we have no records of his activities, but given the work done by his successors in Thrace, we must conclude that there was no major confrontation between his army and the Scordisci. It is possible that he ensured that they were chased from the Roman provinces, but again this is speculation. It has also been argued that the arrival in the region of the migrating Cimbri led the Scordisci to evacuate Roman territory of their own accord in order to face up to this new threat to the north, though there is no direct evidence for this.[161]

It is unclear whether C. Caecilius Metellus retained command of the war for the year 112 BC. Certainly he did not return to Rome to celebrate his triumph until 111, but we know that one of the consuls of 112, M. Livius Drusus, arrived in Macedon and pursued the war against the Scordisci.[162] In fact, we hear nothing about Metellus' activities at all this year. What is clear is that Drusus had far greater success than Metellus:

> Didius, finding them wandering about and dispersed in undisciplined plundering, drove them back into their own land of Thrace. Drusus forced them further still and prevented them from re-crossing the Danube.[163]
>
> Marcus Didius, with great determination, checked these tribes that before had been always invincible and were roaming about without civilization or laws. Drusus confined them within their own bounds.[164]

Despite the omission of Metellus, it seems that Didius checked them in Macedon and Drusus took the fight to them over the border in the non-Roman Balkan region, defeating them and temporarily ending the conflict. Drusus returned to Rome to celebrate a triumph for his activities in 110 BC. It has been argued that Drusus did not actually reach the Danube, which was not done until decades later.[165] Of additional interest is the actual triumph that Drusus celebrated, as it is recorded as being over both the Scordisci and the Macedonians. This latter element has led to speculation that once again a revolt broke out in Macedon against Roman rule, brought about by the Scordiscian invasion, possibly with the two groups allying. Though we have no other details it appears that it was soon crushed. This merely serves to emphasize the possible crisis that Rome faced on its northern borders in this period.

The Northern Wars – The Northwest

Rome's northwestern borders were of a different nature to those of the north-east. In the east Rome held Illyria and Macedon and shared a huge land border with the tribal regions of Europe. In the west, until recently, Rome had formally held nothing on the other side of the Alps and Pyrenees. As noted earlier, the victories in the Gallic War in the 120s gave Rome hegemony over the tribes of southern Gaul. This was reinforced by the creation of the colony of Narbo in 118.[166] This led to the embryonic province of Gallia Narbonensis, but was more of a buffer zone than a Roman province.

Furthermore, whilst Rome had had no formal holding on the far side of the Alps, they had created a series of informal relationships with the various tribes that dwelt within the Alpine region, some established by force and some by diplomacy (backed up by the threat of force). As mentioned above, it was this informal system that alerted the Romans to the impending arrival of the Cimbri in the region. In 115 BC the consul M. Aemilius Scaurus advanced across the Istrian Alps and gained the submission of the local tribe, the Taurisci, an action that was to have important repercussions soon afterwards.[167]

The Cimbric Wars I

The initial problem we face in analysing the early phase of the war is working out the nature of the enemy that Rome was facing. Strabo and the *Periochae of Livy* both state that the migrating tribe was the Cimbri, whilst Appian (whose Gallic War fragment is the largest account of this initial encounter) has them as Teutones. Velleius neatly side-steps the issue by having both tribes present.[168] The problem we face is that until the campaigns of 102–101 BC, the sources do not separate the various tribes. There are two clear possibilities, each equally as valid.

The first view is the view that the three identifiable tribal groups (the Cimbri, Teutones and Ambrones) all migrated at the same time and were one mass and were referred to by one tribal name simply for matters of expediency or ignorance by our sources. The second view is that at this stage, there was only one tribe or people (the Cimbri) who entered the region at this time, and that the others followed later (in the late 100s BC). As will be detailed below, part of this discussion centres on whether it was a whole tribal migration or merely some of the tribes and peoples of the Cimbri. It is possible that, rather than being one event, this tribal migration may have happened over a successive number of years, with certain tribes going one direction and others in another direction. If one tribe found a hospitable region then they may have sent word to those left behind or heading in other directions to draw them to them. Whilst ultimately there is simply insufficient evidence to form a definitive conclusion, the analysis of the events of 104 BC (see Chapter 9), do lend themselves to the theory that the other tribes (of Teutones and Ambrones) did only enter the picture to assist the Cimbric invasion of Italy. For that reason the author prefers the view that at this point it was merely the Cimbri that Rome dealt with and will be solely refered to as such.

The Origins of the Cimbri

The next issues we need to address concern the identity of the Cimbri and their reasons for migrating. Their appearance in 113 BC is the first time they can be found in the surviving historical records, unlike their allies the Teutones, who can be found in the works of the explorer Pytheas.[169] A number of ancient sources who comment on them come up with a number of different possible backgrounds for them.

Plutarch and Strabo present the fullest surviving discussions on the origins of these tribes, though we know of others that existed, such as Poseidonius (see Appendix V). Plutarch argues that they were Germanic, though he acknowledges that others gave them Gallic or even Scythian origin.[170]

The key problem here for our ancient sources was their lack of knowledge concerning both the geography and ethnicity of the tribes of Europe. In the period in question, Rome had penetrated no further north than southern Gaul and had no direct contact with any peoples of the outer-lying regions, other than trade via middle parties. By the time of the Empire, the Romans had penetrated and annexed all of Gaul, Britannia and for a while Germany, thereby gaining greater knowledge of the races that occupied these regions. Therefore, we have accounts written at the time, based on a scant knowledge and those written later with a greater understanding of the geography and ethnicity involved. Furthermore, the Romans had a tendency to see all races of the north as Gauls, certainly the ones who raided southwards. Both the Greeks and the Romans had suffered previously at the hands of Gallic invasions; Rome had been sacked in c.390–386 and Greece had suffered an invasion in 280–279, which resulted in a fresh battle at Thermopylae and an attack on Delphi. Thus for both the Greeks and Romans any such northern invaders summoned up memories of the Gauls and thus all invaders became Gauls.

An added problem is that when Rome did extend their dominion to include Northern Europe, they tended to introduce an artificial boundary between Gallic and Germanic based on the Rhine, but this was an artificial separation not based on any corresponding ethnic boundaries, and the problem with this is that what constitutes a Germanic tribe in the late first century BC and what we more commonly understand as a Germanic tribe of the later Empire and Dark Ages is another matter.

Finding no certainty in our narrative sources, we have to turn to wider fields, such as archaeology, linguistics and ethnography, which have analysed this problem for several centuries. Recently, Faux has produced some excellent compilations of the evidence to date, which all points to the Cimbri being a Celtic tribe, based on their similarities to known Celtic races.[171]

Their history before their encounter with the Romans is another matter and upon that there is no consensus. Some theories, based on accounts found in both Plutarch and Strabo, argue that they were a Gallo-Scythian race and connect them to the Cimmerians as found in Homer and Herodotus,[172] others that they were the survivors of the Gallic attack on Greece in 280–279 who fled north.[173] A more widely-argued theory is that they were part of the main Celtic movement of peoples and that this branch occupied the Jutland Peninsula (modern Denmark) somewhere in the region of the fifth or fourth century BC. Ultimately, it is an argument that will never be solved.

The Cimbric Migration (c.120–113)

As well as the various theories surrounding their origin, we also have to analyse why they moved south en masse and what their aims were. Given the size of the varying estimates of their numbers, 200,000 to 300,000, this was clearly a great migration.[174] The reason most often stated in the sources is one of tribal migration caused by disastrous natural causes, namely rising sea levels. Although Strabo dismisses this theory, arguing that sea levels could not rise unpredictably (based on his limited experience of the Mediterranean), there is some geological evidence to support this. One key problem to this theory, however, is the fact that in Strabo's day, the Cimbri were still to be found living in that region.[175] If the Cimbri were driven from their traditional homes by a natural catastrophe, then what were they still doing there in Augustus' time?

One factor that might help us understand this problem comes from the fact that we regularly talk of the Cimbri as though they were a single homogenous entity. From the descriptions of the battles that take place later in this period (101 BC, see Chapter 10), the sources name a number of different Cimbric chieftains or kings. The most logical explanation for this is that the Cimbri were not one tribe of several hundred thousand, but were a collection of differing tribes of the Cimbric peoples. Thus it seems that a number of the Cimbric tribes migrated from their homeland, either due to rising tide levels or some unknown reason, such as inter-tribal warfare, but a number of the tribes stayed in the region. It is also possible that population growth and overcrowding could have sparked off a mass migration, especially given an earlier example of this, found in Livy from the sixth century.[176]

It is also possible that the tribes that left acted as pathfinders for the whole race and would have summoned their brethren who remained behind once they had secured a new homeland. As they were ultimately defeated, this summons never came and so there were a number of tribes that remained and managed to cope in their old land as best as possible. If this whole migration was caused by rising sea levels or other pressure on natural resources, then the removal of such a large number would have eased the problems and made life more bearable for the remaining tribes.

We do not know when the Cimbric tribes began their migration, but it would have taken them a number of years to move southwards. Strabo preserves details of the route they took, southwards down towards and across the Danube.[177] It has been postulated that the route they chose, which looks unusual to modern eyes, was based on the amber trading routes of tribal Europe.[178] Strabo goes on to say that the Cimbric tribes encountered the Boiii, then the Scordisci, the Teuristae and finally the Taurisci, thus southwards to the Danube and then westwards towards the Alps. Unfortunately, for them, they encountered a hostile reception wherever they went. This is not surprising given that the appearance of several hundred thousand rival tribesmen and women would have gravely alarmed any inhabitants, fearful both of hostile intentions and having to share their resources with such a host. Ultimately, such defeats drove them towards the Alps and they entered the region of Noricum, home to the Taurisci.

As detailed above, the Taurisci were allied to Rome and in this case proved to be highly effective as an early warning system, as they were able to alert Rome to the advance of the Cimbri and request assistance. Not only would the Senate have been honour bound to help one of their allies in the region, but the mere mention of a migrating barbarian horde approaching Rome's sphere of influence would soon have conjured up parallels to the infamous Gallic invasion of Italy in the 390s BC and the Gallic sack of Rome.

It is therefore no surprise that the Senate instructed one of the consuls for 113, C. Papirius Carbo, to take an army to the region to investigate this new arrival, defend their allies and deal with any threat to Rome. Both the Senate and Carbo's initial fears can be seen by Carbo's taking up a defensive position in the Alps, defending Italy from invasion.[179] This was a clear example of the Roman mentality and could hardly be seen as investigating the threat or defending Rome's allies. Upon the arrival of the Cimbri, Carbo then moved his army into Noricum to investigate the situation. What he found apparently did not tally with his concept of a 'barbarian horde'. We are told that, upon hearing of his approach, the Cimbri sent ambassadors to him to apologize for transgressing the territory of the Taurisci, whom they did not know were allies of Rome, and promising to leave their territory and continue their wanderings.[180] This description ties in with the information we have about the Cimbri in this period, namely that they were a migrating tribe looking for a new homeland, avoiding fighting wherever necessary. However, what happened next was to have a profound effect on the nature of their migration.

We will never know whether Papirius Carbo believed the Cimbric ambassadors or not; perhaps he believed it to be a ruse to lure him into lowering his (and Rome's) guard. It is possible that these actions did not fit in with the Roman concept of a 'barbarian', especially in a time of renewed Scordiscian invasions in Macedon. This cultural misunderstanding would have been increased by the Roman paranoia about avoiding another Gallic sack, added to what must have been a personal desire for glory. Having achieved the consulship, the pinnacle of his political career, Carbo was faced with having to return to Rome and report that the 'barbarians' tamely agreed to turn back and wander elsewhere. It was far more attractive to him to defeat them in battle and return home a hero, having saved Rome from a new 'Gallic menace'.

To this end he set about to deal with the Cimbri, despite their protestations of peace. Appian reports that he accepted the ambassadors' offer to move on and even sent guides with them as an act of friendship.[181] However, these guides had been instructed to lead the Cimbri in an unknown direction, but by the longest route possible. He then led his army by a shorter route and ambushed the Cimbri as they were resting; the result was the Battle of Noreia.

The Battle of Noreia (113 BC)

Infuriatingly, we have no details as to how the battle was fought or the size of opposing forces. What we do know is that Carbo turned this ambush into a Roman disaster. It is possible that in his haste to reach the Cimbri he overstretched his own forces, or chose a poor place to attack them, which allowed the greater Cimbric numbers to tell. What was planned as a Roman massacre of the resting Cimbri soon turned into a Cimbric massacre of the Romans, with Carbo's whole army being destroyed. Again, we have no concrete numbers, but Appian reports that those who did survive only did so due to the onset of a large thunderstorm, which provided the Romans with cover to flee in small groups. Of the few who did survive Carbo was amongst them and returned to Rome in shame. His defeat became a byword for Roman military incompetence against the Cimbri, still being used by Plutarch, hundreds of years later.[182]

It is difficult to see how Carbo could have lost this battle so comprehensively, having both the advantage of surprise and having chosen his place of attack. The only two factors which may help to explain this, assuming that his guides did not treacherously warn the Cimbri, are numbers and terrain. It is interesting to note that prior to his attack, it is unlikely that Carbo ever saw the full scale of the Cimbric tribes, having only dealt with ambassadors that came to him. Therefore, he may well have been unaware of the sheer scale of the task he faced (later estimates place Cimbric numbers in the hundreds of thousands). The other factor is terrain. Appian speaks of the Romans fleeing into the woods, and we do not know if he attacked them in an open or wooded area. If he did so then he may have unwittingly foreshowed the later Roman disaster at Teutoburg Forest, which clearly illustrated the legion's limitations in fighting barbarians in a wooded area. Furthermore, we do not know where he attacked the Cimbri. If he did blunder into the middle of the Cimbri then he would soon have found himself surrounded by their far greater numbers.

Whatever the cause, the outcome was another large Roman defeat by a 'barbarian' enemy, following from that of the Scordisci. Whether the Cimbri originally had hostile intentions or not, it is clear that Carbo's actions left Rome nursing a need to avenge the loss and would have certainly soured the Cimbri against Rome. In the short term the defeat left Italy open to Cimbric invasion, though, in keeping with their stated intent, the Cimbri continued their journey northwestwards towards (hopefully) non-hostile territory.[183] Although the immediate danger for Rome had abated, a legacy of bad blood had been created that would come back to haunt Rome.

Summary

We can see that in the years leading up to the outbreak of the Jugurthine War, Rome's focus was clearly on the north. In the space of just two years (114–113 BC) two Roman armies had been destroyed in battle with different barbarian foes: the Scordisci and the Cimbri. In the northeast, Macedon and Greece had been invaded and plundered by a large and persistent tribal enemy, whilst the defeat in the Alps had left Italy itself open to invasion. Once again it showed that despite their military superiority over the so-called more advanced civilizations of the Mediterranean, the Romans were still susceptible to defeat by northern tribes.

Thus, despite the importance given to the Jugurthine War by both the writing and survival of Sallust's pamphlet on the war, for contemporary Romans the priority was their northern borders, assailed as they were by different tribes. Furthermore, it highlighted the fact that the supposedly-superior Roman military machine was not able to stand up to a supposedly 'undisciplined' tribal foe.

War on Two Fronts
(111–105 BC)

Chapter 4

The Jugurthine War:
The Early Campaigns (111–110 BC)

With an examination of the background completed, we can now turn our attention to the Jugurthine War itself. Whilst Sallust's short work provides a good narrative of the war, it does lack in-depth analysis. For this purpose we can break the war down into three phases, each under a different overall commander. This chapter will examine the initial two commanders, L. Calpurnius Bestia and Sp. Postumius Albinus, and the early phases of the war.

Initial Roman Aims

Though Rome had declared war on Jugurtha, as we have seen it was not one that the Senate had desired. As detailed in Chapter 2, the impetus for war had come from the equestrian order and the people, via the tribunes. This being the case, we must focus on the questions of what the Senate desired from this war and what instructions were given to the first commander of the war, L. Calpurnius Bestia.

With regard to the Roman aims, it is important to understand the dilemma which faced both the Senate and the consul responsible for pursuing the war. On the one hand Roman domestic outrage had to be appeased; Jugurtha had flagrantly disobeyed the Senatorial commission's orders to end the Numidian Civil War peacefully and had massacred Italian citizens at Cirta, causing outrage, feigned or real, amongst both the people and the equestrian class. This was being exploited for political capital by a number of tribunes determined to undermine the Senatorial oligarchy and re-opened divides that had been exposed by the Gracchan crises in the previous decades. Thus there was a clear need for Jugurtha to be, or be seen to be, severely punished for his actions.

Yet, when considered from the wider perspectives, the Senate had reason to be cautious. Numidia represented no immediate threat to Roman interests in the region and Jugurtha was an apparently-staunch Roman ally. Certainly there would have been some Senators worried at the prospect of Numidia as the dominant power in North Africa, but given the close ties between the two powers, this would not have been a major concern. If anything, diverting military resources to a war in Africa was exactly the opposite of what current Roman foreign policy demanded. As detailed in Chapter 3, for the previous decade all of Rome's military efforts had been focussed on securing her fragile northern borders from barbarian threats. This was not the time to commit troops overseas when Italy itself was potentially at risk (which given the Cimbric threat, must have been a real concern).

Furthermore, given that Rome already occupied the fertile plains of North Africa, there was no impetus for turning this into a war of conquest. Added to this was the problem of who would rule Numidia, if Jugurtha were to be removed. Adherbal's death in Cirta had removed the last of the triumvirate of Micipsa's children who had been kings of Numidia, though there were a number of other descendants of Massinissa who could have been elevated to the throne, possibly of a freshly-divided Numidia. In fact, given the previous ruling of the Senatorial commission and the fact that if Jugurtha remained sole king then he would have profited by his actions, it is most likely that the re-division of Numidia would have been a desired Roman outcome.

Therefore, for the Senate and its commander this war was to be a punishment campaign, to bring Jugurtha to submission and ensure that the Senate's vision for Numidia be enforced, all to be accomplished in the shortest possible timescale and with the minimum of effort. The nature of Jugurtha's submission is an interesting question, given both his crimes and his previous loyalty to Rome. It is unlikely that the Senate would have considered stripping him of his throne completely, merely humbling him and gaining his public submission.

The Roman Commander - L. Calpurnius Bestia

These were the complicated circumstances which faced the consuls of 111 B.C. The two men elected were P. Cornelius Scipio Nasica and L. Calpurnius Bestia. It is interesting that a Scipio managed to get elected for 111 BC, despite the overall decline in prominence of the family, given their close family ties to the Numidian royal family. If this link was in the mind of the electorate then the lot which decided the consular commands at random denied them their intention, as the command for Africa fell to Calpurnius Bestia. It is no surprise that the other consular command was Italy, covering any possible return of the Cimbri.

Bestia himself was of the plebeian nobility and appears to have been the first of his family to achieve high office. He is the earliest recorded member of his family to achieve an office of the *cursus honorum* and the first to achieve the consulship.[184] He had been a tribune, but we know nothing of his praetorship and thus have no knowledge of his military record to date or how competent an officer he was[185]. On the positive side, we are told that he choose an experienced group of noblemen as his legates for the campaign, which included M. Aemilius Scaurus, the former consul of 115 BC (see Chapter 2).

Again, one of the hallmarks of Sallust' narrative is a lack of military detail. We are not told the size of the army levied by Bestia to take to Africa. However, for the events of the following years we are told that the Roman army was 40,000 strong.[186] Given that Bestia' campaign was only intended to be a punitive expedition, and given concerns elsewhere, notably Italy, it may have been that the army of 111 BC was considerably smaller, but we simply have no firm evidence. We are also informed that the army was freshly levied in Italy, as was the norm.[187]

Initial Jugurthine Aims

It is clear that Jugurtha had not expected Rome to declare war on him for his attack on Cirta. Whether this was due to his financial largesse amongst the Senate or the more prosaic reasons surrounding Roman indifference towards events in Numidia and focus on the north we will never know. What is clear is that even at this stage he hoped to avoid a military confrontation and to these ends he sent an unnamed son as an emissary to Rome to negotiate with the Senate. However, the Senate refused him entry into the city and ordered his party to leave Italy within ten days unless they could offer Jugurtha's unconditional surrender. They left Italy, clearly having not been authorized to make such an offer.

If it was to be war then, given Jugurtha's detailed knowledge of the Roman political and military systems, we must examine what his options and strategies would have been. It is clear from the sending of further emissaries that he realized that although war had been declared, the situation did not necessarily have to result in open warfare. Clearly his best option lay in avoiding full-scale warfare and negotiating a settlement that left him with at least a throne of Numidia, if not the only one. If he engaged Rome in combat, regardless of the outcome, Rome would have no option but to remove him. Thus any Roman invasion would have to be met by a policy of falling back and negotiating a limited submission. Whether this would involve illicit payments to Roman commanders is unclear, but it certainly would have helped.

Again, we have no clear idea of the scale of the Numidian army. What we must acknowledge is that the terrain of Numidia was desert plains, which suited the Numidian light cavalry rather than the Roman heavy infantry.

The Campaign of 111 BC – The Phoney War

Given the above points it is not surprising that the campaign of 111 BC turned into a 'phoney war', with neither side committed to full-scale warfare. Sallust only provides brief details of the campaign. Bestia gathered his army at Rhegium and transferred them from there to Sicily and from Sicily to Roman Africa. Once in Roman Africa he mounted a swift offensive against the nearest Numidian towns, though again we are not told which ones. The only details we are given is that a number of towns were taken by storm, resulting in a large number of prisoners being taken.[188]

This is all we know about the military events of 111 BC. A number of other sources briefly mention the campaign, but nearly all omit even these basic details. However, we should not follow Sallust's lead and dismiss this campaign. In both military and political terms, Bestia was pursuing a sound policy. He had with him an inexperienced army, operating in a region that no Roman soldier had fought in for a generation (since the Third Punic War). Thus, it was imperative that they be blooded in combat without being put at risk, hence some basic siege operations to build up experience and confidence, as well as allowing the opportunity for quick booty. For the purpose of the expedition the sacking of Numidian towns was an excellent method of punishing the Numidian people for the transgressions of Jugurtha. Even Sallust, who seems to have been loath to say anything good about Bestia, admires the swiftness of the initial campaigning.

Following these initial attacks, Jugurtha adopted a familiar tactic and opened negotiations with Bestia. It is here that Sallust immediately condemns Bestia and his deputy Scaurus, a condemnation that has echoed throughout all of the surviving sources. Sallust immediately saw this as nothing more than blatant bribery and lambasts Bestia and Scaurus thus:

> the consul's mind, demoralized as it was by avarice, was easily turned from its purpose. Moreover, he took Scaurus as an accomplice in all his designs: for although at first, even after many in his own party had been seduced, Scaurus had vigorously opposed the king, a huge bribe turned him from honour and virtue to criminality.[189]

As pointed out earlier, negotiating with the Romans was a sound policy for Jugurtha. Despite the Roman invasion of Numidia, full disaster could be averted by submitting to Rome and doing penance for the massacre at Cirta. The only irreversible act would be to engage the Romans in battle. Thus we hear of no Numidian military activity at this time. If some cities had to be sacrificed to the Roman appetite for glory, it was a small price to pay for keeping his head and his throne.

However, given the earlier Roman demand for an unconditional surrender, what can be said of Rome's attitude towards fresh negotiations? Leaving aside Sallust's view that negotiating with Jugurtha was nothing more than blatant corruption, it can be argued that Bestia was actually acting in Rome's best interests. In the first few months of campaigning, Jugurtha had shown no sign of engaging the Roman forces, which raised the clear prospect of a long-drawn-out desert war with the enemy refusing to give battle. This was exactly the type of situation which the Senate would have hoped to avoid. If Jugurtha could be humbled by a show of force and be publicly brought back into the Roman fold, then there was no reason for the war to continue; Roman power and Roman honour would have been satisfied. This is not to say that monies did not change hands between the two parties, merely that it was not the cause of the negotiations and the treaty that followed.

These negotiations led to an armistice and then a settlement. 'Armistice' is a bit of a misnomer given that to date the war had been nothing more than the Romans attacking and plundering towns near the Numidian/Roman African border. The price of the armistice was the gift of grain from the Numidians to the invading Roman troops, which was both logistically astute and an obvious token of submission. With that achieved, Jugurtha appeared before a Roman council of war, formed from amongst the senior commanders of the Roman army, and made his offer of submission and surrender. In practical terms this included thirty elephants, a number of cattle and horses and an amount of silver.

Thus the war appeared to be over in less than a year. Numidia was at peace and Bestia was able to return to Rome to hold the elections for the consuls of 110 BC. This was slightly unusual, but his colleague Scipio, who had been assigned Italy as his province had died and we hear of no suffect consul being elected in his place. For Bestia, the war had been an apparent success; his army had launched a punitive attack on an errant ally and brought him back into line with the submission of the king and the payment of an appropriate indemnity. Thus it was short, successful and profitable. Whether there had been further secret donations provided by Jugurtha, we will never know. Nevertheless, given Bestia's probable instructions for the 'war', he had achieved them admirably.

Matters of War and Peace in Rome

However, it was at this point that the change in Roman domestic politics became apparent. Once again the tribune C. Memmius stirred up the urban populace by claiming that this settlement, which from a logical point of view had achieved the limited Senatorial aims, was a betrayal of the Roman people and the result of Senatorial corruption. Unsurprisingly, this matter is given in great detail by Sallust, who reports what purports to be Memmius' speech on the matter.[190]

Having agitated the urban populace into believing that this was a dis-honourable peace, achieved by foreign bribery, Memmius once again usurped the Senate's control of foreign policy and had the popular assemblies pass a *plebiscitum* ordering the praetor L. Cassius to go to Numidia to bring Jugurtha back to Rome to give evidence against the nobles accused of accepting his 'bribes'. Thus, the war against Numidia and the peace negotiations were put on hold and Jugurtha, who had been declaimed as an enemy of Rome by Memmius, was now being called as a witness to substantiate his accusations. Thus it is clear that foreign affairs were now clearly at the mercy of the domestic clashes between the Senate and other sections of the population. It was a clear indicator of things to come and though Memmius was the first to manipulate the Numidian crisis for his own ends, he was not to be the last.

Sallust reports the effect that this unorthodox delay had on the Roman army in Numidia, with reports of desertion, attacks on the locals and the sale of the donated elephants back to the Numidians.[191] Once again it appears that the much-vaunted Roman military discipline was breaking down. What effect the arrival of Cassius had on Jugurtha we can only speculate. The Romans had declared war on him, invaded Numidia, attacked his towns, forced his surrender and were now calling him as a witness in a corruption hearing. The latter placed him in a highly awkward position. He clearly needed both the Senate and People to ratify his peace treaty, but could not afford to antagonize either of them. Certainly, even if there was bribery, he could not implicate his own allies within the Senate.

Fortunately for Jugurtha, this situation was salvaged when a tribunician colleague of Memmius, C. Babeius, utilized his right to intervene (*intercessio*) to prevent the king from speaking. As is to be expected, Sallust attributes this intervention to a large Jugurthan bribe, but in reality there were a number of senators who would have not wished potentially-damning evidence to be given. Thus the year ended with stalemate, both in military terms in Numidia and political terms in Rome, with one being beholden to the other.

This uneasy peace between Rome and Numidia was shattered by one act: the murder of a Numidian prince, Massiva, who was reportedly being touted as a rival candidate to Jugurtha for the Numidian throne. Massiva was a son of the Numidian co-regent, Gulassa, brother of King Micipsa, and thus a cousin to Jugurtha. We know nothing about his age or upbringing, but he had clearly been excluded from Micipsa's plans for the succession. Sallust tells us that during the Numidian Civil War he was a supporter of Adherbal, who had fled to Rome after the latter's murder. With war between Rome and Jugurtha, attention turned to him as a possible new co-regent of Numidia or a straight replacement for Jugurtha.[192]

These hopes were apparently fostered by Sp. Postumius Albinus, who was elected as one of the consuls of 110 BC and who had received Numidia in the lot for provinces. Here we again see the drawback of Rome's annual system of rotating command. L. Calpurnius Bestia had successfully led a punitive campaign and brought about Jugurtha's submission. His successor, eager for glory himself and without an approved peace between Rome and Numidia, appeared to be eager to renew the war.

It appears that as Massiva had been in Rome since 112 BC, and it is likely that he had been advocating his own elevation to either the sole or joint kingship for some time, what he now had was consular backing for this desire. Sallust reports that a proposal making Massiva king of Numidia (though whether this was as sole or joint king is unclear) was apparently in preparation to be brought before the Senate.[193] Certainly, Massiva's elevation would have allowed the Senate to return to their earlier settlement and divide Numidia once more, most probably with Massiva receiving Adherbal's kingdom of Eastern Numidia.

This action or even rumoured action would have placed Jugurtha in a terrible position. If he did nothing, at best he would return to the position of 118 BC, and at worst he would be ousted altogether. Yet he had spent months in Rome witnessing the chaos that Rome's political system had descended into. Therefore, he took a gamble and ordered a subordinate (Bomilcar) to arrange the murder of Massiva. The murder succeeded, but the gamble failed when the assassin was caught and confessed, with Bomilcar duly being put on trial. Here Jugurtha made his final fateful decision, and chose to protect his subordinate by secreting him back to Numidia. This proved to be the final break with the Senate who ordered Jugurtha out of Italy and a renewal of hostilities. As Jugurtha left Sallust has him looking back and saying, 'A city for sale and doomed to speedy destruction if it finds a purchaser,' though this is more likely to have been Sallust's view rather than Jugurtha's.

The Campaign of 110 BC – Renewal of War and Roman Disaster

Roman Aims

With the breakdown of negotiations and the blatant act of treachery committed in their own midst, the Senate would have had no option but to be committed to a full-scale war in Numidia with the aim of removing Jugurtha. Despite Massiva's assassination there were enough members of the Numidian ruling family from whom a pliable client-king could be found. Thus it was only in 110 BC, nearly eighteen months after war had been declared, the Roman state was fully committed to the war.

The Roman Commander – Sp. Postumius Albinus

The new Roman commander hailed from a patrician family which had a record of consulships dating back to the fourth century BC and a distinguished (if unspectacular) military record. It is clear from his actions in Rome that he was committed to a war in Numidia, which he would have been seen as an opportunity for personal military glory. Thus the war now had a fully committed Roman commander with clear aims.

Jugurthan Aims

For Jugurtha, the murder of Massiva and facilitating the escape of the organiser of the plot from Roman justice had been a step too far. This was a clear affront to Roman dignity and one which would have been difficult to justify. Yet even at this point, he would have had a clear sense that he still had a number of factors in his favour. The terrain suited the fast 'hit and run' type of warfare favoured by the Numidians, with their light cavalry. Furthermore, knowing the Roman military as he did, it was clear that he would have to avoid a full-scale pitched battle and frustrate the enemy. Albinus' command was only for a year and then Jugurtha would be facing a fresh Roman consul, who may have been more open to negotiation/bribery (at least in Jugurtha's mind).

The Campaign of 110 BC

Postumius arrived in Numidia to take charge of the army stationed there, along with fresh pay and supplies, but no fresh troops. We are not told what measures he took to restore discipline, but it seems unlikely there were major changes given the events that followed. Once again Sallust is light on the details of the campaign of 110 BC, but what is clear is that it followed the familiar pattern of vigorous thrusts from Postumius' forces being met with a Numidian refusal to give battle.[194] It can be said that Jugurtha copied the classic Roman 'Fabian tactic' of refusing to give battle when faced with a superior fighting force.[195] At the same time as refusing to give battle, Jugurtha continued with his offers to negotiate a settlement, whilst harrying the Roman forces with lightning raids. These would have served a two-fold purpose: to frustrate the Roman forces and convince them that there would be no military solution to the war, whilst bolstering the morale of his own forces, showing them how slow and ineffectual the Roman method of warfare was.

Again, here we have a perfect example of the flaws in the Roman military machine; when faced with a static enemy, such as an opposing army or a town, the Roman heavy infantry had no equal. When faced with a guerrilla army, be it in the forests of Spain or the deserts of North Africa, the Romans had little response. The recent defeats suffered at the hand of the Scordisci and Cimbri highlighted the Roman vulnerability to foes that did not give battle in the same manner.

For Postumius it was a frustrating campaign, with the Numidians refusing to give battle and prevaricating over submission. This in turn resulted in dissatisfaction in Rome about the time it was taking to finish what was meant to be an easy war. As the year passed by, we can easily understand Postumius' growing frustration, knowing that with the election of fresh consuls, he would lose his chance for victory and his consulship would end in relative failure. Obviously frustrated and feeling the pressure from Rome, Postumius left Africa to conduct the consular elections for 109 BC, leaving his forces in camp under the command of his brother A. Postumius Albinus.

However, Spurius' absence turned out to be longer than expected, again resulting from trouble in Rome with tribunes. This time it was P. Licinius Lucullus and L. Annius who were attempting to seek re-election to the tribunate, which, whilst not illegal, was strenuously opposed by many who sought to avoid entrenched tribunes and a return to the days of the Gracchi.[196] In the deadlock that followed, all elections for 109 BC were delayed, with Sp. Postumius remaining in Rome. Once again Roman military activities in Numidia became beholden to domestic political infighting, centred on the tribunes.

The Battle of Suthul

In his brother's absence, Aulus Postumius saw an opportunity to restore his family's glory (and his own) and planned a knockout blow at Jugurtha by moving to attack his treasury, at the town of Suthul, during the winter of 110/109 BC.[197] However, the town's defences proved to be formidable and the initial assault failed, with the Roman army digging in for a winter siege. It was at this point that Jugurtha made a fateful decision and one which changed the course of the war. Abandoning his previous policy of not engaging the Romans in battle, and seeing the opportunity of a weak Roman army, led by an in-experienced commander, he decided to commit his forces fully to the war and attack the Roman forces.

In secret, he amassed his own forces and marched them to a position near Suthul, then sent emissaries to Aulus Postumius promising a favourable settle-ment. Using these promises he got Aulus to break his siege of Suthul and lead his army into following Jugurtha's. Why Aulus did this will never be known. The most plausible explanation is that he shadowed Jugurtha's army, hoping that if the offer of a settlement proved to be false, he could at least engage Jugurtha's army in battle. Thus Aulus allowed himself to be led straight into a trap. The key problem for the Romans here being that the most experienced Roman commander was leading the Numidian army not the Roman one. As the two armies shadowed each other, Jugurtha put his knowledge of the Roman soldiers to good use and sent agents amongst apparently disaffected Roman forces. Such disaffection is easy to understand, given that they were now coming to the end of a second year with little to show for their efforts, apart from a collapsed peace treaty of the previous year and another year spent chasing shadows around the desert.

At a set time (again we are not told when), Jugurtha sprung his trap. As the Romans made camp for the night, Jugurtha was able to secretly surround them with a large Numidian force, catching them unawares. From Sallust's descrip-tion the Numidian attack on the Roman camp turned into an utter Roman rout; unprepared, inexperienced and suffering from a number of either pre-planned or spontaneous desertions, Aulus' army fled from the camp with little resis-tance, seeking shelter in the nearby hills.[198] The attack was a spectacular victory for Jugurtha who had routed a Roman invading army with minimum casualties. Once again he stuck to his policy of not meeting the Romans in open battle and defeated a force of 40,000 Romans (if we are to believe the figures provided by Orosius[199]), though we are not given Roman casualties.

The next day, Jugurtha sent an emissary to Aulus Postumius and made clear his terms. In return for their lives, Aulus would agree to evacuate all Roman forces from Numidia and the survivors of his army would have to pass under the yoke as a sign of submission. Faced with little alternative and no real chance of resisting, Aulus agreed to the shameful terms and agreed a treaty with Jugurtha. Thus the winter of 110/109 BC saw the complete defeat of the Roman invasion of Numidia and a Roman commander agreeing to a unconditional surrender to Jugurtha rather than the other way around.

Summary of the Early Campaigns – Rome

Although we posses little detail of the military campaigns of the first two years, there can be no denying that the Romans had a poor start to the war. A number of factors can be seen throughout these first two years. First and foremost is that Rome appears to have had no clear plan of what they were hoping to achieve in the war and this is reflected in their military activities. This lack of direction was a direct result of the circumstances surrounding the outbreak of the war; was Jugurtha an enemy of Rome or an errant ally?

At no point did either Calpurnius Bestia or the Postumii Albinii treat the war as though they intended to defeat Jugurtha and ensure his capture, as they would with an outright enemy king. All three commanders acted as though they were on punitive expeditions designed to bring Jugurtha to heel. The people, or at least a section of them stirred by the tribune Memmius, may have wanted an aggressive war with Jugurtha, but the Senate did not. Jugurtha and Numidia had always been allies of Rome and in the Senate's view there were more pressing issues. In 111 BC Jugurtha appeared to have agreed with the Roman view and soon negotiated himself into an armistice. After the events of 110 BC in Rome, the matter became more serious, but as the disaster with Aulus Postumius showed, Jugurtha was still not seen as an implacable enemy of Rome. With the defeat and humiliation of a Roman army however, this was bound to change.

This lack of a clear plan for the war was supported by the chaotic political situation in Rome during both years, which only contributed to the uncertainty. In 111 BC Memmius stoked up the desire to treat Jugurtha as an enemy of Rome and then called him to Rome under the protection of the people, as a witness in a political witch-hunt. The following year, the chaos surrounding the tribunician elections kept the consul in Rome for far longer than he was meant to be, which left his army in the command of his even more inexperienced brother.

This brings us onto our third point, the quality of the commanders chosen to face Jugurtha. Although both Calpurnius and Postumius seem to have been perfectly competent commanders in their own rights, both were inferior in military experience and tactics to Jugurtha. In fact Jugurtha probably had more experience in Roman warfare than either of his two opponents, having served though the Numantine War (though we do not know where either man served prior to their consulships).

The next obvious point concerns the quality of the Roman army in Numidia. Despite Sallust's work on the war, he provides little in the way of military details. The only clear figure we have for troop numbers comes from Orosius, writing in the fifth century AD (though he may have used Livy – see Appendix V), who puts Postumius' Roman forces at 40,000 strong, which is perhaps a higher figure than we would expect for a campaign of this nature, at this time. The only other detail comes from Sallust who states that the Third Legion was present at the Roman defeat in 110. However, aside from the numbers and identities, the most important observation regarding the Roman army in Numidia concerns their quality, or lack thereof.

Both during the winter of 111/110 BC and the winter campaign of 110/109, the sources report that discipline, both in camp and in the face of the enemy, was poor.

In the first winter we have reports of desertions, banditry and collusion with the enemy, whilst in the following year, even allowing for Sallust's usual charges of bribery, there was desertion and flight in the face of the enemy, and the ineptitude (or bribery) involved in allowing the Numidians to draw up a large force to attack the Roman camp undetected. In short, this was a continuation of the poor quality and training of the recruits that had been seen in the Numantine War some twenty years before. In this case, it contributed to the Romans withdrawing from Numidia in defeat and disgrace.

Summary of the Early Campaigns – Numidia

For the Numidians, at first glance the war to date had been a complete success. The Roman invasion of 111 BC had soon been blunted by negotiation and its renewal in 110 BC had resulted in a complete Roman defeat. However, as Jugurtha would have well known, the point of no return had been passed in the winter of 110/109 BC. As pointed out above, for the majority of the first two campaigns the Romans did not know what type of war they were pursuing and this was partly down to Jugurtha's skill in not overtly appearing as Rome's enemy. This was aided by his sensible decision not to face the Romans in battle, knowing only too well their military superiority in face-to-face conflict and their weaknesses when faced with a guerrilla campaign (of the type he had witnessed first-hand in Numantia). This policy meant that even by the winter of 110/109, he was still not an implacable enemy of Rome and that is the main reason why Aulus Postumius was still willing to negotiate, rather than solely due to the familiar allegations of bribery.

However, in attacking and routing a Roman army, not to mention forcing them under the yoke, he had clearly abandoned this previous policy and crossed the line into becoming a full-blown enemy of Rome. He would have known only too well what the reaction in Rome would have been and that now he truly was at war with Rome. There are two possible reasons for this change of tactic. Firstly, he saw an unparalleled opportunity to inflict an easy defeat on Rome, which would not come again nor could be easily passed up. Secondly, it was likely that he was under pressure at home to stand up to the Romans rather than prevaricating, however successful it had been. For the Numidians as a whole, they had just gone through a long civil war and now had Roman armies attacking their cities, ostensibly for the actions of their king. It is entirely possible that Jugurtha was under pressure to deliver, which he did in spectacular form. Orosius notes that following this victory he consolidated his position in North Africa by adding a number of smaller territories to his own, but no details are given.[200] Certainly, this victory would have enhanced his reputation as a great African leader.

This leaves us with the question of what his long-term aims were now that he had crossed the line and gone into direct conflict with Rome. Jugurtha would have been only too well aware that ultimately he could not win a war against Rome, given the massive disparity in resources. Yet, he possessed a good understanding of the Roman mentality (or at least that of the Senatorial elite). The war was unpopular in the Senate and if he could make it as uncomfortable as possible, by denying them quick victories and using hit-and-run tactics then it was just possible to arrange a negotiated settlement, especially if he could hold out until the barbarian crisis became more acute. However, weighing heavily against this option was his defeat and humiliation of Aulus' army and the reaction of the forces opposed to the Senate in Rome.

Backlash at Rome

When news of the defeat and humiliating treaty reached Rome, the shock and outrage was understandable. In the Senate, focus immediately shifted to the treaty Aulus Postumius had agreed to and whether the Senate would ratify it. Naturally, this placed the consul Sp. Postumius in an impossible decision. Supporting his brother meant supporting his treaty, which no Roman would ever agree to. Unsurprisingly, the Senate refused to ratify the treaty, using the dubious excuse that no treaty could be binding without the agreement of the Senate and People of Rome. Spurius then made attempts to recover the situation in Africa by raising fresh forces in Rome and from the allies. However, unnamed tribunes prevented him from taking them to Africa.[201] He thus returned to the Roman province of Africa himself, to try to rebuild his army, but could take no immediate action against Jugurtha.[202]

However expected the reactions of the Senate were, the tribunes went a stage further. Not only did they prevent fresh reinforcements from reaching the province, but one tribune, C. Mamilius Limetanus, proposed an extraordinary piece of legislation which created a special court to try those deemed to have aided Jugurtha, either directly or indirectly. Sallust gives examples of those soldiers and officers who sold the Numidian elephants back to Jugurtha, those who deserted the army and Aulus Postumius himself, who had agreed to the disgraceful treaty. This was the first such special court to try those who were suspected of betraying Rome and the looseness of the wording brought all those who were suspected of having been bribed by Jugurtha under its remit.[203]

Chapter 5

The Jugurthine War:
The Metellan Campaigns (109–107 BC)

It was in this poisonous atmosphere that the delayed elections for the consuls for 109 BC were held, with Q. Caecilius Metellus and M. Iunius Silanus being elected. Given the nature of the crisis, both at home and in Africa, the two consuls agreed amongst themselves that Metellus should take charge of the Jugurthine War and we hear of no complaints concerning this breach of usual practice.[204]

The Roman Commander – Q. Caecilius Metellus

Q. Caecilius Metellus hailed from Rome's leading family in this period. Between 123 and 109 BC, six different members of the family held the consulship, culminating in the aforementioned double Metellan triumph in 111 BC (see Appendix IV for a fuller description of the Metelli in this period). Thus unlike the two previous Roman commanders, the consul of 109 came from the most prominent Roman military family of the day. This gave Metellus a natural advantage in terms of financial and political support in the Senate. Furthermore, it would have been expected that his command would not have been simply for the year of his consulship, as with the previous two commanders, but that he would take pro-consular authority and retain his command in Africa as long as the war lasted. This was what initially happened in 108 BC and would have continued to have been the case, had it not been for an extraordinary set of circumstances. Given his position he took with him a highly-experienced command staff, which included the veterans C. Marius and P. Rutilius Rufus. His staff also included at least one member of the Numidian royal family, Gauda, a half-brother of Jugurtha.[205]

The Campaign of 109 BC

Finally, with a high-profile commander and with the humiliation of Suthul fresh in their minds, the Jugurthine War effort took centre stage for Rome. As would have been expected Metellus began meticulous preparations for the war, starting with levying a large army from both Roman citizens, allies and the overseas allies. Once again, however, we are given no precise figures for the size of Metellus' army. Upon arriving in Roman Africa to take over from Sp. Albinus, Sallust reports that Metellus found the province and the remaining Roman forces in disarray. Discipline throughout the army had apparently collapsed, from Sp. Albinus himself to the lowest Roman soldier. Military regulations had been abandoned with the troops supporting themselves by plundering the local population.

Metellus was thus faced with a difficult position, despite his undoubted advantages. Much of the campaigning season had been lost due to his late election to the consulship, with the elections having been postponed from 110 to 109, and the time it had taken to assemble a fresh army in Italy. Furthermore, the Roman forces in North Africa were in disarray and it would have taken some time to restore discipline and integrate the forces in Africa with his fresh troops, all of whom would need further training before seeing action. Acting against this, however, was the weight of expectation that came with him. Given his social and political position and the urgency with which the Senate and People would have expected him to avenge the loss at Suthul, Metellus was under considerable pressure to deliver a quick result. Nevertheless, he went about the initial preparations meticulously; discipline was restored and the legions were trained hard, with forced marches and conditions made to simulate being in hostile territory.

For Metellus, his aims for the war were far clearer than those which had faced his predecessors, namely total victory. Yet, this in itself presented a number of problems. This was still not a war of conquest, but was a war against one man, Jugurtha and the war would not end until Jugurtha had been captured or killed. As detailed earlier, the territory favoured the Numidians, mountains and deserts to hide in and wide open plains on which to use the Numidian light cavalry. For Jugurtha, this new campaign must have presented him with an interesting dilemma. He was at the highpoint of his monarchy, king of a unified Numidia, having utterly defeated the invading Roman armies and, as we are told, embarking on a campaign to enlarge his kingdom at the expense of the neighbouring states and tribes. Yet, given his knowledge of the Romans, he must have realized that under Metellus the situation would be totally different. Here was the scion of Rome's leading family, the position that the Scipios had been in generations earlier. He must have known that Metellus would have settled for nothing less than complete victory and that, after humiliating Rome both militarily with the victory at Suthul, and politically, with the Romans going under the yoke and agreeing a withdrawal, Rome would never have settled for a negotiated peace.

Nevertheless, we are told that he continued with the tried and tested tactic of sending envoys to discuss peace whilst preparing for renewed conflict. This time, however, it appears that he had met his match, as Metellus adopted the same strategy. A Roman invasion of Numidia was accompanied by attempts to turn the Numidian envoys, persuading them to either assassinate or capture Jugurtha. The Roman invasion met with no initial resistance whatsoever, and Jugurtha had the border towns offering tokens of submission to the Romans and supplies for their army. Metellus used this goodwill to take the town of Vaga as a forward base, placing a garrison here and a forward supply centre. Jugurtha once again sent envoys to negotiate, whom Metellus once again attempted to turn to the Roman cause.[206] With the preliminaries aside Jugurtha determined to defeat this Roman invasion and set about selecting a position to face the Romans in battle. The place he chose was near to the Muthul River.[207]

The Battle of Muthul River (109 BC)

If we can see one characteristic of Jugurtha's military expertise, it comes through his careful selection of his battle sites. In both 110 at Suthul and at Muthul in 109, he used his knowledge of his kingdom's geography to select sites that maximised his army's strengths and exploited the Roman weaknesses. At no point had he been forced or panicked into going to battle, and on both occasions, the Romans fought at a location he had selected.

Sallust, for once, provides us with an excellent description of the battle site:

> In the part of Numidia which the partition had given to Adherbal there was a river flowing from the south called the Muthul, and about twenty miles from it was a naturally desolate and uncultivated range of hills running parallel with the river. From about the middle of this range an elevation branched off and extended for a long distance, covered with wild olive, myrtles, and other varieties of trees which grow in a dry and sandy soil. The intervening plain (between the spur and the river) was uninhabited from the lack of water except the parts along the river, which were covered with shrubs and frequented by cattle and farmers.
>
> On the hill then, which flanked the Romans' line of march, Jugurtha took his position with his line greatly extended. He gave command of the elephants and a part of the infantry to Bomilcar and placed his own

men nearer the mountain with all his cavalry and the best of his infantry.[208]

Thus Jugurtha had chosen an ideal place for an ambush, occupying the higher ground and potentially trapping the Roman army between his own forces and the river (see battle diagram). Furthermore, his army was utilizing the cover of thickets on the hill to conceal his force's true size from the enemy. However, Metellus, an able commander soon spotted the Numidian army and brought his force to a halt and altered formation to meet the 'surprise' attack:

I. The Battle of Muthul River (109 BC), Stage 1

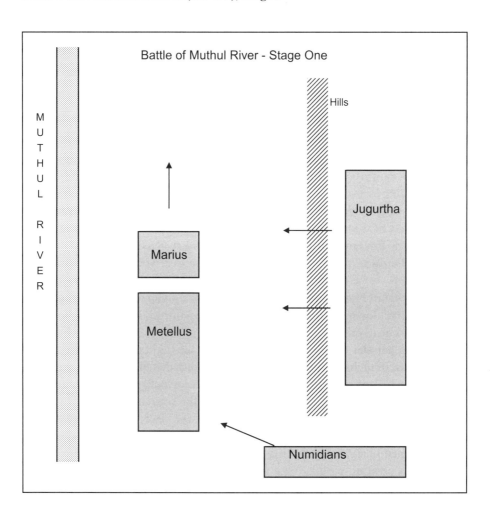

His right flank, which was nearest the enemy, he strengthened with three lines of reserves. Between the maniples he placed the slingers and archers, while on the wings he stationed all the cavalry and after a brief address, which was all that there was time for, led the army down into the plain in its new formation, with what had been its front, marching at right angles to the direction of the enemy.[209]

As the Romans marched down into the plain, the Numidians held their ground. This led Metellus to believe that Jugurtha planned a series of skirmishes to wear down the army rather than an outright attack. To secure his position he sent Rutilius Rufus and a force of cavalry and lightly armed troops to secure a site by the river for a camp, should one be necessary overnight, thus giving the army access to fresh water. Metellus remained in command of the cavalry at the head of the column, with Marius in command of the main force behind him. Once Metellus' army had entered the plain, Jugurtha sent a force of 2,000 infantry to block the route the Romans had come from and prevent a possible retreat.

With the trap now in place Jugurtha's forces attacked:

> The rear of Metellus' column suffered heavy casualties, and both flanks were harassed by mobile assailants who pressed home their attacks and spread great confusion in the Roman ranks. For even the men who resisted with the most courage were disconcerted by the irregular manner of the fighting, in which they were wounded at long range without being able to strike back or come to grips with their enemy.
>
> Jugurtha's horsemen had been given careful instructions beforehand. Whenever a squadron of Roman cavalry began a charge, instead of retreating in one body, they scattered as widely as possible. In this way they could take advantage of their numerical superiority. If they failed to stop their enemy's charge, they would wait until the Romans lost their formation, and then cut them off by attacks in the rear and on their flanks.[210]

Thus, we can see the key to Jugurtha's strategy: to harass the Romans at distance, by shot and cavalry and deny them their superiority in close quarter infantry combat. Furthermore, the widespread attacks and the terrain acted to disrupt the Roman battle discipline and tight combat formation. We do not know how long this struggle went on for, but the impression Sallust gives is that it continued for some time. As Sallust himself comments, the Romans had both superior quality and number of soldiers, but the Numidians had the ground in their favour and the style of combat played to their strengths.[211]

Nevertheless, the key to the Numidian victory would have been the collapse of the Roman formation and an attempted withdrawal. Effectively the Romans were boxed-in, with Numidians ahead and to the right, as well as blocking the route behind them, with the river to their left. Had the Roman troops broken they would have been massacred. Sallust points out that this point was not lost on Metellus who wasted no time in informing his men that retreat was not an option.[212] Furthermore, the Numidian attack was a series of strikes rather than close-order combat. With this in mind, Metellus ordered an advance uphill towards the Numidians, to force them to fight in close quarters or retreat. Faced with a Roman advance and not wanting to engage the legionaries at close quarters, the Numidians broke and scattered into the mountains.

Attention now shifted to Rutilius' force by the river. At some point before battle had started, Jugurtha dispatched his lieutenant, Bomilcar, along with a force of forty-four elephants and accompanying infantry to attack the Roman advance force, now making camp by the river. Sallust states that Bomilcar attempted to launch a surprise attack on the Romans using the cover of the wooded region between the two forces. Given that his force had over forty elephants in it, a surprise attack does seem unlikely to have succeeded, especially given the presence of Roman pickets. Upon seeing the massive cloud of dust kicked up by Bomilcar's force, Rutilius gathered his men into formation and charged out to meet the enemy.

This almost-comic Numidian attack ended as almost as soon as it started when the elephants became entangled in the undergrowth between the two forces, disrupting the Numidian advance. The accompanying Numidian infantry apparently broke and fled for the safety of higher ground leaving the elephants to be slaughtered. Here Sallust provides the only figures for the battle, with forty Numidian elephants killed and four captured.[213] With Bomilcar routed, Rutilius then set off to rejoin the main force, by which time night had fallen. Sallust increased the drama of his narrative by having both Roman forces mistaking the approach of the other for the enemy; with battle narrowly being averted thanks to the scouts sent out by both sides. Following the battle we are told that Metellus remained in camp for four days, to rebuild his army, whilst Jugurtha set about raising a fresh one.

What are we to make of the second battle of the Jugurthine War and the first one to receive anything approaching a detailed description in Sallust? It is clear that despite having chosen his ground and tactics perfectly, Jugurtha and the Numidians had been clearly defeated by Metellus, thanks to the quality of the Roman forces. Despite a superior position and the excellent use of his missile weapons (bows and slings) and cavalry on both occasions when faced with Roman legionaries in close quarters, the Numidian troops fled from the battle-field. Naturally, this was aided by the calm and steady leadership of Metellus

II. The Battle of the Muthul River - Stage 2

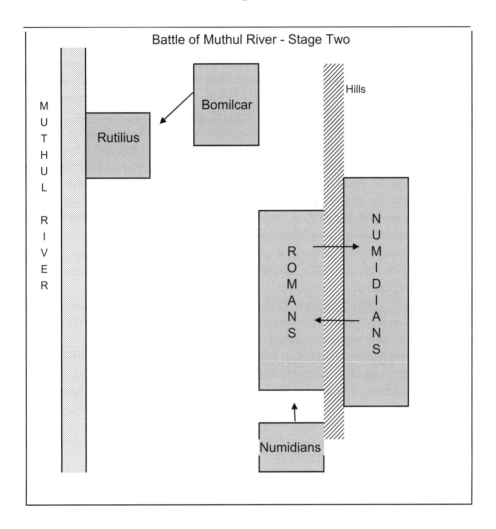

Battle of Muthul River - Stage Two

who had confidence in the superiority of his own forces and the knowledge that this would tell in the final outcome.

The overall effect is interesting to consider. One the one hand, the Romans had won a clear victory, restoring Roman pride and the balance of power between the respective forces. The superiority of the Roman military machine had clearly been demonstrated and the weaknesses of the Numidian one made all too plain to see. Nevertheless, we must ask ourselves just how bitter a defeat was it for Jugurtha? Although we have no figures for casualties, Sallust's narrative makes it clear that the bulk of his forces survived, although he did lose a considerable force of elephants. More importantly, as long as the king himself remained free then the war would continue. However, Sallust does make one important but odd point as a postscript to the battle. He states that despite the reactively low Numidian casualties, the majority deserted Jugurtha, who had to recruit a force of untrained peasants to rebuild his army. Sallust ascribes this to being a quirk of the Numidian culture.[214] However, it would perhaps be more logical to see it as the first signs that, although Jugurtha intended to fight on, the Numidian military knew when they were beaten.

Nevertheless, despite his victory, Metellus was left with a serious problem, namely how to bring the war to a speedy conclusion. Jugurtha had been defeated militarily, but until he was in Roman hands the war would continue. In many respects this was the type of warfare that most vexed the Romans; the enemy had been defeated militarily, but the figurehead remained. With Hannibal, they had forced him into exile and, after two decades on the run, eventual suicide; whilst with Viriathus, they had resorted to assassination. With no other option, Metellus began a campaign of denying Jugurtha access to the resources of Numidia, by the country's total subjugation. This process is best described by Sallust:

> He (Metellus) therefore marched into the most fertile parts of Numidia, laid waste the country, captured and burned many strong-holds and towns which had hurriedly been fortified or left without defenders, ordered the death of all the adults and gave everything else to his soldiers as booty. In this way he caused such terror that many men were given to the Romans as hostages, grain and other necessities were furnished in abundance and garrisons were admitted wherever Metellus thought it advisable.[215]

Although this was an admirable strategy in terms of denying Jugurtha access to resources, it would have turned the Numidians against Rome, especially when you consider that Metellus had started this campaign being welcomed by the local inhabitants. Furthermore, if anything, it would have increased support for the flagging campaign of Jugurtha. Another side effect of this policy was that it spread Metellus' forces over a wide area. This presented an opportunity for Jugurtha, who responded by shadowing Metellus' main force and mounting lightning strikes with his cavalry against any stray Roman units he came upon. Sallust records that one such unit was ambushed and slaughtered.[216] This tactic forced Metellus to adopt more caution when campaigning in the Numidian countryside, with his army split into two main forces, one commanded by him, and one by Marius, with the two shadowing each other. This set the tone for the rest of the campaign of 109 with Metellus and Marius' forces attacking the various Numidian towns and Jugurtha shadowing them with his cavalry and impeding the Roman progress whenever he could, through spoiling crops or poisoning water sources, but not giving battle.

Thus, once again, the Roman army became bogged down in a long and drawn-out war against an 'invisible' guerrilla enemy. The effects on Roman morale can be seen by Sallust again referring to the existence of groups of Roman deserters. Metellus determined to bring Jugurtha to battle once more by attacking the city of Zama, which he hoped would force Jugurtha to make a stand to save the city. It has to be said that this was a vain hope at best and showed just how lacking in ideas the Romans had become. Unfortunately for Metellus, Jugurtha learnt of this plan from a group of Roman deserters who had switched sides and was able to use his greater speed to reach Zama first and make preparations. Zama's defences were duly bolstered, aided by the presence of the Roman deserters to defend the town. Jugurtha, however, had no intention of being pinned down in one location and swiftly took his cavalry force back into the hills.

Once again, Jugurtha's superior military intelligence showed through, as he learnt that Marius had taken a small force to the nearby town of Sicca to gain additional supplies. He therefore moved his cavalry force and ambushed Marius as he was leaving the town, planning to surround Marius by having the inhabitants of the town attack Marius from the rear. Marius though, kept his head and advanced swiftly at the enemy, thus escaping from being surrounded and again testing the nerve of the Numidians in front of him. Again, when faced with Roman soldiers charging them, the Numidians broke, and the ambush failed, with few casualties on either side.[217]

Once more, a familiar pattern was repeated, with Jugurtha's brilliant tactical ability being negated by the poor quality of his troops.

Despite losing the element of surprise, Metellus continued with his siege of Zama. Jugurtha again, however, proved to be a master of the unexpected and attacked the lightly-defended Roman camp behind Metellus' army. Once again this resulted in initial success with the Roman guards scattering rather than standing and fighting, the majority of whom were slaughtered. However, Sallust reports that just forty men held firm and defended a ridge or hill-top, long enough for Metellus and Marius to realize the situation and come to their aid.[218] Jugurtha, after surprising and embarrassing the Romans once more, had to retreat when faced with overwhelming odds and thus the stalemate continued.

The war continued in this vein, with Metellus continuing with the siege of Zama and Jugurtha ambushing and harrying the Roman lines wherever he could. Sallust preserves a good account of the siege, obviously taken from a first-hand account. In many ways the siege of Zama became a microcosm for the war itself. Overwhelming Roman military might was not enough to take the city, and Jugurtha continued to ambush the Roman forces without being brought to battle and continued to be driven off. In the end, with the onset of winter, Metellus was forced to abandon the siege of Zama and took the bulk of his army back to Roman Africa to winter there. He naturally left garrisons in a number of Numidian towns.

Thus, the campaign of 109, despite the brilliant victory at Muthul River, had ended in stalemate and the war dragged on into a fourth year, with still no obvious Roman success in sight. As on so many occasions, Roman military superiority, in both numbers and quality, could not defeat an enemy who refused to give battle and continued to harry them. Certainly, Metellus had restored Roman pride and military superiority in battle, but had no obvious military strategy to bring the war to an end.

Therefore, with no other option, Metellus once again attempted to end the war by diplomacy through the subversion of Jugurtha' deputy, Bomilcar, whose position, as he fully understood, was a precarious one. As Sallust points out, Bomilcar, having been Jugurtha's agent in the murder of the Numidian prince Massiva in Rome, would have been handed over for Roman justice if there were any settlement between Rome and Jugurtha then Bomilcar.[219] Furthermore, he must have realized that ultimately the Numidians would not win this war and again he would find himself at the mercy of Roman justice. Therefore, a separate deal between himself and the Romans was the only way of ensuring his own survival. Bomilcar thus attempted to persuade Jugurtha to come to terms with the Romans, successfully as it appears, and negotiations were opened.

We have to question whether Jugurtha had suddenly had a change of heart brought about by Bomilcar or whether this was nothing more than a continuation of his earlier tactic of negotiating with the Romans to muddy the waters. Metellus convened a council of his senior men and sent initial terms to Jugurtha of 200,000 pounds of silver, all his elephants and a number of horses and weapons, along with the return of all Roman deserters, all of which were complied with. It was only when Jugurtha himself was ordered to appear before the Romans, at Tisidium, that he broke off negotiations.

Given that he handed over a considerable portion of his resources to Metellus, we have to consider that Jugurtha was genuinely trying to seek a settlement with Rome. However, following his victory and humiliation of the Romans at Suthul, he must have known that the Romans would never have allowed him to remain as King of Numidia, and in fact it was unlikely that the Romans would have let him remain alive at all. What this incident shows, if anything is that both sides were tiring of this war, with no victory in sight for either party. Thus the war continued into a fourth year (108 BC) with Metellus remaining in command of the campaign as proconsul, which was hardly a surprise given his reputation, accomplishments and formidable political support in the Senate.

Treachery in the Winter of 109/108 BC

However, this support back in Rome came in contrast to his position in Africa. Another year had passed and Jugurtha, despite the set-piece defeat, was still in the field with his army and could act with impunity, striking against the Romans seemingly at random. The war was to drag on into a fourth year, with no obvious military solution in sight and negotiations for a peace had broken down once again. Added to that was the military failure to capture the city of Zama. On the ground, this lacklustre Roman performance had resulted in desertions, as we have seen. With a number of deserters being handed over by Jugurtha, Metellus was at least able to make an example of them and discourage any further such actions. However, it was at a higher level that Metellus faced the most danger, when this discontent found a figurehead, in the shape of his own deputy, Caius Marius. Marius' background will be examined shortly (Chapter 7), but at this particular time he found himself in an ideal position. That Rome would win the war was inevitable, at least in a military sense, yet the campaign was dragging on and Marius found himself in a position that many deputies find themselves in, being convinced that he could do a better job than his superior.

With the Roman army wintering in the province of Africa, Marius apparently requested of Metellus that he be given leave to return to Rome and stand for consul. For Metellus there were a number of obvious reasons to refuse such a request. For a start Marius was a serving officer on an important campaign and should not be released for personal political reasons. Secondly, it was obvious that Marius was angling to take Metellus' own command away from him. Thirdly, was the fact that, as Metellus saw it, Marius did not possess the attributes to be elected consul and would fail utterly. Despite his military and political record, he had no real powerbase or allies of his own and had only achieved what he had through being a client of the Metelli. Furthermore, he was an Italian nobleman (albeit with Roman citizenship) but was not a Roman one, an important distinction in the eyes of the Roman aristocracy. For these reasons, it is not a surprise that Metellus refused Marius' request. Nonetheless, Metellus was now faced with a potentially rebellious deputy to contend with as well.

With the failure of the negotiations, the Romans spent the rest of the winter in their African province, regrouping their forces for the next campaign. This left Jugurtha a relatively free hand in Numidia (Roman garrisons excepted) and he used it to his advantage. He assembled a new army and spent the rest of time trying to win back the towns and cities that had gone over to the Romans (mostly unwillingly) and even trying to subvert the Roman garrisons left behind in a number of towns. Success came in the form of the town of Vaga, one of the first Numidian towns to turn to Metellus in 109 and with a Roman garrison. During a public festival the officers of the garrison were invited to dine with the town's dignitaries, during which they were murdered. With the garrison leaderless the townspeople attacked the soldiers, cut them off from their citadel and fell upon them in the streets, massacring them. Suspiciously only the Roman commander, T. Turpilius Silanus survived.[220]

Upon hearing of the disaster at Vaga, Metellus set out at once and crossed the border with a large Roman force intent of avenging the loss. Upon reaching the town, the inhabitants made a fatal mistake. Metellus' force contained a large number of Numidian cavalry, which had gone over into Roman service (itself a clear sign of Numidian discontent). As the cavalry reached the town before the Roman infantry, the townspeople assumed that they were from Jugurtha and opened the gates and went out to greet them. Naturally, taking advantage of this stroke of fortune the Romano-Numidian cavalry slaughtered the inhabitants and took the gates before they could be closed. Despite some resistance the town fell easily, with inhabitants being slaughtered and the survivors enslaved. Sallust dates the whole rebellion to two days in length.[221]

The most prominent victim was the garrison commander T. Turpilius Silanus, who was condemned by a military tribunal and scourged and executed.[222] What made the matter worse was that Turpilius was a friend of Metellus and only there at his request. Plutarch claims that at the tribunal, Marius pushed for Metellus to sentence his friend to death, which Metellus reluctantly had to do. Plutarch claims that this increased the tension between Metellus and Marius. He then goes onto add that soon after the execution the charge was found to be false and Turpilius was actually innocent. Thus, for Plutarch at least, Marius had got Metellus to execute his friend on trumped-up charges.[223] Exactly how Turpilius could be innocent is never stated by Plutarch, nor could we imagine how it could be the case. Even if he did not conspire with the inhabitants then he was at least guilty of gross negligence. As we find none of this in Sallust's account, we must exercise caution.

Though the rebellion had been swiftly and brutally crushed, ensuring that a repetition was unlikely, it did show the weakness of the Roman position and was another setback for Metellus, showing the danger of Roman inactivity during the winter months.

Jugurtha, however, still faced discontent within his own ranks, again in the form of Bomilcar. Still fearful of his own position and the inevitability of a

Numidian defeat, he plotted to remove Jugurtha in a coup. To these ends, he enlisted the help of a Numidian nobleman and army commander, Nabdalsa, who commanded the Numidian forces on the border of Roman Africa. However, on the appointed day Nabdalsa's nerve cracked and he withdrew from the plot. Bomilcar compounded this failure by writing a letter to him, berating him for his lack of nerve and entreating him to join his plot as it was inevitable that Jugurtha would lose the war. As usually happens in these cases, the letter found its way into the hands of another, Nabdalsa's secretary, who took it straight to the king. When Nabdalsa found out about the letter's loss he managed to make it to Jugurtha first and admitted the whole plot. Bomilcar and the rest of his conspirators were rounded up and executed immediately. Nabdalsa was spared, probably due to his position and Jugurtha's desire to limit the spread of this rebellion. We know the details of this plot thanks to Numidian deserters, probably some of those associated with the plot itself, who made their way to the Roman lines.[224] Though the plot had been dealt with, Jugurtha's weak position in Numidia had been clearly exposed. The inevitability of his defeat seemed to be widely accepted, yet he could not surrender nor could the Romans bring the war to an end.

Thus the campaign of 108 BC began with both sides facing internal divisions and the prospect of another year of stalemate. Whilst Jugurtha rid himself of Bomilcar by a swift execution, Metellus rid himself of Marius by finally acceding to his demand to return to Rome, accepting that it was better to remove a source of discontent from Africa than to let it fester. He did this safe in the knowledge that there was no real chance of Marius being elected consul. Unfortunately for him, however, this safety was only in his own mind, as will be detailed in the next chapter.

The Campaign of 108 BC and the 'Second Metellan Battle'

The campaigning for 108 began, as was usual, with a Roman invasion of Numidia, yet on this occasion Jugurtha gave battle. Once again Sallust's limitations as a historian come to the fore as the details of this battle are relegated to just a handful of lines.

> Metellus unexpectedly appeared with his army; whereupon Jugurtha made ready and drew up his Numidians as well as time allowed. Then the battle began. Wherever the king was present in person, there was some show of resistance; everywhere else his soldiers broke and fled at the first charge. The Romans captured a considerable number of standards and arms, but few prisoners.[225]

We are given no reason as to why Jugurtha gave battle. Sallust's implication is that Metellus was able to surprise him and left him with no choice; yet given both the superior intelligence Jugurtha had access to as well as the speed of his forces compared to the Romans, this seemed unlikely. Sallust does state that Jugurtha was growing increasingly paranoid following the conspiracy of his officers and it is perhaps possible that he sought battle to restore flagging Numidian morale. Standing against this possibility, however, was the inevitable outcome, which Jugurtha must have been aware of: when faced with superior Roman infantry, the Numidians once again broke and fled.

The other possibility is that Metellus was able to corner Jugurtha, yet the speed with which this was accomplished is baffling, given that he had spent the previous year failing to do just that. It is perhaps worth remembering that a number of Numidians had deserted to the Roman side over the winter of 108. We are not told of their rank, but given the strong possibility that they were involved in the attempted coup described above, then it is more than likely that they were a number of senior-ranking Numidians and brought with them considerable intelligence on Jugurtha's plans. With this knowledge we can speculate that Metellus was able to finally surprise Jugurtha. Nevertheless, with the little evidence we have all we can do is speculate upon this.

Whatever the cause of the battle, the result was clear enough. The Numidians were defeated and Jugurtha fled deeper in Numidia, taking refuge at the royal stronghold of Thala. Metellus swiftly followed up his victory with a dash to Thala in an attempt to capture the king. Despite this swift advance, Jugurtha was able to flee once more, with his children and his treasury. Nonetheless, Metellus determined to capture the stronghold and set about another siege. On this occasion the town fell after a forty-day siege. However, the gains were minimal as the town's leading citizens fled to the royal palace, taking their treasures with them. After a feast, which included large amounts of wine, these citizens then set fire to the palace, with themselves in it, in an apparent act of mass suicide (though a drunken accident cannot be ruled out).

Unfortunately, this is all that we know of the campaign of 108 BC, the battle and the siege, with Sallust skipping over the rest of the year, perhaps on account of there being little to report. Once again, it appears that although the Romans had defeated Jugurtha once again in 108, the war seemed to be no nearer a conclusion. On the positive side, most of Numidia now lay in Roman hands and Jugurtha was apparently on the run with only a small retinue.

The African War

However, it was at this point, just when he seemed to be at his lowest ebb, that Jugurtha showed his superb diplomatic and tactical abilities and pulled off a coup which resulted in a massive escalation of the war for Rome. Having been cut off from his Numidian resources, Jugurtha widened his influence and gained allies and forces from outside of Numidia, namely the Gaetulians to the south and the Mauri to the west. The Gaetulians were a collection of tribes who lived to the south of the Numidians, by the Atlas Mountains. In the few Roman sources that do mention them they are usually collected together as one race, though the reality was far more complicated.[226] Sallust exhibits a typical Roman reaction to the Gaetulians when he describes them as:

> a wild and uncivilized race of men who at the time had never heard of Rome. He (Jugurtha) mustered their population in one place and gradually trained them to keep rank, follow the standards, obey orders and perform the other duties of soldiers.[227]

Aside from overlooking the incredible amount of time it would have taken Jugurtha to train a barbarous people from scratch in the art of 'western' warfare, we have a reference from Livy that Gaetulians were to be found in Hannibal's army and can conclude that they had long been used as mercenaries, and thus were well acquainted both with Rome and an organized form of warfare.[228] Given this, we can assume that far from being a case of Jugurtha wandering out of the wilderness, as Sallust paints it, it would haven been more the case that Jugurtha's money appealed to them.

Further help came from the west in the form of Bocchus, King of the Mauri, a tribal people in the very northwest of Africa (Mauretania). Bocchus was related to Jugurtha by marriage and thus it seems that Jugurtha was able to appeal to family ties, liberally aided by substantial monies, to bring Bocchus to his aid.[229] Furthermore, it appears that Bocchus had been snubbed by the Romans when he had approached them for a treaty of alliance at the outbreak of the war (though the date and the Roman commander are not given[230]). Jugurtha was also able to play upon Bocchus' fear of the Roman intentions, with them now in control of Numidia. Such a fear may also have been a strong motivating factor in the decision of the Gaetulian tribes to follow Jugurtha.

Thus, at a stroke, Jugurtha had gone from being a fleeing refugee to being the head of a somewhat untested two-nation African alliance against Rome. We must always be cautious in following the apparent short timescales given by our surviving sources and it is more than possible that Jugurtha had been working on these alliances for some time. Nevertheless, for Rome the situation had become potentially grave; where previously they had been facing one king, who did not have the whole support of his nation, they now faced two armies, of Gaetulians and Mauri, commanded by Jugurtha and Bocchus. This latter point has often been overlooked in the histories, with too great a focus on Jugurtha himself. Nevertheless, we must be cautious as to how reliable these new allies were to Jugurtha.

This new hybrid force (which again we have no numbers for) then invaded Numidia and made for Cirta, the site of the siege that had initially caused the war, which by this point of 108 BC was now apparently in Roman hands, though we are not given any details about how it came to be so. By this point Metellus had turned Cirta into a temporary headquarters, housing the Roman supplies, prisoners and captured loot, perhaps for the winter.

One major problem we have with our surviving record concerns the chronology of events.[231] Sallust condenses the events in Numidia in a few short sections.[232] We do not know when in the year the unnamed 'Second Battle' took place. Nor do we have a timescale for Jugurtha's creation of the Gaetulian–Mauri alliance. The clear implication is that Metellus had turned Cirta into a headquarters to spend the winter, rather than evacuating Numidia once again and losing control. After the siege of Thala we are given no indication of Metellus' activities in Numidia, and given the sudden appearance of Cirta in Roman hands, we can speculate that Metellus used this time to consolidate the Roman control of Numidia. Thus when Bocchus and Jugurtha invaded Numidia, the onset of winter was approaching.

Metellus, aware of the advance, established a fortified camp near Cirta to await the arrival of this invading army. It was at this point that he received the unexpected news, that not only had Marius been elected to a consulship for 107 BC, but that the assembly had voted him the province of Numidia and the command against Jugurtha, overriding the Senatorial prerogative (see Chapter 7). We do not need Sallust to imagine how Metellus felt at this betrayal, to be replaced by his own deputy and, even worse, one who was a social inferior and a client. For the Roman campaign, this news could not have come at a worse time. When faced with a massive escalation of the war and an invasion by a combined Mauri-Gaetulian army, the last thing the Romans needed was to have their field commander undermined and de-motivated in such a manner.

Metellus responded by use of diplomacy, in an attempt to break up the alliance between Bocchus and Jugurtha. He sent emissaries to Bocchus to convince him that he did not need to become an enemy of Rome or to support Jugurtha's doomed cause. Unfortunately, Sallust' narrative of the rest of the 108 campaign tails off at this point, with his interest taken by events in Rome involving Marius.[233] This joint attack by Bocchus and Jugurtha on Cirta fails to materialize, perhaps due to Metellus' diplomacy making Bocchus think twice.

When Marius arrives in Africa in 107 BC (again we are given no clear timescale), the command of the army is handed over to him by P. Rutilius Rufus, at Utica (in Roman Africa). Metellus had understandably refused to hand over command as tradition dictated. Thus by 107 BC, the Roman army was back in the Roman province of Africa, again leaving Jugurtha and Bocchus apparently in charge of Numidia. The gaps in our sources do not give us any detail of how this occurred. As far as they are concerned, Bocchus and Jugurtha suddenly stopped their attack on Cirta and sat around for six months waiting for Marius to arrive and take command of the war, and then restarted their campaigns in early to mid–107, at exactly the same point they had left off. Once again, Roman military history falls foul of the priority given to domestic politics. Had we still had the relevant books of Livy intact, this would not be the case (see Appendix V).

Even if Bocchus had been dissuaded from attacking the Romans, Jugurtha was still in command of the Gaetulian army and Cirta made a tempting target. We are unfortunately left with a series of questions, which, for the foreseeable future, will never be answered: did Jugurtha attack Cirta or did Metellus withdraw all of his forces back to Roman Africa?

We can perhaps find some help in the actions of Marius in the campaign of 107 BC. On the one hand we are told that Jugurtha was attacking towns in Numidia still allied to Rome, but on the other that there were numerous strongholds still in Jugurthan hands.[234] It is most likely that no serious fighting took place between Metellus and Jugurtha in late 108/early 107, though whether this was the result of Jugurthan or Metellan indifference is impossible to tell. We cannot even be certain that Cirta remained in Roman hands, though this seems most likely from the later context of the campaigns of 107 BC. It is possible that Metellus left Cirta and a number of towns garrisoned and withdrew the bulk of the army back into Roman Africa. Faced with a strong Roman defence and an uncertain ally, it is also possible that Jugurtha was not able to successfully besiege Cirta and when he realized that Metellus was not going to be drawn into battle, gave up the attack and concentrated on bringing the rest of Numidia back to his rule.

Summary – The Metellan Campaigns

i) Rome

In the face of it, the Metellan campaigns were an obvious success for Rome. When Metellus took command in 109 the Romans had just been defeated and humiliated and had been driven from Numidia. In the period that followed the

Romans fought two pitched battles against the Numidians, at Muthul River and the so-called 'Second Battle', and comprehensively won both, gaining complete control of Numidia and forcing Jugurtha to flee. Yet by 107 BC the situation had, if anything, become potentially more dangerous for Rome than in 109, for two main reasons.

Firstly, despite overwhelming military superiority, the war continued with no obvious end in sight. If anything, Jugurtha was showing the tenacity of the Romans, in the fact that every time he was defeated in battle, he raised a fresh army and continued to fight. Florus drew the parallel to Hannibal, but when Hannibal was defeated in 202 at Zama, Carthage sued for peace and he had to lay down his arms.[235] As the undisputed king of Numidia, Jugurtha was able to continue the war, though as noted below his control over Numidia wavered with every defeat. Furthermore, the Roman grip on Numidia itself appeared to be tenuous. Certainly, cities such as Thala, Vaga and Cirta could be taken, by siege if necessary, but the Roman hold on them was tenuous at best, with the ever present danger of a native rebellion. Furthermore, the Roman writ of control only extended to the towns and cities they garrisoned, with the country-side uncontrolled and potentially hostile. This was especially the case when Jugurtha reverted to his guerrilla tactics. With regard to this last point the Metellan campaigns had again shown that although superior in battle, the Roman army was not able to win a war when the enemy refused to come to terms and fought on.

As noted earlier, the war that had broken out centred on the figure of Jugurtha himself, even if there were sound strategic reasons for wanting to limit the power of Numidia. Until he came to terms, was killed or captured, the war would continue. Given the strains at Rome both domestically and with regard to the situation in the north, the Senate needed a speedy conclusion to the war. When, after eighteen months, it looked as though Metellus was not able to deliver this result, these tensions spilled over and saw the extraordinary election of Marius to the consulship and then the command in Numidia.

The second reason was the rise of the Mauri-Gaetulian alliance, which saw a significant escalation of the war. Instead of fighting the Numidians, who had been shown to be militarily of poorer quality, the Romans now faced a coalition of the three main North African races, the Numidians, the Mauri and the Gaetulians, which, if unchecked, threatened Rome's domination of the North African region. Furthermore, at the same time as Rome faced this alliance, the issue of instability of command was raised once more, with Metellus being undermined by his deputy, and stripped of the command altogether. Although the sources are not clear, this may have resulted in the Roman army failing to engage this new invading North African army and retiring to Roman territory.

Nevertheless, we have to ask ourselves, how much of this situation was down to Metellus. In just eighteen months he had restored Roman discipline and shown the superior Roman military ability in two set-piece battles. Jugurtha had been expelled from Numidia and the country was under nominal Roman suzerainty. Certainly, Jugurtha had re-invaded at the head of a new pan-African army, but this did not mean that either the Mauri or the Gaetulians would prove to be any more of a challenge in battle than the Numidians were.

Thus, it can be argued that the position Metellus left in the beginning of 107 BC was far stronger than the one which he had inherited two years earlier. That the situation had the potential to become worse for Rome did not mean that it would, especially given the Roman military superiority in set-piece battles. Nonetheless, there were no clear signs that the war would come to a speedy conclusion and for that Metellus lost his command.

ii) Jugurtha

For Jugurtha the campaigns of 109–108 BC had been a clear setback. During the winter of 110 he is reported to have been on the offensive, engaging in wars to enlarge his kingdom, which may have included subduing the Gaetulians, having defeated and humiliated the Roman army. By the summer of 108, he had been defeated twice in battle and been driven from his kingdom. His campaigns show both his individual brilliance as a commander and the inherent weaknesses of his position. Both at Muthul River and Thala, he forced the Romans to fight on his terms, using his tactics on his ground. Yet this tactical brilliance was not matched by the quality of the men under his command, who proved to be no match for a Roman legion and usually fled when faced by one at close quarters.

His leadership skills were ably demonstrated by the 'grand alliance' he created in 108 BC, as joint head of an army of Gaetulians and Mauri. Yet, if he could not rely on his own countrymen, what chance did he have with mercenaries and untrustworthy allies? Both the Gaetulians and Mauri had been weaker than the Numidians at the start of the war; if the Numidians were no match for Rome then would these new allies prove to be any better?

Nevertheless, his tenacity in continuing to fight was both a result of his character and his desperate position. His actions both at Rome, but especially at Suthul, had ensured that Roman public opinion would brook no peace terms that did not end in his being paraded though Rome. Furthermore, his own position in Numidia was weak, undermined by the seemingly-inevitable Roman victory. The aborted coup of 109/108 BC also showed the weakness of his grip on Numidia, with most Numidians realizing that the war, and all of its associated misery would only end with him killed or captured. If his own countrymen were not trustworthy then the Gaetulians and Mauri were less so. Bocchus had already been open to negotiating with the Romans and the Gaetulians were mercenaries at best and would not be reliable following their first defeat.

Thus as 107 opened, Jugurtha had no option but to keep fighting and had just one glimmer of hope of emerging from the war intact. Defeating the Romans was logistically impossible; they had a far superior military and a near-endless supply of men and commanders. Whilst the Senate may have seen the logic of coming to a negotiated settlement with him, the Roman people, however, were another case. From the outset, this war had been driven by Roman public opinion, usually manifesting itself in the actions of the tribunes. By 107 BC this had resulted in an outsider being elected consul and the Senate having their prerogative of selecting Rome's military commanders stolen away from them. It is clear that with the circumstances as they were and Jugurtha being the focus of the wrath of the Roman people, peace was impossible. Yet if the circumstances changed and this war became an unnecessary distraction in the face of a greater threat, then peace may indeed have been possible.

Chapter 6

The Northern Wars: Victory in Thrace, Defeat in Gaul (111–107 BC)

Before we turn our attention to Marius, we must first consider the events that had occurred on Rome's northern borders during the period of 111–107 BC, to see how Rome was faring in the Northern Wars. When we last examined the situation, in the northeast the Scordisci had been driven from Greece and Roman armies were operating in Thracian territory, whereas in the northwest, Roman forces had been destroyed at the Battle of Noreia.

The Cimbric Wars II (109–108 BC)

Between the years 113 to 109 we have no trace of the Cimbri. The surviving Roman sources simply dismiss them as having continued their wanderings once more. Yet to dismiss them so easily diminishes their role as a genuine opponent for Rome, some mythical bogeymen that appear out of nowhere every few years. If anything, the Battle of Noreia merely confirmed an existing pattern for the Cimbri, of finding a hostile reception wherever they went. Even though on this occasion they were victorious, the Cimbri apparently decided that the region was unsuitable for peaceful settlement or would require too great a war to be worth their while, and continued their westward quest, which would take them into the fertile regions of Gaul. We do not know their route, or whether these years were a continued migration or whether they found somewhere to settle, even temporarily. By 109 BC, however, the Cimbri had begun to penetrate the Rhone valley and once again appeared on the fringes of Roman influence.

Again, we only have scant details for the events of 109–108 BC and even then the exact chronology is not clear. Furthermore, the details of Florus and the *Periochae of Livy* are at odds with each other. Of the two consuls of 109 BC, we have already discussed Q. Caecilius Metellus; the other consul was M. Iunius Silanus.

The surviving narrative histories give us two principle versions of the events of 109/108 BC. Firstly, there is the version given by Florus:

> The Cimbri, Teutones and Tigurini, fugitives from the extreme parts of Gaul, since the ocean had inundated their territories, began to seek new settlements throughout the world, and excluded from Gaul and Spain, descended into Italy and sent representatives to the camp of Silanus and thence to the Senate asking that 'the people of Mars (Rome) should give them some land by way of pay and use their hands and weapons for any purpose it wished'. But what land could the Roman people give them when they were on the eve of a struggle amongst themselves about agrarian legislation? Thus repulsed they began to seek by force of arms what they had failed to obtain by entreaties. Silanus could not withstand the first attack of the barbarians.[236]

Secondly we have the shorter *Periochae of Livy*:

> consul Marcus Iunius Silanus lost a battle to the Cimbri. The Senate refused the demand of the envoy of the Cimbri for a home and land on which to settle.[237]

References to Silanus' defeat can be found scattered throughout the remaining sources, including Velleius, who states that the battle took place in Gaul, and Eutropius who makes the unusual claim that Silanus defeated the Cimbri in Gaul.[238] Given the varying accounts, what are the main differences? In the first place, there are the key questions of where the battle took place and who the Romans were actually fighting.

Florus places the battle in Italy, whilst the others place it in Gaul. Given the Roman loss in the battle, we would expect to hear far more about it had it taken place in Italy, as such a defeat would be on a par with Hannibal and would have left Rome defenceless. Thus we can accept that the encounter took place in Gaul. The other issue we have is with the identities of the enemies facing Rome. Florus believes that Rome was faced with an alliance of the Cimbri, an existing threat, and the Teutones and Tigurini as well, whereas the *Periochae of Livy* has just the Cimbri returning. Throughout Florus' account we see this grand alliance of 'differing tribes', whereas the other accounts only feature the Cimbri, until c.102 BC (see Chapter 9).

Although the lack of a detailed surviving narrative means we can never rule out the possibility that the other tribes were present, the balance of probability suggests that it was just the Cimbric tribes involved in these early stages.

The next issue concerns the Cimbric embassy, which asked the Senate for land to settle on (foreshadowing what eventually became Roman policy hundreds of years later in the late Imperial period). Florus would place this before the battle, with Silanus waiting for an answer from the Senate. The *Periochae of Livy* seems to place this after the battle. What is clear is that at some point in 109 BC, the wanderings of the Cimbri brought them back to Rome's northern borders. Silanus, as consul, was dispatched to Gaul to intercept them. Given the fate of his predecessor Carbo, at the Battle of Noreia, it is possible that Silanus initially received the Cimbric envoys and forwarded them onto the Senate. For the Cimbri, seeking Roman permission to settle in Gaul, on Rome's borders, would avoid further bloodshed. For Silanus, there was perhaps benefit in seeing whether the Senate would consider the request, despite the bad blood between the two sides. If nothing else it would allow him time to plan a battle were one needed.

It was almost inevitable that the Senate rejected the Cimbric demands, acceptance of which, given the earlier loss at Noreia in 113 BC, would only be taken as a sign of Roman weakness and encourage further uprisings in the region. Once again, we have no description of this crucial second battle against the Cimbri, other than that it was another Roman disaster. Silanus returned to Rome and was left alone for a while until in 104 he was prosecuted for his actions in the defeat, though he was acquitted.[239] We are not even sure of the year that the battle took place, with the sources being vague and allowing it to be dated to either 109 or 108 BC. Recently, Evans has speculated that it took place to the northwest of the Alps near Lake Geneva, but there is no clear evidence for such an identification.[240]

If we are to follow the *Periochae of Livy*, after the victory the Cimbri sent the demand for land to the Senate, yet we hear no more about it; the conclusion drawn from the sources is that they continued their wanderings. Yet we have to ask ourselves whether this was the case. Twice now the Cimbri had defeated the Romans in battle and southern Gaul was a potentially excellent homeland for them. Given that they had already moved away from southern Gaul after the Battle of Noreia only to be forced back to the region, it does seem that they again left the region having once more proved their military superiority over the Romans. Frustratingly, we are left with nothing more than idle speculation centred on the Cimbri not wishing to remain in a region where there were hostile powers, even ones they could defeat.

We have no record of any activity in the north by the consuls of 108 BC, which lends weight to the theory that this unnamed battle took place in this year. The year 107 BC saw the situation become much worse for Rome. Being defeated twice in succession by the Cimbri clearly undermined Rome's status as the hegemon of the region and it appears that the balance of power began shifting away from them. The Cimbric victory apparently stirred a number of local tribes against Rome, though whether this was through deliberate Cimbric agitation is unclear. A new threat to Rome arose in the form of the Tigurini, who came from Helvetia (Switzerland) and invaded the territory of the Nitiobroges, Roman allies in the region. As can be seen, the Tigurini travelled some distance from the Alps to the Atlantic, most probably via the Garonne River valley.[241] Thus we see that the Roman control over the region was disintegrating.

Of the two consuls of 107, Marius received Numidia (as we will see in Chapter 7), whilst L. Cassius Longinus received Gaul, with orders to suppress these revolts and defeat the Tigurini. Orosius preserves the fullest report of Cassius' campaign:

> the consul L. Cassius, who was in Gaul, pursued the Tigurini as far as the Ocean (the Atlantic). When he was on his way back, he was surrounded and slain in an ambush laid by the enemy. Lucius Piso, a man of consular rank and at the time the legate of the consul Cassius, was also killed. The other legate, C. Publius, in accordance with the terms of a most disgraceful treaty, handed over to the Tigurini hostages and a half share of all the Roman baggage. This was done in order to save the surviving part of the army, which had fled for refuge to the camp. On returning to Rome, Publius was summoned to trial by the plebeian tribune Coelius on the charge that he had given hostages to the Tigurini. Consequently he had to flee into exile.[242]

If this was not enough, Caesar adds that the survivors were made to go under the yoke as a token of submission.[243] Thus, for a second year in succession a Roman army had been slaughtered by a tribal enemy, this time the Tigurini. Again we have no other details of the battle, such as a location, or how Cassius and his army were able to be ambushed. Once again, we have a tribal army ambushing a Roman one and again we are reminded of the Teutoburg Forest massacre. Not only this, but for the second time in four years, a defeated Roman army had to submit to the yoke.

Thus the Cimbri and the Tigurini roamed free in Gaul, Rome's military reputation was in ruins, and then we hear that the Volcae, Roman allies in southern Gaul rose up in revolt. As 107 BC ended, the war in Numidia seemed to be a growing irrelevance, with the threat from the north being the main cause of instability. Two Roman armies in two years had been defeated by two different invading barbarian enemies. As yet there was no direct threat to Italy, but given the apparent ease with which the tribes could defeat Roman armies and the collapse of the 'Pax Romana' in southern Gaul, it is clear where the real danger to Rome lay.

The Military Reforms of 109 BC

There is a further brief but highly interesting note on the domestic activities of the consuls of 109 BC. Asconius, in his commentary on one of Cicero's speeches (the *pro Cornelio*), reports the following Cicero quote:

> Gentleman of the jury, there are generally four ways in which a decision about a law can be traditionally taken by the Senate; one of these is a proposal to repeal a law, enacted during the consulship of Q. Caecilius and M. Iunius, in the case of laws which obstructed the military effort.

To which Asconius adds his own note:

> He is referring to Q. Caecilius Metellus Numidicus and M. Iunius Silanus, who were consuls at the time of the war against the Cimbri, a war being conducted inefficiently and unproductively; indeed Iunius himself had little success against the enemy. So he repealed a number of laws passed during this time by the people, which had reduced the length of military service.[244]

This brief statement is of enormous interest as it appears that the consuls, faced with the renewal of the Cimbric threat in the north and the continuation of the war in Numidia, attempted to increase the pool of available manpower by over-turning tribunician laws that restricted military service.

We have no further details as to which laws were repealed, or any resistance to these proposals from the serving tribunes. These issues will be explored in greater depth in Appendix III. What is clear is that the military strain Rome was under, fighting in Gaul, Thrace and Numidia, was forcing the ruling elites to look at ways to increase the available military manpower. Given what occurred under Marius in 107 BC, it is interesting to see an earlier attempt being made in 109 BC.

The Scordiscian Wars II (110–107 BC)

Although the war in the northwest saw a lull between 113 and 109, in the north-east, in Macedon and Thrace it was another matter. Rome's victories against the Scordisci in 112–111 BC (see Chapter 1) again proved only to be a temporary lull in the fighting. The other consul of 110 BC, M. Minucius Rufus, was sent to Macedon and remained there until 106 and fighting the Scordisci once more, again earning himself a triumph (in 106 BC). Thus, even with war raging in Numidia, Rome was still engaged in wars with the Scordisci in Macedon and Thrace throughout this period.

We have three different types of evidence for Minucius' activities: from the narrative sources, inscriptions in Greece and from the *Fasti triumphales*.

The surviving narrative histories inform us of the following:

> Minucius laid waste all the country [Thrace] along the Hebrus [the modern river Maritsa/Evros[245]], losing, however, many of his men as they rode across a river covered with treacherous ice.[246]
>
> Minucius utterly defeated them in a battle near the River Hebrus, which flows from the high mountains of the Odrysae, and after these the survivors were completely annihilated by the proconsul Appius Claudius in a hot fight.[247]
>
> Minucius crushed them on the frozen Hebrus.[248]
>
> The general Minucius Rufus, hard pressed by the Scordiscans and Dacians, for whom he was no match in numbers, sent his brother and a small squadron of cavalry on ahead, along with a detachment of trumpeters, directing him, as soon as he should see the battle begin, to show himself suddenly from the opposite quarter and to order the trumpeters to blow their horns. Then, when the hill-tops re-echoed with the sound, the impression of a huge multitude was borne in upon the enemy, who fled in terror.[249]
>
> About the same time [c.108 BC] took place the famous triumph over the Scordisci of Minucius,[250]
>
> Proconsul M. Minucius fought successfully against the Thracians.[251]
>
> [Who were defeated], as were the Scordisci and Triballi in Macedonia by Minucius Rufus.[252]

Archaeology has revealed that Minucius was awarded an equestrian statue by the people of Delphi, the base of which, and its inscription, still survives:

> Marcus Minucius, son of Quintus Rufus, imperator after the Gauls,

Scordisci, and Bessi, Thracians were defeated, because of his merits, was dedicated by the people of Delphi.[253]

Furthermore, the triumphal inscription for Minucius reveals that he triumphed over both the Scordisci and the Thracians.

Thus it is clear that Minucius fought and won a battle against the Scordisci and their allies on the River Hebrus, though at what point we do not know. It appears that this battle was a decisive one and a great Roman victory. Certainly, we hear no more of the Scordisci until the 80s BC, which given their persistence throughout the previous decade must show the size of the defeat. Once again we have the problem that we know almost nothing about the great battles the Romans fought in this region, though the Frontinus extract does give us some details. The Romans were heavily outnumbered by the Scordisci and their allies, but Minucius was able to fool them with a bluff into thinking that they were trapped between two Roman armies and they broke. Furthermore, we know that the battle took place in winter, due to the ice, an unusual occurrence for the Roman military. We do not know when the battle was fought but given that Minucius returned to Rome in 106 for his triumph, it should be placed either in the winter of 108/107 or 107/106. Given that he would need to rest and ensure order back in Macedon before his return to Rome, a longer timescale is the more likely, making 108/107 the most probable date. Thus the wars in the northeast, which had been continuing for over a decade, were brought to an end at the Battle of the Hebrus. This brought to a close one of the three major battle fronts that Rome was fighting on during this period.

Chapter 7

The Jugurthine War: The Marian Campaigns (107–105 BC)

As Marius comes to dominate the period that follows, it is clear that we need to see what type of man he was and so we need to examine his background prior to his bid for a consulship of 107 BC. Plutarch provides us with a biography of Marius and a number of other references can be found to his early activities. Evans also provides an excellent summary of his early career.[254] Nevertheless, there are a number of elements of his background that remain unclear.

Background and Early Career

Marius famously did not hail from the Roman nobility, but came from an Italian background.[255] He was born c.157 BC in the region of Arpinium (as later did Cicero). Plutarch chose to portray Marius as coming from a humble background, but there is much to argue against this. His parents are only named as Marius and Fulcinia, both of whom may have been related to Senatorial aristocracy.[256] Thus it is likely that Marius grew up as Italian nobility, albeit crucially with Roman citizenship, which allowed him entry into Roman politics. Throughout the Republic, but especially in the later centuries (such as the second century BC), it was common for Italian nobles to join the Roman aristocracy, bringing fresh blood, becoming so-called *novi homines* (new men).[257] In this respect, Marius appears to have followed the standard pattern for this: military service, followed by junior political office sponsored by a powerful Roman patron.

Marius undertook his military service in Spain, during the Numantine War (see chapter one), though the exact dates are a matter of conjecture. According to Plutarch, he eventually came to the notice of Scipio Aemilianus, who apparently noted his qualities.[258] Whether it was a coincidence or a dramatic contrast that both Marius and Jugurtha came to Scipio's attention we will never know. It is perhaps ironic that both men fought for Rome in the same war and would have at least met, though thankfully we are spared any such dramatic stories of this meeting in our surviving sources.

Such distinguished military service would have given Marius the chance to enter Roman politics, albeit at a low level. Here the sources present us with an issue, as Marius appears to disappear for much of the 120s BC. Evans argues that he spent the time between the end of the Numantine War and his first datable political office (the tribunate of 119 BC) engaged in building up the funds and contacts necessary to pursue a political career.[259] The chronology of his earliest attempts at office is hopelessly confused. Sallust speaks of a military tribunate that he was easily elected to, following his exploits in Spain, so this would place it in the early 120s (c.130/129).[260] Valerius Maximus also tells us that he failed in gaining elected office back in Arpinium, so this could account for some of the intervening years.[261] Valerius tells us that Marius, once back in Rome, then stood for the Quaestorship, which according to an inscription from a monument in Rome he succeed in obtaining.[262] All this came against the backdrop of the Gracchan tribunates (see chapter one).

His first datable office was as a tribune in 119 BC, though we are told that he only succeeded at being elected at the second attempt.[263] Plutarch adds that at this point he was being sponsored by the Caecilii Metelli, Rome's leading political family (see appendix four).[264] His tribunate is noted for two main actions: for proposing a law and opposing another. He proposed a law on what seems to be an obscure voting technicality, the width of the passages of the voting pens in judicial cases, through which the citizens of Rome passed. Cicero considers it to have been a sensible move aimed at reducing the potential for the corruption of voters and lets it pass without much comment.[265] In Plutarch, however, the law is a deliberate populist measure, in the vein of the Gracchi, aimed at reducing the influence of the nobility.[266]

Certainly Marius' law was opposed by many in the Senate and the two consuls, one of whom was a Metellus and thus from the family that sponsored him.[267] The Senate voted against the law, purely as an expression of their opinion, as they had no formal veto on legislation. When Marius appeared before them he apparently threatened both consuls with imprisonment unless the Senate's vote was reversed.[268] When he received the support of his nine tribunician colleagues, the consuls and the Senate backed down. This would have given Marius a certain notoriety with the people, but cannot have impressed his sponsors. Perhaps in an attempt to redeem himself he successfully opposed one of his colleague's proposals for the distribution of grain to the people.[269]

Thus, on one occasion he had threatened to imprison the consuls over a law which technically favoured the people, though would have been obscure to many, whilst on the other he blocked what would have been a popular grain distribution law. Although we have no other information to assess these actions on, it does show a certain opportunism. What is clear is that, in the short term, there was little electoral advantage as he is reported to have failed to be elected to either the Curule or Plebeian Aedileships (though these were highly competitive positions, given the low number of places).[270]

However, Marius was able to bounce back in 116 when he secured election to the Praetorship for 115 at the first attempt, albeit in last place. A prosecution for bribery soon followed his election, though he mange to secure acquittal.[271] Such prosecutions were the norm, especially in tight elections and against the lowest ranking successful candidate. To a *novus homo* such as Marius, a Praetorship was a major achievement and ranked him as a rising star. Whilst it may be a coincidence that his election coincided with that of a Metellus as consul and another as censor (see Appendix IV), it appears that he had again been sponsored by the Metelli, having patched up any rift caused by his actions in 119 BC. An uneventful Praetorship was followed by an equally uneventful governorship of *Hispania Ulterior* (Farther Spain), where all he could claim was to have relieved the province of banditry.[272] Nevertheless, it would have opened up opportunities for business contacts in the region and a certain level of profit.[273]

The period of 113–109 presents us with another gap in his life.[274] The most obvious next step for an ex-Praetor back from his province would have been a campaign for the consulship, probably in 112 or 111 BC, but our sources are silent on this. We do know that his political connections improved via a marriage to a Roman noblewoman named Iulia, who hailed from the Iulii Caesares, tying him into one of the oldest yet obscure patrician families.[275] A consequence of this marriage is that Marius became uncle to the future C. Iulius Caesar. With the marriage somewhere in the region of 113–110, it has been argued that he campaigned for the consulship in this period, now with additional backers, though this remains conjecture.[276]

In any event, by 109 BC, his career had stalled at the Praetorship and he accepted the offer by Q. Caecilius Metellus to join him in Numidia as a legate in 109 BC. Nonetheless, we must not overlook his achievements to date. From provincial aristocracy to Roman Praetor was a great achievement. He had close ties with the Metelli, Rome's leading family and was married into the old aristocracy. The Marii were now present in Roman politics and under normal circumstances his son could look forward to taking the family to the heights of the consulship. As events turned out, however, Marius was not finished and soon developed other ideas.

Marius and the consulship of 107 BC

One key question that faces us is whether Marius had this plan in mind from the beginning of his legateship or whether he developed it when in Africa. Given his position in 109 BC, having reached the praetorship, but stalled in a bid for the consulate, and in his late forties, the best he could have hoped for was more military success and greater wealth. Despite his being in Africa throughout 109 and some of 108, it is clear that he appreciated how things had changed in Rome in the period after 110 BC. The disaster at Suthul led to the creation of the Mamilian Commission and a witchunt against prominent Senators.[277] Not only were failed commanders being prosecuted, but a number of prominent anti-Gracchans also fell under its scope as well. As Farney points out, this did not merely create the atmosphere for running on an anti-Senatorial ticket, but also the opportunity, given that several men who may have expected to run for the consulship had now been removed from the picture,[278] though we are not informed who Marius did actually run against, aside from his eventual colleague, L. Cassius Longinus.

It is also clear from both Sallust's and Plutarch's accounts that Marius had begun a long-term whispering campaign amongst elements of the Roman army and wider community in North Africa.[279] When he started this is impossible to date, but it is most likely to have occurred after the Roman victory at Muthul River, when it was clear that a military victory in battle was not going to end the war. The elation that the Romans must have felt at defeating Jugurtha would have soon turned into disappointment as the war still dragged on. Sallust details two particular sections of the Roman community that were targeted by Marius: the soldiers and the traders, both of which groups would have been eager for the war to end.[280] For the soldiers, a chance to return home, and for the business community, a chance to restore what had been a profitable area of trade. Furthermore, as we have already noted, Marius in particular played up to the Numidian prince Gauda, present in Metellus' army, most likely offering him a clear chance to rule in place of Jugurtha.

It is interesting to note that once more Marius appears to have had a template for these actions in Scipio Aemilianus. Appian informs us that Scipio benefited from the soldiers serving at Carthage to send back word to their friends and relatives in Rome that he would make a better commander than the ones they were presently serving under.[281] As is often the case when dealing with Marius, the shadow of his old commander Scipio Aemilianus is present.

Thus, we can see that Marius, despite being in Africa, was able to use the winter break of 109/108 to get these elements to send back word to Rome that Metellus was merely more of the same and that someone fresh would be needed. However, there is one key issue here which we must not overlook.

Harbouring a desire for one last run at the consulship is understandable enough, but that would not automatically bring with it command in Numidia. Metellus had already had his command in Numidia made proconsular and thus would run at the Senate's discretion, which given the dominant Metellan position within the Senate, would be for as long as Metellus himself wanted. Under normal circumstances foreign affairs were a matter for the Senate and it alone, though Tiberius Gracchus had infamously infringed on this right with the kingdom of Pergamum in 133 BC. Thus for Marius to be considering gaining both a consulship and the Numidian command, he must have already formulated the radical step which would grant him both: getting the people to vote him the command.

To run for the consulship on such an anti-Senatorial ticket was a bold step in itself, especially against the leading Senatorial faction, but to then propose removing their power to allocate provincial commands, even on this one occasion, was truly either genius or insanity. Luckily for him, it worked.

It is clear that Metellus was all too aware of his subordinate's ambitions and manoeuvring against him. It also seems clear that he did not give him much hope; even if Marius could gain a consulship, then his command would have been safe, assured by the Metellan faction in the Senate. Perhaps he considered that Marius would gain a command against the northern barbarians and fare no better than any previous commander. From Plutarch's account it appears that the condemnation of Turpillius for his role in the mutiny at Vaga was the final straw in relations between Metellus and Marius (see Chapter 5).[282] Whatever the exact circumstances, Metellus reasoned that he was better off without Marius' disruptions, which was a fair assumption at the time.

Once at Rome, Marius swung into action and ran for the consulship on a promise of ending the war, which, he argued, was being unnecessarily prolonged by either Senatorial incompetence, corruption or both. Given the atmosphere created by the Mamilian Commission and the growing threat from the north, it was a campaign which would have resonated well with the people of Rome. Furthermore, it seems that he had allies amongst the tribunes of 108, who agitated for his election, even accusing Metellus of treason at one point.[283] In such a charged anti-Senatorial atmosphere, we must not forget that Marius himself had been serving senator for well over a decade at this point and probably had a number of allies there. Nevertheless, it is clear that he stressed his position as an outsider, from his Italian background to repulses at elections, which could be blamed on Roman noble jealousy. Clearly, though it must have paid to have kept his marriage alliance with the patrician Iulii as quiet as possible at this time.

An interesting question is how his friends, family and allies viewed this move. Although Sallust reports a particularly virulent anti-Senatorial speech made before an assembly of the people, we must exercise caution as it may be Sallust rather than Marius' words.[284] We can legitimately ask whether such a tactic, of playing to the people against your own supposed colleagues was that unique. Clearly, Tiberius Gracchus had led the way by seeming to side with the people against Senate, whilst maintaining a healthy number of allies within it. The Metelli, though powerful, were bound to have a number of opponents, who did not relish the prospect of another Metellan victory to add to their tally. Ultimately, though, the sources do not stretch this far.

It is clear though that Marius judged the public mood in Rome to perfection and was elected one of the consuls for 107 (the other being an L. Cassius Longinus). We do not know who was defeated or what Longinus' attitude or connections in all of this were. Nevertheless, the first stage had been completed, and at fifty years of age, Marius had achieved his dream of becoming consul.

Marius as consul

We do not know what provinces had originally been assigned to Marius for 107 BC, but as Longinus gained Gaul, where he was killed fighting the Tigurini, it is likely that Marius was given Italy. We have little detail on the events that surrounded the re-assignment of the Numidian command, only that a tribune, T. Manlius Mancinus, proposed a law (*plebiscitum*) to the assembly proposing that Marius be given command in Numidia and that there is no reference to any of the other nine tribunes opposing it. What the Senate made of it is unclear. Marius had run on a programme of ending the war in Numidia, yet we hear that the Senate snubbed this by re-affirming Metellus as commander shortly before it was put to a vote. Given the timing, it is probable that Marius only put it to a vote when snubbed by the Senate. Cicero presents the whole affair in a more ordered light.[285]

At a stroke Marius had utilized the theory of popular sovereignty that under-pinned the unwritten Roman constitution (though usually buried very deep). The assemblies could vote on whatever they liked regardless of Senatorial prerogative. Marius now placed the military commands in the hands of the tribunes, a step far greater than either of the Gracchi in this respect, though one which had a forebear, if not direct precedent, in Scipio Aemilianus' actions over the Numantine command in 134 BC (see Chapter 1). Nevertheless, such an outright move was an important and deadly precedent; one which sparked-off the First Civil War in 88 BC and was utilized with great skill by Pompey in later years. Yet, the whole incident is missing from Plutarch's account.

What Marius did next was just as important, but far more contentious historically. Both Sallust and Plutarch agree that Marius determined to raise fresh forces in order to enlarge the army in Numidia and end the war with a surge. Sallust reports that he called for more troops from Rome's allies and clients across the Mediterranean, corroborated by the fragments of Diodorus, which provide us with an excellent insight into this process. Diodorus add that he requested military aid from Nicomedes of Bithynia.[286] Nicomedes initially refused on the grounds that large numbers of his people had been enslaved by the Roman tax collectors from Asia. This resulted in a decree banning the enslavement of any citizen of an allied state, which was to have its own consequences. Whilst Nicomedes' excuse can rightly be treated as dubious, this incident does show that Rome had to bargain from a position of weakness for help from her allies.

As well as reinforcements from overseas, Sallust informs us that he recruited a number of men from Latium and initiated a programme of recruiting veterans back into the army.[287] However, all of these methods of recruiting fresh forces are eclipsed, at least in the ancient sources, as well as a number of modern ones, by the report in both Sallust and Plutarch that Marius initiated the process of recruiting troops from the poorest classes of Roman society, those without land. This has become the most infamous of Marius' military reforms, the alleged abolition of the land qualification for military service. This issue is paradoxically one of the most important in Roman history, whilst being of minimal impact in the short-term analysis of the war. For those reasons it will be analysed and discussed more fully in a later section on Marius' military reforms (Chapter 11). For now we can content ourselves with the fact that Marius engaged in a number of recruiting methods designed to bolster his forces for the upcoming campaign surge.

One important aspect about the whole recruitment issue, as noted by Evans, is the speed with which this was to be accomplished.[288] Whilst he was still recruiting his infantry reinforcements Marius sent a legate, A. Manlius, to Africa to prepare for his arrival and left Italy whilst another legate, L. Cornelius Sulla, was still recruiting the cavalry reinforcements. Clearly, he wished to make as early a start as possible in the campaign against Jugurtha, which is hardly surprising given that he was elected on a mandate of a swift end to the war. Furthermore, he had seen how much time had been lost from the 109 campaign during the handover between commanders, nor did he know how well Metellus would take the news of his being replaced by his deputy.

The Campaigns of 107 and 106 BC.

When trying to assess the Marian campaigns of 107 and 106 BC, we are faced with two problems presented by our surviving sources. The first one is the apparent absence of any detail of the events between Jugurtha's invasion of Numidia in late 108 BC and the arrival of Marius in late 107 BC. Furthermore, not only is there an absence of detail, but Sallust's narrative picks up where it left off, giving us the impression that whilst events at Rome were taking place, events in Numidia were frozen until Sallust turns his attention to them once more. The second problem concerns the merging of the campaigns of 107 and 106 BC into one, sandwiched between two sieges at opposite ends of Numidia.

If we are to understand the events that occurred, then these two problems must be explored first. As 108 BC drew to a close, Jugurtha had invaded Numidia at the head of a 'grand alliance' of Mauri and Gaetulians and was threatening to undo the Roman achievements to date. Sallust then breaks off his campaign narrative for the election of Marius and the recruitment of his new army, which would have taken at least the first half of 107 BC. His narrative resumes, where he left off, yet screams the following question: What was Jugurtha doing in the months when Sallust is captivated by events in Rome? It is almost as if Jugurtha freezes where he is and waits patiently for the domestic situation in Rome to work itself out. This is always an issue in this period of Roman history, when our sources are far more concerned with domestic events than foreign affairs.

Upon his arrival in Africa, Marius formally took command of the Roman army there. As mentioned previously, he did so from P. Rutilius Rufus as Q. Caecilius Metellus apparently refused to meet with Marius, which is hardly surprising given the circumstances, Marius having usurped his command. Thus we apparently find the Roman army still in the province of Africa half way through 107 BC. Whilst it was normal for them to withdraw from Numidia during winter, it appears that their break continued throughout the early part of 107, whilst waiting for a change of commander, a situation exacerbated by the enmity between Metellus and Marius. Furthermore, this coincided with a renewed Jugurthan invasion of Numidia, which aside from an unknown number of garrisoned towns and cities was open to him. Once again, it appears that the Roman domestic political situation cost them crucial momentum in the war.

Therefore, it was almost as if the clock had been turned back and the war had to begin afresh. Yet although the situation in 107 may superficially resemble that of 111 and 109 BC there were significant differences. The primary one is that the Numidians had already been defeated in battle. Jugurtha himself may not have accepted this fact, but it is clear that the country and people as a whole had, hence Jugurtha's reliance on an army of Gaetulians. Numidian armies had been easily defeated by Roman armies, and their cities occupied and in some cases laid waste. Nor was this a Roman war of conquest, but rather a war focussed primarily upon the figure of the king. The plotting amongst the

Numidian nobles reveals that they saw Jugurtha as the key obstacle to peace in the kingdom. This was further exacerbated by the presence of a clear rival to Jugurtha on the Roman side, namely his half-brother Gauda. Here was a Numidian prince of the house of Masinissa, who was allied to the Romans and with the apparent full backing of the new Roman commander Marius.

Thus, the war against Numidia had effectively been won. For the rest of the war it was to be relegated to merely being the battleground for two invading armies, the Romans from the east and the Mauri and Gaetulians from the west. All that Jugurtha could call on was the support of a few garrisoned forts and handful of towns still loyal to him. Though as had already been seen, loyalty in a war such as this tended to be sold to the side with the nearest army. Without Numidian backing, Jugurtha was reliant on the Mauri and the Gaetulians, which contained considerable risks. The Mauri were led by their king Bocchus, who despite the marriage alliance had already shown himself to be reticent about bringing the wrath of Rome upon his own kingdom, and in short was unreliable at best. Although Jugurtha had personal command of the Gaetulians, at most they were a mercenary army and like all mercenary armies were reliant upon regular payment. Furthermore, they were operating in Jugurtha's own country, which brought with it a host of issues concerning foraging and discipline. Finally, they had not been tested in battle against the Romans and there was no guarantee that they would fare any better than the previous Numidian armies.

As if the weaknesses of his own side were not bad enough, Jugurtha was faced by a greatly-increased Roman army. As is usual for this period, we are given no figures, but Marius raised a fresh army in Italy and combined it with Metellus' army already in Africa. This gave him far greater manpower and far greater ability to conduct wider ranging campaigns in Numidia. The only downside for Marius was that he was light on cavalry, which was still being assembled in Italy by his deputy, L. Cornelius Sulla.

For Marius, his aims were twofold. Having been raised to power on his promise to end the war swiftly, he needed quick results. In short this meant the death or capture of Jugurtha. In a wider context he also had to consider the Roman position in North Africa and ensure that the war did not escalate into a full-blown war against the Mauri and Gaetulians, but was contained to Numidia. If it were not, not only would this weaken the Roman position, but it would undermine his need for a swift resolution. For Jugurtha, this escalation was his only hope. Negotiation was impossible, given that the only terms acceptable to Rome were his head. He had lost the support of the vast majority of the Numidians and was reliant on two other neighbouring powers for his survival. Nevertheless, he had already survived for four years and had seen off three Roman commanders. If the Romans could be ensnared in a long-drawn-out affair in North Africa then it was possible that events in Rome or in Gaul would ensure his survival, which at this point is all he could hope for.

In terms of strategy, despite the enlarged army, Marius had few other options than the ones that faced Metellus in the previous years: bring Jugurtha to battle and kill him, ensure that he had nowhere left to run and handed himself over, or induce others to hand him over. Given that he had high expectations to live up to, the military option was the preferred route. Therefore, it is no surprise that Marius' strategy consisted of reducing the few strongholds and towns that were still doggedly pro-Jugurthan, either by siege or intimidation. This would further have the effect of reducing Jugurtha's bases of operations and sources of money, both essential with a non-native army at his side. Furthermore, it would test the mettle of his allies.

Such a strategy is what ultimately Sallust provides us with details of, albeit in a particularly-unhelpful manner. The reported siege was at Capsa (modern Gafsa) in the southeast of Numidia. In military terms the attack is noted for the cunning manner in which it was staged, marching his troops at night to catch the town unawares, and the brutal manner in which the town was dealt. Marius' forces attacked the townspeople just after dawn and caught them defenceless and with the city gates open. Despite their apparent offer of surrender, the male population was massacred and the women and children enslaved, with the town being burnt. Sallust notes that such an act was '*contra ius belli*' or against the laws of war, but then goes onto highlight the startling effect this massacre had on the other remaining Jugurthan strongholds in the region.[289] Thus we have a perfect example of early 'shock and awe' tactics, with the destruction of one town ensuring the compliance of the others.

The Sallustian narrative then switches to the other side of the country. By this point one of the few remaining Jugurthan strongholds was an unnamed fortress near the Muluccha River , which formed the border of Numidia and the kingdom of the Mauri.[290] Once again we have a full description of the siege including a colourful story of how a Roman soldier, whilst out hunting snails to eat, discovered an unguarded approach to the mountain-top fortress.[291] The key problem we have is that there is no chronology in Sallust's' accounts, a problem exacerbated by the fact that these two sieges took place on opposite sides of the country. To reach the fortress at Muluccha, Marius would have had to cross the 800-mile length of Numidia, which is done in total silence in Sallust's account.

At this point it would be helpful to turn to our supplementary sources for the war, notably Orosius and Plutarch's life of Marius. However, here we are to be disappointed once more. Plutarch's accounts of the Marian campaigns cuts from Marius arriving in Africa to the final capture of Jugurtha, completely missing out any details of the intervening campaigns or battles.[292] Orosius is little better, giving these campaigns just one sentence:

> Marius gave an excellent example of this trait [his astuteness], when he outwitted the enemy and captured the city of Capsa, which, they say, was founded by the Phoenician Hercules and which now was filled with royal treasure.[293]

Thus we are forced to return to Sallust and try to make sense of the campaigns and their chronology. This subject has been argued over by many a historian and the consensus can be detailed as follows.[294] Upon invading Numidia, Marius began a programme of giving his untrained troops combat experience by low-level attacks on Jugurthan strongholds and a number of skirmishes with Jugurtha's Gaetulian forces (as detailed below), which will have taken place in late 107 BC. Either then or in early 106 BC he moved into the southeast of the country and destroyed the town of Capsa. This makes excellent strategic sense and would have secured the east of Numidia under Roman control. Throughout 106 he undertook a systematic march across Numidia, re-securing the country for Rome and storming any remaining Jugurthan towns or forts. By late 106, this process had taken Marius across the length of Numidia, until he reached the Muluccha River and the siege of the nearby fortress.[295]

With this issue dealt with, there are still two unanswered questions. Firstly, how successful a strategy was this for the Romans, and secondly, just what were Jugurtha and Bocchus doing all this time? Upon Marius' invasion of Numidia (in late 107), Sallust explicitly states that Jugurtha and Bocchus were still together with their respective armies. Faced with the invading Roman force, we are told that the two monarchs separated and withdrew into the Numidian interior. Sallust ascribes this to a desire to avoid open combat and force Marius to divide his forces into two, thus weakening his overall position. Not only did Marius not apparently do this, but we hear no more of Bocchus or his army in Numidia.[296] In fact, following the fall of the fortress at Muluccha, Bocchus and his forces are in fact back in his own kingdom without having fired a shot in anger.

It is clear from this that at some point soon after Marius' invasion of Numidia, Bocchus and his forces retried back to his own kingdom, without either formally allying with Rome or breaking off his alliance with Jugurtha; clearly Bocchus was playing a waiting game. Although, on his own, Jugurtha's defeat may have looked inevitable, aided by the full resources of the Mauri victory was still possible, at least in the short term. Bocchus clearly formed a third side to this war, playing both sides off against the other for maximum advantage. Jugurtha may have been a native African prince, but the Numidians had been the dominant power in North Africa. Thanks to this war, however, the tables had been turned and Numidia was now weaker than the Mauri. On the other hand, a Roman conquest of Numidia would put Bocchus' own position in jeopardy. Thus we can understand Bocchus' reluctance to commit to one side or another.

This left Jugurtha on his own in Numidia, with his Gaetulian army. Sallust does inform us of a number of small encounters between the Roman and Gaetulian forces in the initial stages of the Marian campaign:

> He [Marius] made frequent attacks on Jugurtha and the Gaetulians, while they were plundering our allies [the Numidians], routing them and compelling the king's own troops to throw away their arms not far from Cirta.[297]

Although only a brief passage, we learn two interesting facts. Firstly, Jugurtha's Gaetulian army was living off the land, thus further alienating his own people. This was countered by the Romans defending the Numidians from the Gaetulians. Thus it was clear that Marius was winning the 'hearts and minds' of the native population, but at the cost of tying up his own forces. If anything, it was Jugurtha and his army that were being seen as the invaders. Secondly, at some point in late 107 BC, Jugurtha and Marius clashed in the vicinity of Cirta, the old Numidian capital.[298] Thanks to the gaps in Sallust's narrative we are not even aware who held Cirta at this time, the two possibilities being that there was still a Roman garrison there, left by Metellus in 108 BC, or that it had been abandoned by the Romans under Metellus, when he withdrew back to Africa in late 108. Nevertheless, the clash (it is not described as a full-scale battle) left Jugurtha on the run and Cirta securely in Roman hands.

The mention of Cirta leads us back to the figure of Gauda, the Numidian prince in the Roman army, and ally of Marius. Although the issue of the government of Numidia is not touched on in the sources until the end of the war, it is tempting to speculate that Marius installed Gauda as a temporary monarch, based in the traditional Numidian capital of Cirta, to provide an alternative source of authority to Jugurtha and the semblance of a normal ruling authority. Thus the war would have become Numidia and Rome fighting together against Jugurtha, a renegade and deposed ruler, rather than Rome fighting Numidia. This may explain Marius' early move to Cirta in 107, to install Gauda as a 'legitimate' ruler of Numidia, although this act would have ultimately needed to have been sanctioned by the Senate and People of Rome.

After these clashes between Jugurtha and Marius in 107 BC, Jugurtha then disappears from the narrative until the fall of the fortress at Muluccha. We can speculate that he could only look on impotently as his few remaining strongholds fell to the Romans, and he was reduced to skulking around the Numidian deserts living off the land with his foreign army. It was only with the fall of the fortress at Muluccha, that Jugurtha attempted a last throw of the dice and planned to defeat the Romans in battle. For this, it was clear that he needed the combined might of the Gaetulian and Mauri armies. Thus he turned to Bocchus once more and made him a more substantial offer (other than marriage ties and mutual threat from Rome). Jugurtha offered Bocchus one whole third of Numidia to be added to his kingdom, as an inducement to commit to his side.[299] Such an act would have greatly enlarged Bocchus' kingdom and made him the pre-eminent native power in North Africa.

This offer shows the desperate straights that Jugurtha had been reduced to, which in turn leads us back to our earlier question of how successful Marius' strategy had been. Following the siege near Muluccha, as 106 BC drew to a close, two years had elapsed since Marius' election as consul, promising a swift end to the war. Certainly much of the first year had been lost in waiting to take up his consulship, passing the necessary legislation and recruiting and blooding a new army, but on the face of it, was he proving to be any more successful than Metellus?

We hear little of events in Rome during this period. On the one hand, Marius' supporters had secured a prolongation of his command, from consular to pro-consular and we hear of no attempts by the Senate to block this. On the other hand, there was the return of Metellus and the celebration of a triumph (in 106 BC) to mark his 'victory' in Numidia. As has been seen in the Northern Wars, such a triumph being celebrated whilst the war continued was normal practice, yet this one also resulted in Metellus being given the cognomen of Numidicus, thus becoming Q. Caecilius Metellus Numidicus. This was a clear provocation to Marius' position and a sign that the Metelli, who were after all the dominant family/faction within the Senate, would not take Marius' usurpation of the command lightly. Sallust reports Metellus' return to Rome, but not his triumph, stating that he was hailed by the Senate and People (which is surprising, given that they had humiliatingly voted him out of his command in an unprecedented manner).[300] In any event, a triumph would always have been enthusiastically welcomed by the people, whoever was celebrating it, giving them a public celebration and feast, marking a Roman military success, which would have been especially welcome given the losses in the north.

Ultimately though, despite the time it had taken, Marius' strategy of reducing Jugurtha's remaining strongholds and forcing him into a corner paid off, with the latter determining on a final military confrontation. Having taken the fortress at Muluccha, Marius determined to retire for the winter to the nearby Numidian coastal towns. Jugurtha was able to move his Gaetulian force to the border to meet up with Bocchus' army entering Numidia from the west, a feat that was managed without alerting the Romans. This combined force then moved towards the Roman army, which was in the region of the city of Cirta.

What followed were two battles between these armies. However, unusually for this war, we have two separate and somewhat divergent accounts of these battles from two different sources, Sallust and Orosius. To appreciate the problem, we need to examine both of these accounts.

The First Battle of Cirta (Sallust)

Sallust presents us with a detailed account of the battle:

> Then, at the very moment that the consul learned from his scouts of the presence of the enemy, they appeared, and before the army could be drawn up or the baggage piled, in fact before any signal or order could be given, the Mauri and Gaetulian cavalry fell upon the Romans, not in order or with any plan of battle, but in swarms, just as chance had brought them together.
>
> Our men were all bewildered by the unseen danger, but nevertheless did not forget their valour. Some took arms, while others kept off the enemy from their comrades who were arming; a part mounted their horses and charged the foe. The combat was more like an attack of brigands than a battle. Without standards and in disorder, horse and foot massed together, some gave ground, others slew their opponents; many who were bravely fighting against the enemy were surrounded from the rear. Valour and arms were no sufficient protection against a foe who were superior in numbers and attacked on every side. At last the Romans, both the raw recruits and the veterans, who as such were skilled in warfare, if the nature of the ground brought any of them together, formed a circle, thus protecting themselves on every side and presenting an orderly front to the attacks of the enemy.
>
> In so dangerous a crisis Marius was neither frightened nor less confident than before, but with the bodyguard of his cavalry, which he had formed of the bravest soldiers, rather than of his friends, went from place to place, now aiding those of his men who were in difficulty, now charging the enemy where they were pressing on in greatest numbers. He directed the soldiers by gestures, since in the general confusion his orders could not be heard. The day was now ending, yet the barbarians did not at all ease their efforts but thinking that the darkness would favour them, as the kings had declared, they attacked with greater vigour.
>
> Then Marius, adapting his tactics to the situation and wishing to provide a place of refuge for his men, took possession of two neighbouring hills, one of which was too small for a camp, but had a large

spring of water, while the other was better adapted to his purpose because it was the most part high and steep and required little fortification. He ordered Sulla to pass the night with the cavalry beside the spring, while he gradually rallied his scattered forces and the enemy were in no less disorder, and then led them all at the quick march to the hill. Thus the kings were compelled by the strength of the position to cease the battle. However, they did not allow their men to go far away, but encompassed both hills with their huge army, they camped in loose order.

Marius, who was especially heartened by the enemy's lack of discipline, ordered the utmost possible silence to be kept and not even the customary signals to be sounded to mark the night watches. Then, as daylight was drawing near and the enemy having at length become exhausted just beginning to sleep, he [Marius] suddenly ordered the watch and at the same time the horn-blowers of the cohorts of the cavalry and of the legions to sound the signal together, and the soldiers to raise a shout and burst forth from the gates of the camps. The Mauri and Gaetulians, being suddenly awakened by this strange and terrible sound, were incapable of feeling or of arming themselves, or indeed taking any action at all. Their enemy was upon them and no help was at hand. The shouting and din, the confusion and the terror had made them frantic with fear. In the end they were completely routed. Most of their arms and standards were taken, and more were killed than in any previous battle; for they were too tired and too much dazed by the surprise to make good their escape.[301]

The First Battle of Cirta (Orosius)

Orosius on the other hand presents us with the following account, which is longer than the rest of his account of the whole war:

Greatly strengthened by the cavalry contingents of the latter [Bocchus], he [Jugurtha] harassed the Marian army by frequent raids. Finally at Cirta, an ancient city, the capital of Masinissa, he encountered the Romans, who were preparing an assault upon that city. He drew up his forces in battle array with a cavalry force numbering 60,000. No battle was ever more turbulent or more harrowing to a Roman soldier. A cloud of dust, raised by the galloping and snorting of the horses as they circled about in attack, veiled the heavens, shut out

III. The First Battle of Cirta (105 BC), Stage 1

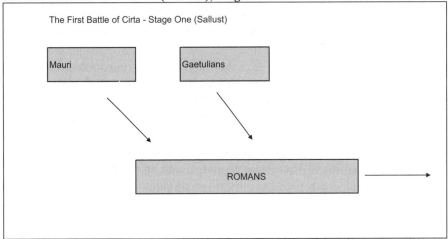

IV. The First Battle of Cirta, Stage 2

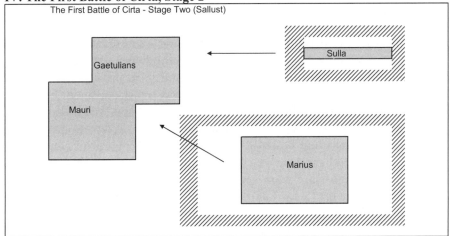

the daylight, and brought on darkness. So great a shower of missiles poured down upon the Romans that no part of the body was safe. Moreover, the density of the atmosphere prevented them from seeing any distance ahead, while their great numbers, as they crowded together, made manoeuvres for defending themselves difficult to execute.

The Mauri and Numidian [Gaetulian] cavalry did not have to exert themselves much to carry out a well-timed javelin attack designed to break up the ranks of their opponents who were occupying a favourable position. They kept on discharging their darts blindly in the confident assurance that the missiles must of necessity strike their mark. Driven into one space, the Roman infantrymen pressed closely together against one another.

Night afforded the Romans a temporary relief from their perilous situation, but the next day the same conditions of war and of danger prevailed. It was useless for a soldier to rush against the enemy with drawn sword, for he would be driven back by darts hurled from a distance. The infantrymen could not flee, since the cavalry, which had completely hemmed them in, could swiftly overtake them. When the third day came and there was no help from any source, the dread appearance of death presented itself on all sides. Finally, the consul Marius offered a means of escape by undertaking a brave and desperate move. His entire army in battle formation rushed forth simultaneously from valley and open plain and offered battle everywhere at the same time. The enemy, again circling around them, not only cut to pieces the flanks of the line, but also kept overwhelming the centre with darts that reached their mark, though hurled from a distance. Furthermore, the heat of the sun, unbearable thirst, and the presence of death all around them exhausted the disorganized Romans and reduced them to a state of complete despair.

At this point a storm of wind and rain was sent from the heavens against the Africans. This kind of assistance, which was well known to the Romans, brought unexpected deliverance. The sudden downpour cooled the thirsty and heated Romans and gave them a drink, but so far as the Numidians were concerned, it made the shafts of their darts slippery, which they were accustomed to hurl with their hands without *ammenta* [a leather thong tied to the shaft to assist the thrower]. Thus their darts became useless. The shields too, which they usually carried and which were made from stretched and toughened elephant hide, though easy to handle and offering adequate protection, were of such a nature that they absorbed the rain like a sponge. This added weight rendering them unmanageable and quite useless in affording protection, since they could not be manipulated with ease. When the Mauri and Numidians (Gaetulians) had thus been unexpectedly thrown into confusion and rendered helpless, Bocchus and Jugurtha took flight.[302]

The Key Differences and Similarities

Thus, we can see that the two accounts contain some notable differences, indicating the use of different sources for the battle. The first clear difference concerns the location of the battle and the initial encounter. In Sallust, Marius is leading his army to their winter quarters at Cirta when he is attacked at dusk, in a classic Jugurthan ambush. In Orosius, Marius is laying siege to Cirta (or intending to) and the attack was preceded by a number of enemy raids upon the Roman army. It seems highly unlikely to say the least that Cirta was still in Jugurtha's hands by late 106 BC, especially given that Marius had spent the preceding year reducing every remaining Jugurthan fortress in Numidia and that we are told he was in the vicinity of Cirta in late 107 BC. It is this last point that may help to throw some light on Orosius' account. We know from Sallust that Marius and Jugurtha were in the vicinity of Cirta in late 107 BC and that there were indeed skirmishes between the two sides. Thus, it is entirely possible that Orosius or his source have condensed these two separate events into one account. If this is what has happened, and at this stage we can only speculate, then it actually throws light on Sallust's account of the campaign of late 107, as it seems that the Romans were forced to lay siege to Cirta, which must have fallen into Jugurthan hands, when Metellus evacuated Numidia in late 106 BC. Thus Cirta fell to Marius in late 107 BC and remained in Roman hands throughout 106 BC.

Both Sallust and Orosius do agree that the battle was initially a disaster for the Romans. If they were indeed attacked by 60,000 Mauri and Gaetulian cavalry and it was indeed at dusk in an ambush, then we can see the Roman plight. Aside from Orosius' literary flourish of the skies turning dark with arrows (highly reminiscent of the Battle of Thermopylae), the next major difference was the length of the encounter. In Sallust the battle starts at dusk and ends at dawn the next day. In Orosius, we are given no start time, but the battle dragged on for three days. Orosius makes no mention of the hills that Marius defended in Sallust's account, but if the Romans did take up a defensive position then the battle could have dragged on, as Orosius suggest, with Jugurtha's army unable to get to grips with the Romans at close quarters and the Romans unable to break out.

Orosius' account is the more detailed for the Mauri/Gaetulian tactics and this fits in well with previous Jugurthan tactics and his analysis of their strengths and Roman weaknesses. Once again Jugurtha chose to utilize weapons of distance and speed, cavalry and javelins, to avoid engaging the Romans at close quarters. On this occasion, if he did have them surrounded and pinned down in a defensive position, then, unlike the Battle of Muthul River, the Romans would find it difficult to charge forwards and engage the enemy.

The biggest difference between the two accounts comes with the ending of the battle. In Sallust we are presented with a clear-cut example of Roman discipline and barbarian indiscipline, with the highly-improbable account of the Mauri and Gaetulians completely losing all sense of discipline, not to mention common sense, and celebrating when the Romans were trapped in a defensive position and then falling prey to a dawn counterattack, which any half-decent commander could have anticipated. In Orosius, it is chance, or divine intervention, which saves the Roman army, when a ferocious downpour soaks the Mauri/Gaetulian weapons and renders then unable to engage with the Romans. Furthermore, in Sallust the armies of Jugurtha and Bocchus are completely defeated and in Orosius they retreat and regroup, with the Romans skulking off in a hasty withdrawal (though retreat might be a more apt description). Given that Jugurtha and Bocchus were apparently able to mount a second attack just a few days later, withdrawal rather than defeat seems the most likely outcome.

In both accounts though, it is Marius who engineers this Roman breakout. The only difference being that in Sallust he is aided by the Mauri and Gaetulian indiscipline and in Orosius by the elements. In both accounts Marius is the saviour of the Roman army, though we must question how they got into such a mess in the first place. On both occasions, however, Marius is greatly assisted by what look suspiciously like standard Roman prejudices: barbarian indiscipline and divine favour. The question of which account is more accurate is an impossible one to answer, as we cannot even be sure that either is an accurate description. It is entirely possible that both may have been in circulation at the time and both contain many fabulous elements to turn them into good stories for public consumption.

What is clear is that the result was inconclusive, with both sides withdrawing and regrouping for a further encounter. On this occasion, although we have another two accounts, Orosius has clearly exhausted himself and relegated the final battle to just a sentence, whilst Sallust again gives us a highly dramatized account.

The Second Battle of Cirta (Sallust)

With his opponents scattered, Marius continued the army's march towards their winter quarters, rather than following up the victory. This is not as strange as it first seems. Although the enemy had been defeated, it is clear from later events that they had not been destroyed as Sallust claims. Furthermore, this battle had been a close run thing and had shown the vulnerability of Marius' army. Thus, regrouping over winter would have been a priority, as opposed to chasing down Jugurtha. Sallust goes into great detail about the precautions Marius' army now took on their march, to prevent a repeat of the ambush they had suffered, by marching in battle formation. This clearly indicates that the enemy was still a viable threat and that Marius was in effect attempting to retreat from hostile territory. Marius' fears were confirmed as the Mauri and Gaetulians attacked on the fourth day of the march, having obviously regrouped under their commanders.

Once again, Jugurtha apparently demonstrated his superb tactical abilities when he drew up his combined armies into four separate forces, planning on attacking the Romans from all sides. On this occasion Marius' scouts were apparently able to warn him of this ambush and he drew his army up in square formation to meet this threat. Once again Sallust details the battle:

> Meanwhile, Sulla, whom the enemy had reached first, after encouraging his men, attacked the Mauri with a part of his force, charging by squadrons and in close order as possible; the rest of his troops held their ground, protecting themselves from the javelins which were hurled at long range, and slaying all who succeeded in reaching them. While the cavalry were thus engaged, Bocchus, with his infantry being brought up by his son Volux, who had been delayed on the way and had not taken part in the previous battle, charged the Roman rear.
>
> Marius at the time was busy at the front of the battle, since Jugurtha was their with the greater part of his forces. Then Jugurtha, on learning of the arrival of Bocchus, made his way secretly with a few men to meet up with him. When he reached them, he cried out in Latin, which he had leaned to speak when at Numantia, that our [Roman] men were fighting in vain, since he had a short time before killed Marius with his own hand.[303] With these words he displayed a sword smeared with blood, which he made so during the battle by killing a Roman infantryman. When our men heard this they were shocked, rather by the horror of the deed than because they believed the report, while at the same time the barbarians were encouraged and charged upon the stunned Romans with greater vigour.
>
> Our men were just at the point of flight when Sulla, who had routed his opponents, returned and fell upon the flank of the Mauri. Bocchus at once gave way. As for Jugurtha, while he was trying to hold his men and secure the victory which he had all but won, was surrounded by the [Roman] cavalry, but though all, on his right and left were slain, he broke through alone, escaping amid a shower of weapons.
>
> Marius in the meantime, after putting the cavalry to flight, was hastening to the aid of his men, of whose imminent defeat he had now heard. Finally, the enemy were routed in all parts of the battlefield.

Then there was a fearful sight in the open plains; of pursuit, slaughter or capture. Horses and men were thrown to the ground, many of them wounded, without the strength to escape or the will to remain still, struggled to get up, only to collapse immediately. As far as the eye could see, the battlefield was strewn with weapons, armour and corpses, with patches of bloodied earth showing between them.[304]

V. The Second Battle of Cirta (105 BC), Stage 1

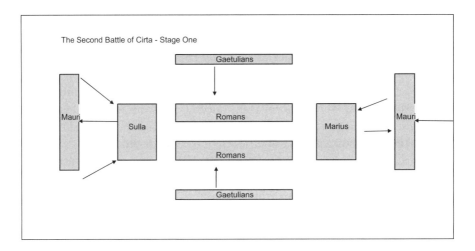

VI. The Second Battle of Cirta (105 BC), Stage 2

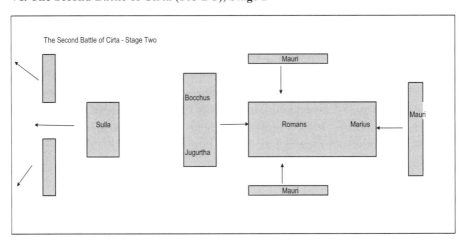

VII. The Second Battle of Cirta (105 BC), Stage 3

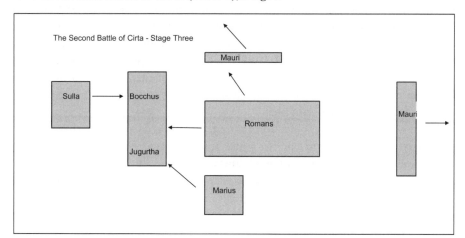

The Second Battle of Cirta (Orosius)

In comparison, Orosius presents only a brief description of the battle:

> Later, however, these same kings (Jugurtha and Bocchus) threw 90,000 soldiers into a final struggle. When the Romans conquered them, their forces it is said, were slaughtered almost to the last man.[305]

The Second Battle of Cirta – Analysis

Both authors agree that for Jugurtha and Bocchus this attack was the last throw of the dice. They committed their full forces, cavalry and foot, in an all-out attempt to defeat the Romans, with Orosius again providing a figure for Jugurtha's forces, of 90,000. Overlooking the more dramatic elements, such as Jugurtha's bluff in Latin we can see the following. Whilst we have no figure for the Roman army, it is clear that they were outnumbered. Such a figure for the Jugurthan forces is a high one, but he was utilizing the manpower of two nations and his forces would have included a huge number of poorly-armed men as well as fully-equipped soldiers.

There were several differences between the first battle and the second. In the first battle Jugurtha utilized his two strengths, surprise and distance, whilst in the second he had neither, just sheer weight of numbers. In addition, he attacked from all sides hoping to break the Roman army down. In such a case, had they lost heart and broken they would have been slaughtered. However, it is clear that the Roman army maintained its discipline and held firm, again showing their superior close-quarter fighting ability. Whilst they held firm, the tide of the battle was turned by the victory of the Roman cavalry under Sulla, who, after driving off the Mauri cavalry (at least in his sector) then returned to the fray to support the infantry and catch the Mauri from behind. With Bocchus and Jugurtha fleeing, their armies' discipline broke and the battle turned into a rout and a slaughter.

What is clear from these accounts is that, surprisingly perhaps, these battles could have gone either way, showing just how the situation had been altered by the addition of the Mauri and Gaetulian forces. This allowed Jugurtha to field armies, probably twice the size of the Roman one. Once again, Jugurtha showed his awareness of his troops' inferior quality and always attempted to overcome this by using elements such as surprise and distance. The first battle, despite Sallust's positive presentation, looks for all intents and purposes to have been a stalemate, with the Romans only just being able to extricate themselves from what could have been a massacre. Thus, even after six years of warfare, Jugurtha was still able to engineer a position which could have resulted in military victory. Had he done so then, given events in the north, this could have turned the tide of the whole war in his favour. Here we can clearly see the quality of his military abilities. His ultimate failure once again rested in the poor quality of his soldiers, when face-to-face with the Roman legion. Ultimately, we can see a case of a great commander saddled with inferior troops.

For Marius, however, these battles reveal both positive and negative aspects of his command. On the positive side, his policy had finally paid off and he had forced Jugurtha to give battle, allowing him the chance of defeating the pan-African alliance and clearly demonstrating Rome's military superiority to the races of North Africa. The Battles of Cirta clearly established Rome's military dominance of North Africa, which was not to be challenged for over a century. The battles also revealed Marius' steady leadership abilities, cool head and clear thinking in battle, marshalling his forces to utilize their strength: close-quarter superiority.

On the negative side, on both occasions he allowed Jugurtha to choose his ground and time of attack, disastrously so in the first battle. On the first occasion it appears that Jugurtha was able to catch the Romans completely unawares, though we must always exercise caution when Sallust is decrying Marius' military abilities. On the second occasion, the Roman scouts alerted the army in time and allowed Marius the time to prepare his army and blunt Jugurtha's tactics.

Overall we have to consider whether these Roman victories were a result of the finest quality of general being victorious or the finest quality of army. Had

Jugurtha been in command of Roman forces, we must suspect that the outcome would be quite different. Ultimately, however, this once again reveals the underlying strength of the Roman system, which allowed it to defeat individual generals of quality, men such as Hannibal, Mithridates or Jugurtha. As for Marius, these battles reveal that, although initially placed on the back foot in terms of pre-battle planning, his clear strengths came to the fore in the midst of battle, which ultimately brought about victory.

The Abduction of Jugurtha and the End of the War in Africa

Despite the closeness of these two battles, the end result was clear: a complete military victory for the Romans. Yet, once again, this did not mean that the war itself was over. By the end of 106, the Romans had defeated the armies of three entire nations – the Numidians, the Mauri and the Gaetulians – yet while Jugurtha lived and was free, the war would not end. Marius was now faced with the same problem that had beguiled Metellus in 108 BC, namely how to turn victory on the battlefield into an end to the war.

Whilst Jugurtha would never surrender to the Romans, the focus shifted to Bocchus, who had gambled and lost heavily. Allying with Jugurtha against the Romans had always been a risk, but the lure of enlarging his kingdom at Numidia's expense had been too tempting to resist. Now, however, with his army destroyed at the Second Battle of Cirta, his kingdom was the next logical target for Roman anger. It was at this point that Bocchus sought to recover by diplomacy what had been lost by force and just four days after the battle of Cirta, he sent word to Marius to open negotiations. What followed was a protracted series of negotiations between Bocchus and Marius, with the former offering friendship and allegiance to Rome, in much the same position that Jugurtha had once been. What Bocchus ultimately had to offer was of paramount interest to Marius and Rome, namely Jugurtha himself.

As a precursor to any deal, Bocchus received Marius' permission to send a three-man delegation to the Senate to express his forgiveness for taking up arms against them, and naturally blaming Jugurtha. Sallust records the Senate's reply to the petition:

> The Senate and People of Rome do not forget either service or injuries.
> However, since Bocchus repents, they forgive his offence; he shall have
> a treaty of friendship when he has earned it.[306]

Thus for Bocchus, the situation was clear. Not only could he avert Roman invasion, but could get himself into Roman favour; the price was Jugurtha. To negotiate the deal, Marius sent his deputy, L. Cornelius Sulla, to Bocchus' court. Sallust reports that Sulla's column was intercepted en route by Volux, Bocchus' son, with a warning that Jugurtha was attempting to intercept him.[307] Forewarned, Sulla was apparently able to evade the ambush. It is clear that Jugurtha must have been aware of Bocchus' manoeuvrings, which were only logical, though we must always be aware of the possibility that the whole incident was staged by Bocchus to publicly demonstrate his new loyalty to Rome. Even if Jugurtha had been preparing an ambush, it is entirely possible that the news was leaked by Bocchus.

Sallust gives these events his usual dramatic flourish and states that, even at this stage, Bocchus was vacillating between Jugurtha and Rome.[308] This is highly unlikely given the relative power of the two sides; Bocchus would have been clearly aware that his future and that of his kingdom depended on the delivery of Jugurtha and, in short, it was a case of Jugurtha or him. That did not mean that he could not protract the situation for his maximum benefit, with an eye on the post-war settlement of the region.

Jugurtha, meanwhile, was apparently being kept appraised of the situation by his representative at Bocchus' court, a man named Asper. According to Sallust, Jugurtha was negotiating with Bocchus to kidnap Sulla and use him as a hostage to negotiate a peace treaty with Rome.[309] This interpretation relies heavily upon the figure that Sulla became, not the man he was in 105 BC, a deputy commander from an ancient but obscure Roman family. Neither Marius nor the Senate would have concluded a peace treaty with Jugurtha under any circumstance, never mind the holding of such a minor hostage. Again according to Sallust, Bocchus agreed to Jugurtha's plan and arranged to meet with him and hand Sulla over to him. When Jugurtha and his party arrived, the inevitable happened, and Bocchus' men attacked and overpowered them, murdering all but Jugurtha, who was handed over to Sulla, and then to Marius and ultimately Rome.[310]

What we have to ask ourselves is why Jugurtha walked into such a trap. He knew about Bocchus' negotiations with the Senate and must have realized that Bocchus' only way out would be to betray him. Given Bocchus' patchy record of allegiance in the past few years, he could hardly have expected loyalty from the man. Sallust's notion of taking Sulla ransom is possible, but Jugurtha would have realized that such a minor hostage was of limited use to him. Ultimately, we have to admit that we will never know what enticements Bocchus used to get Jugurtha to attend that meeting. In the end, it perhaps came down to the fact that Jugurtha had finally run out of options.

Jugurtha was conveyed to Rome and paraded in Marius' triumph on the 1 January 104 BC. According to Orosius, he was accompanied by his two sons, a detail omitted by Sallust. For his final fate, Plutarch has the following:

But we are told that when he [Jugurtha] had been led in triumph he lost his reason; and that when, after the triumph, he was cast into prison, where some tore the tunic from his body, and others were so eager to snatch away his golden earring that they tore off with it the lobe of his ear, and when he had been thrust down naked into the dungeon pit, in utter bewilderment and with a grin on his lips he said 'Hercules! How cold this Roman bath is!' But the wretch, after struggling with hunger for six days and up to the last moment clinging to the desire for life, paid the penalty which his crimes deserved.[311]

Orosius, meanwhile, states that he died a more prosaic death, executed in his cell by strangulation.[312] In any event, it was an ignominious end for a man who had successfully challenged Roman might for so long.

Africa after the War

Following Jugurtha's capture, Marius' post-war settlement was a conservative one. Bocchus was confirmed as king of the Mauri and an ally of the Roman People. In addition, he received the western third of Numidia, which had been promised him by Jugurtha, and which reduced the power of Numidia. The rest of Numidia was kept as one kingdom and Gauda, Jugurtha's half-brother, was confirmed as the new king. The Gaetulians were made independent from Numidia also.[313]

Numidia soon turned back to a prosperous trading nation, but became entangled in Rome's First and Second Civil Wars. As a result of backing the Pompeians against Caesar in 46 BC, Juba I, the king of Numidia, committed suicide and Numidia was partitioned, with the eastern part being added to the province of Africa and the western part remaining independent under a non-native king. Juba's son, Juba II, briefly ruled the reduced Numidian Kingdom between 29–27 BC as a client of Octavian, but was given the kingdom of the Mauri to rule and married off to Cleopatra Selene, daughter of M. Antonius and Cleopatra VII. Their son Ptolemy became king, but was murdered by the Emperor Caius (Caligula) in AD 40 and the kingdom annexed and divided into two new Roman provinces (of Mauretania).

Considering he initially backed the wrong side, Bocchus came out of the war rather well. In 112 his kingdom was a minor one, dwarfed by the power and connections of Numidia, yet by 105 BC he was a staunch ally of Rome, with friends in high places and possessing an enlarged and more powerful kingdom. The Mauri continued to prosper as Roman allies, managing to avoid the entanglements that cost Numidia so dear during the Roman Civil Wars. Ironically, when Bocchus II died in the late 30s BC he willed his kingdom to Rome, but this merely saw a Numidian prince become king of the Mauri. As noted above, the kingdom of the Mauri was annexed by Rome in AD 44.

The Gaetulians too became caught up in the Roman Civil Wars, but they initially benefited from backing Caesar against the Numidians and supporters of Pompey. However, the expansion of the Roman Empire into Numidia saw the Gaetulians go to war with the Rome in c.AD 3–6, which saw them defeated and added to the Mauri kingdom. When that too was annexed, they finally passed into formal Roman control.

Conclusion – The Jugurthine War

What are we to make of this war? The Romans initially became embroiled in a domestic dispute of one of her allies on her southern-most border and got themselves bogged down in an unnecessary and distracting seven-year war. In military terms, they suffered one humiliating defeat and tied up valuable manpower and resources at a time when it was most needed elsewhere, for little apparent return.

Although Rome appeared to gain little as a result of the war, we must look beyond the formal notions of empire. Throughout their history the Romans had no black-and-white concept of a formal division between Roman and non-Roman territory. Although on a modern map, the only Roman possession was the province of Africa itself, the war had seen a massive extension of Roman power in the African continent, north of the Sahara. By 105 BC, not only had Numidia been defeated and humbled, but so had the Mauri and the Gaetulians, who seven years earlier had been completely absent from Roman consideration. Thus Roman might and domination now covered the whole of North Africa, from Libya to the Atlantic coast. Over the late Republic and early Empire this domination slowly turned into formal empire, a situation that remained until the Vandal invasions of the fifth century AD.

Although the Romans had once again emerged victorious and greatly strengthened their grip on North Africa, the domestic repercussions had been serious. Their failure to act decisively in the first place had seen the tribunes and assemblies intervene on the Senate's prerogative of deciding Roman foreign policy, by forcing the declaration of war. The failure of the first two consular commanders had led to the Mamilian Commission being established and a witch-hunt being conducted by the assemblies against the Senatorial commanders. The perceived failure of Metellus had led to Marius, a relative outsider, not only being elected consul, but using the tribunate and the assemblies to trample over another Senatorial prerogative, that of choosing consular provinces. All the Senate could hope for would be that once the war was over, they could restore some measure of control over the domestic situation. However, events soon occurred that threw these hopes into disarray.

Three key Romans came out of this war with their reputations enhanced. The first was L. Caecilius Metellus 'Numidicus', who despite being replaced, had defeated Jugurtha militarily and had effectively put Numidia out of the war, forcing Jugurtha to rely on ultimately-untrustworthy allies. As well as having his military reputation enhanced, he registered his claim to having won the war by taking the cognomen Numidicus. He remained a key member of the most powerful faction in the Senate, the Metelli, who continued their domestic pre-eminence, with both censors of 102–101 being Metelli, one of whom was Numidicus himself (see Appendix IV). Furthermore, his treatment at the hands of Marius and the assembly would have enhanced his standing within the Senate. This being the case, Metellus could look forward to settling the score with Marius when he returned to Rome after the war.

The second man was L. Cornelius Sulla, who had acquired an excellent military reputation in battle and now could, and indeed did, claim to have ended the war by organizing the capture Jugurtha himself. Sulla famously had a ring made depicting the handover of Jugurtha to him (later depicted in coin by his son). In addition, during the 90s BC Bocchus paid for a group of statues depicting this scene on the Capitol.[314] Both were later to be bones of contention between Sulla and Marius, though this was not immediately clear. He had clearly established himself as a man to watch and a good prospect for returning his obscure patrician family to the consulship.

Finally, comes the figure of C. Marius himself. From being a loyal and aged deputy he had managed not only to become consul, but to overturn a key senatorial power, the right to decide consular commands. He had constructed an alliance of the people and the equestrian order to propel him to the pinnacle of the Roman political ladder and provide him with the power to alter the Roman system of recruitment. This gave him a prominent position to end the war in Africa and gain military glory for himself.

It has often been argued as to which of the three men had the greater influence in winning the war.[315] Of the three, the easiest to dismiss is Sulla, as, although he was the officer in charge at the handover of Jugurtha, the whole thing had been arranged by Bocchus and was the inevitable price of his peace with Rome. Sallust makes a great attempt to enlarge Sulla's role in this process, no doubt encouraged by Sulla's own memoirs and the reputation of the man he was to become.

This leaves us with Metellus and Marius. Metellus clearly did much to restore the Roman position in Numidia after the disasters of 110 BC. His competent generalship and use of the superior Roman military might at his disposal effectively led to the defeat of Numidia, but not of Jugurtha, thus deserving him the title of Numidicus. However, it was under his command that Jugurtha was able to escalate the war into a pan-African one, which so nearly cost Rome during the Battles of Cirta. Furthermore, it is apparent that when faced with the Mauri/Gaetulian invasion of Numidia in 106 BC, combined with the news of Marius' usurpation of his command, he slackened the pace of the Roman military effort to a considerable extent. Nevertheless, he did give Marius a base on which to build.

Then we come to Marius' own contribution. He arrived in 107 with the largest Roman army yet in the war and with the Numidians defeated. For the next year he conducted an uninspiring but competent campaign of reducing Jugurtha's remaining powerbase and ultimately his options. However, he too could not prevent the reformation of Jugurtha's 'grand alliance' with Bocchus, which so nearly led to disaster at the Battles of Cirta. Furthermore, despite his apparent calm leadership in battle, Sallust's account at least leaves him facing a charge of incompetence for getting his army ambushed in such a manner. It is highly possible that neither of the accounts of the battles was intended to flatter Marius and the true picture, now lost, may have been far less fraught than depicted. Nevertheless, it is interesting to note how close Rome came to being defeated in the war, even as late as 106 BC. Had the Roman army been destroyed at Cirta, given the war in the north, it was unlikely that they could have mounted any serious opposition for several years, leaving North Africa in the hands of Jugurtha and Bocchus.

This brings us to the final figure to consider, that of Jugurtha himself. Here is a man of contradictions, clearly a superb general, albeit one encumbered with an inferior army for the majority of the war. Furthermore, his recklessness in the political field led to a war against Rome and one that neither side wanted, nor one that in normal circumstances he would have ever been able to win, given the disparity of resources. This recklessness, however, was tempered by the creation of the grand alliance of North African races, which was always a bold and risky move, albeit one that nearly paid off. In the end, he paid for this recklessness with his life, but forever earned himself a position as a tenacious enemy of Rome and one that brought about significant changes within the Roman political and military systems. These changes may have happened anyway, but Jugurtha proved to be a catalyst for them.

For Marius, the end of the war should have been his crowning glory, a return to Rome followed by a triumph, which would be the apex of his career, at the age of around 52. Once his command expired he would become a private citizen again and would have to face the domestic consequences of his actions in 107 BC. From the people this would be short lived-adulation, from the equestrian order, long-term support, and in the Senate, hostility from the established Roman families and especially the Metelli. However, events transpired elsewhere to make the Jugurthine War merely the launching pad to an even greater and unprecedented role in the Roman Republic. For Rome, 105 BC saw the ending of one crisis but the worsening of another.

Chapter 8

The Northern Wars: Disaster at Arausio (106–105 BC)

With the Jugurthine War ended we can now turn our sole focus to the Northern Wars. Although the conflicts on Rome's northern borders had been simmering since 113 BC, from 105 BC onwards they escalated to a far more intense level. In many ways, these conflicts reflect the Jugurthine War. Both began as relatively minor issues, a domestic dispute in Africa and a migrating tribe in Gaul, but both escalated into full-blown conflicts that threatened Rome's empire.

As we saw earlier, repeated defeats at the hands of the Cimbri (113 & 109 BC) had apparently led to a collapse of Roman authority in the region. Even with our few meagre surviving sources, we hear of the revolt of the Volcae against Rome and the invasion of the Tigurini and Toygeni from Helvetia (Switzerland).

The Gallic War (106 BC)

Again, with the focus of our surviving sources on the actions of Marius in Africa, we have few details for the campaigns of 106 BC. What we do know is that once again Rome suffered no obvious effects from the defeat at the hands of the Tigurini. In many ways, this is hardly a surprise. The Romans still had the Alps as a barrier and the Tigurini were more intent on plundering the tribes of southern Gaul, in the absence of Roman authority than challenging Rome directly by invading her own territory.

The absence of a direct threat to Italy from either the Tigurini or the Cimbri allowed the Romans time to recover their position in southern Gaul. Of the two consuls that year, Q. Servilius Caepio and C. Atilius Serranus, Caepio received Gaul as a province and began the process and bringing Rome's rebellious allies back under Roman authority. The only clear details we have of this process are the capture of the town of Tolossa (Toulouse), which is widely commented on, though not for purely military reasons. When the town was sacked, the Romans came to control a vast hoard of treasure. Orosius says that it came from a

Temple to Apollo, Strabo (quoting Poseidonius and Timagenes) argued that the treasure found at Tolossa ultimately came from the Temple of Delphi, supposedly sacked by the Gauls in 279.[316] In any event, it was a vast sum, which then mysteriously vanished, whilst under guard and en-route to Massilia.[317]

The best account of the campaign is by Dio:

> Tolossa, which had formerly been in alliance with the Romans, but had revolted, as a result of the hopes placed in the Cimbri, even to the point of keeping the garrison in chains, was suddenly occupied at night by the Romans, after they had been admitted by their friends. They plundered the temples and obtained much money besides; for the place was wealthy from old, containing among other things the offerings which the Gauls under the leadership of Brennus has once plundered from Delphi. However, no treasure of importance reached Rome, but the soldiers themselves stole most of it, and for this a number were called to account.[318]

In addition to Dio, the majority of sources name Caepio himself as being complicit in the theft, but at the time his command was extended to a proconsulship for 105 BC.

However, such a focus on treasure comes at the expense of any other details of the year's campaigning. We have no details of any activities by or against the Tigurini in this year. They barely feature in the rest of the war, aside from a supporting role in the Cimbric invasion of Italy in 101 BC.

The Cimbric War (105 BC)

Once again, after having defeated a Roman army, it appears that the Cimbri moved away from southern Gaul, and made no move towards Italy, having been rebuffed in their apparent request to settle there. Once again, we are faced with their disappearance from our surviving accounts. Given that Roman armies were continuing to operate in southern Gaul during this period, they did not encounter the Cimbri for another four years. It has been speculated that they moved northeastwards again towards the River Main and founded settlements, but there is little evidence to support this. Once again, we have to admit to our ignorance of their movements. Clearly, whatever settlement plans they had in this period failed once more, as by 106 the Cimbri, possibly joined by their allies, moved southwards towards Roman territory for the third time.

Here we must analyse the pattern of continued battles with Rome interspersed by periods of absence. In 113, when the Cimbri first encountered

Rome, this happened in the east of the Alps and apparently by chance. In 109 the Cimbri approached Roman territory from the west and this time sought permission to settle in Italy. By 106 BC, the Cimbri would have been fully acquainted with the Roman hegemony over southern Gaul, and deliberately moved towards their territory, clearly knowing the response they would receive. Rather than taking a Romano-centric view that they were only 'barbarians', who only obeyed natural instinct and had no grater desire other than conquest, we have to ask ourselves why they approached Rome this third time and whether their tactics had changed.

One aspect that is apparent is that seven years after initially fighting Rome they had still not found a region to settle in peacefully. Given the attrition rates of battle, and disease and the need to find enough food for several hundred thousand people, clearly some element of frustration and desperation must have set in. As events showed, the Cimbri were clearly not intent on invading Italy at this point, nor is there any clear evidence of an alliance with any other tribes, such as the Teutones and Ambrones. Furthermore, there is no evidence of a formal pact between the Cimbri and Tigurini in this period either, despite the fact that both had a common enemy. What must have been clear to the Cimbri is that they would not be able to settle in southern Gaul or Spain until Roman influence had been removed from north of the Alps. In the period that followed 109 BC, this looked as though it may have been accomplished, with the Tigurini invading the region and defeating a Roman army and revolts amongst the native cities and tribes under Roman suzerainty.

However, within a few years it appeared that Roman influence had not been eliminated, and in fact the Romans began to re-assert themselves in the region. It may have been down to random chance that the Cimbri fought Rome for a third time in 105 BC, or it may have been connected to Rome beginning to reassert her dominance in the region. Thus there is an argument that this third clash was not the result of random wanderings at all but a deliberate attempt by the Cimbri to eliminate Roman influence north of the Alps and thus allow them to carve out land for themselves. To do this they would require a further and comprehensive victory over the Roman army, removing them from the Gallic theatre of operations altogether.

This line of argument allows us to develop the seemingly-random Cimbric clashes with Rome into a more logical sequence and allows for the evolution of the Cimbric attitude towards Rome. It began with an initial unplanned encounter, which then turned into a military confrontation. This was followed by a Cimbric request to settle again, which led to another battle. Growing increasingly impatient, the Cimbri then waited for the collapse of Roman power north of the Alps, set in motion by the earlier victory, and when this failed to materialize they then took a more positive step to ensure the removal of Roman

early-modern depiction of the handover of Jugurtha by Bocchus to Sulla. Artistic depictions of
 handover were a source of tension between Sulla and his commander Marius in the years that
owed the war. Sulla commissioned and wore a ring depicting the scene and, during the 90s,
chus commissioned a series of statues depicting the scene on the Capitol, later destroyed by
rius. Such artistic representations allowed Sulla to claim the credit for ending the war and
ance his own aspiring career. His son released a famous coin bearing the scene, decades later.
hor's collection)

A bust of Sulla, who at the time of the wars was one of Marius' many junior officers, though he was to later become a deadly rival. (© *Philip Matyszak, used with thanks*)

An early-modern representation of the Gracchi (Tiberius and Caius), whose tribunates were the catalyst for the political turmoil in Rome during this period. (*Author's collection*)

The ruins of the Republican Forum of Rome, as viewed from the Capitol, site of Marius' clash with Saturninus. (*Author's collection*)

Numantia, site of the war in Spain where both Marius and Jugurtha served under Scipio Aemilianus and learnt much of their respective military prowess. (*Author's collection*)

Modern Constantine (ancient Cirta) in North Africa, the capital of the unified Numidian kingdom and key site of the Jugurthine War. (*Author's collection*)

Three reliefs taken from the 'Altar of Domitius Ahenobarbus', depicting a Roman cavalryman, officer and pair of legionaries of the period. These reliefs were found in Rome and have generally been attributed to a monument commissioned by Cn. Domitius Ahenobarbus, consul of 122 BC and victor of the Gallic wars of the 120s. If this is the case then they show a contemporaneous depiction of the Roman military in this period. (© *Adrian Goldsworthy, used with thanks*)

rtist's impression of a Roman Republican legionary from the period. In addition to his sword
ladius) he would have carried one or two javelins (*pila*). (© *Philip Sidnell*)

Artist's impression of a Numidian horseman from the period. The Numidians were renowned for their horsemanship, riding bareback and without the aid of a bridle, the only tack being a simple neck-strap. (© *Philip Sidnell*)

The Dying Gaul; a Roman statue, believed to be a copy of a Hellenistic original depicting a Gallic warrior. The 'Gauls' always remained the apotheosis of barbarian threat to both Greek and Roman civilizations throughout the period, and for the Romans always conjured up the image of the Gallic sack of Rome. In reality the term 'Gaul' was a blanket one, used to cover a multitude of races. (*Author's collection*)

Artist's impression of a 'Gallic' warrior from the period. While there are references to Gauls fighting naked as depicted in the statue, possibly out of bravado, they would have been in the minority. This warrior's shield and helmet differs little from contemporary Roman types, but his sword is much longer and he is armed with a stout spear as his primary weapon. The wealthiest warriors wore mail shirts.
(© *Philip Sidnell*)

Bust of Juba I, King of Numidia throughout the mid-first century BC. He was a staunch ally of Pompey the Great and supported him during the Second Civil War, against Caesar (nephew of Marius). The Civil War in North Africa went badly for Juba (in a manner similar to Jugurthine War), when Bocchus II, King of the Mauri, allied to Caesar, invaded Numidia. Viewing the situation as hopeless Juba committed suicide and Numidia was finally annexed by Rome (under the leadership of Marius' nephew). (*Author's collection*)

Bust of Juba II, Son of Juba I, he grew up as a captive Numidian prince in Rome, before becoming a friend and ally of Caesar's son Octavian. When Octavian became the first Emperor Augustus, Juba II was restored to the Numidian throne, but soon transferred to the throne of the Mauri (Mauretania). This represented the final triumph of the house of Masinissa, taking over the throne once held by Bocchus, who betrayed Jugurtha to Rome. He was also married to Cleopatra Selene, daughter of Mark Antony and Cleopatra VII. (*Author's collection*)

Bust of Ptolemy I, Son of Juba II, grandson of Antony and Cleopatra. He was named in honour of the Ptolemaic dynasty that ruled Egypt from the death of Alexander the Great to Cleopatra. Upon his father's death he inherited the throne of Mauretania and remained a staunch Roman ally all his life. On a visit to Rome in AD 40 he was murdered by the Emperor Caius (Caligula). Although Mauretania revolted, this was soon crushed and the Emperor Claudius annexed it to the Roman Empire. Thus Ptolemy was the last surviving ruler of the house of Masinissa and his death signalled the end of an independent North Africa. (*Author's collection*)

influence north of the Alps, by militarily emasculating them. Whilst the above theory is an attractive one, as ever it needs to be clearly stated that it is merely a speculative one, for which there exists no positive evidence. Nonetheless, it does allow for a more nuanced and evolved consideration of the seemingly-random clashes between the Cimbri and the Romans. As always it is up to the reader to draw their own conclusions.

The Battle of Arausio (105 BC)

The Battle of Arausio represents one of the greatest defeats the Romans ever suffered, and is one of the least known. On the face of it, the Romans and their allies lost between 60,000 and 80,000 soldiers. This makes it a far greater defeat than those suffered at Teutoburg Forest and Carrhae, and on a par with the defeat to Hannibal at Cannae. Yet whilst these other battles are all well known, Arausio remains in the background by comparison. This is due to the fact that we have no surviving narrative that covers the battle, thus minimizing its modern historiographical impact. However, we should be under no illusion as to its impact at the time.

We have no clear timetable of events that led up to Arausio, but we can piece together some fragments. It appears that at some point in early 105 BC, the wanderings of the Cimbri and their allies (whether together or independently) brought them back into southern Gaul. With the memories of the defeats of 113 and 109 still fresh and with Roman armies apparently pacifying southern Gaul, it appears that a concerted effort was made to finish the tribal threat once and for all. This renewed threat was perhaps made even graver by the possible first appearance of the Teutones, along with the Cimbri.

In any event, to bolster the Roman military presence in Gaul, one of the consuls of 105 BC, Cn. Mallius Maximus, was dispatched with a fresh Roman army. We are given no size for this army. The ancient sources quote the two armies as being between 60,000 and 80,000 men. Brunt estimated that the number of Roman legions involved was four, two from each Roman army. He estimated the size of each Roman army at 11,000 Roman and 22,000 allied infantry and cavalry, utilizing a postulated ratio of 2:1 allied to Roman. Thus he places the total Roman strength at around 66,000 men.[319]

Thus Rome had two armies in Gaul, one under the proconsul Caepio and one under the new consul, Mallius. Rather than combining their forces, the two men were assigned different provinces. We are not explicitly told which, but the Rhone was the dividing line between the two men's commands. By Roman tradition, Caepio as proconsul would have been outranked by Mallius as serving consul, yet both men had separate provinces to maintain the distinction between them. Added to this was the fact that neither got on well with the other. Dio reports that Caepio was resentful of being outranked by Mallius, especially as Gaul had been his sole command.[320]

It appears that prior to the battle there was an initial encounter between the Romans and the Cimbri. Serving under Mallius, as a legate, was M. Aurelius Scaurus, who had been suffect consul in 108, and was obviously serving under Mallius to bring some experience to his general staff. A number of sources report that Scaurus and a Roman force fought a battle with the Cimbri, during which the Romans were routed and Scaurus captured. Both the *Periochae of Livy* and Licinianus report a story that Scaurus faced a council of Cimbric leaders and demanded that they desist from crossing the Alps and invading Italy.[321] Following his argument he was murdered by a Cimbri named Boiorix, whom Plutarch believes was a king or chieftain.[322] We naturally have to ask ourselves how the Romans learnt of this story, given the non-Roman audience (though it is possible that it came from prisoners later captured). Furthermore, we have to consider the language barrier, with Scaurus only speaking Latin (as well as Greek) and the Cimbri their own native tongue (though it is possible that they had bi-lingual guides from the local tribes with them). All we can say for sure is that the encounter cost Scaurus his life.

Orosius places this incident during the Battle of Arausio itself, yet there is good evidence to argue that it preceded the battle by some period of time.[323] Firstly, although the *Periochae of Livy* has the two events following each other, the passage covers several years' worth of events and does not indicate that they occurred at the same time. In fact, this usually indicates an elapse of time. Secondly, both Licinianus and a fragment of Dio (see below) indicate an elapse of time between Scaurus' death and the main battle.

Thus it appears that Scaurus' force met the Cimbri on its own, separate from the two main Roman armies, and was easily routed, being outnumbered. The most obvious explanation is that Scaurus' force was on a scouting mission to locate the main Cimbric army, which unfortunately for him was a mission he accomplished only too well.

With the enemy located, the two Roman armies drew up on the banks of the Rhone, near to the town of Arausio (now the town of Orange) on what now equates to 6 October 105 BC.[324] We have no surviving detailed account of the battle; all we can do is analyse the surviving fragments:

Granius Licinianus

> The ex-consul M. Aurelius Scaurus was thrown from his horse and captured. When they [the Cimbri] summoned him to a council, he

neither did nor said anything which was unworthy of a Roman, who had held such great honours. Because of this he was killed, although he could have escaped; he refused their request to act as their leader, out of shame that he should survive after the loss of his army. The consul Mallius was alarmed by this victory of the Cimbri, and sent a letter begging Caepio to join forces with him and confront the Gauls with a large combined army; but Caepio refused. Caepio crossed the Rhone and boasted to his soldiers that he would bring help to the frightened consul; but he did not even want to discuss with him how to conduct the war, and he disdained to listen to the envoys whom the Senate sent, asking the generals to co-operate and jointly to protect the state. The Cimbri sent envoys to arrange a peace and to ask for land and for corn to sow, but he dismissed them so brusquely that they attacked the next day. His camp was situated not far away from Mallius' camp, but he could not be persuaded, though he was so close, to join together their armies.

The greater part of the army was destroyed . . . on the day before the *nones* of October. Rutilius Rufus says that at least 70,000 regular troops and light-armed troops perished on this one day . . . [325]

Dio Cassius

After the death of Scaurus, Mallius has sent for Servilius [Caepio]; but the latter replied that each of them ought to guard their own province. Then, suspecting that Mallius might gain some success by himself, he [Caepio] grew jealous of him, fearing that he might secure the glory alone, and went to him; yet he neither camped in the same place nor entered into any common plan, but took up a position between Mallius and the Cimbri, with the evident intention of being the first to join the battle and so of winning all the glory of the war. Even thus they [the Romans] inspired their enemies with dread from the outset, as long as their quarrel was concealed, to such an extent that they were brought to desire peace; but when the Cimbri made overtures to Mallius, as consul, Servilius [Caepio] became indignant that they had not directed their embassy to him, gave them no conciliatory reply, and actually came near to slaying the envoys. The soldiers forced Servilius [Caepio] to go to Mallius and consult with him about the situation. But far from reaching an accord, as a result of the meeting, they became even more hostile than before, and parted in a disgraceful fashion.[326]

Orosius

In this battle, M. Aemilius [Aurelius Scaurus], who was of consular rank, was captured and killed, and the two sons of the consuls were slain. Antias writes that 80,000 of the Romans and their allies were slaughtered in that disaster and that 40,000 servants and camp followers were killed. Of the entire army it is said that only ten men survived. Having gained possession of camps and a huge amount of booty, the enemy seemed driven by some strange and unusual urge. They completely destroyed everything they had captured; clothing was cut to pieces and strewn about, gold and silver were thrown into the river, the breastplates of the men were hacked to pieces, the trappings of the horse were ruined, the horses themselves were drowned in whirlpools and men, with nooses fastened around their necks, were hanged from trees.[327]

Livy

At Arausio these same enemies conquered in battle Cn. Manlius (Mallius) the consul and Q. Servilius Caepio, the proconsul stripped them both of their camps and killed 80,000 soldiers and 40,000 servants and camp followers, according to Valerius Antias.[328]

Eutropius

M. Manlius and Q. Caepio were defeated by the Cimbri, Teutones, Tigurini and Ambrones, nations of Germans and Gauls, near the River Rhone, and being reduced by a terrible slaughter lost their very camp as well as the greater part of the army.[329]

Vegetius

The Cimbri destroyed the legions of Caepio and Mallius inside Gaul. The remnants were taken up by C. Marius, who trained them in the knowledge and art of warfare.[330]

Plutarch

He [Sertorius] had his first experience of war under Caepio during the campaign in which the Cimbri and Teutones broke into Gaul, when the Romans suffered a crushing defeat and their army was routed.

VIII. The Battle of Arausio (105 BC), Stage 1

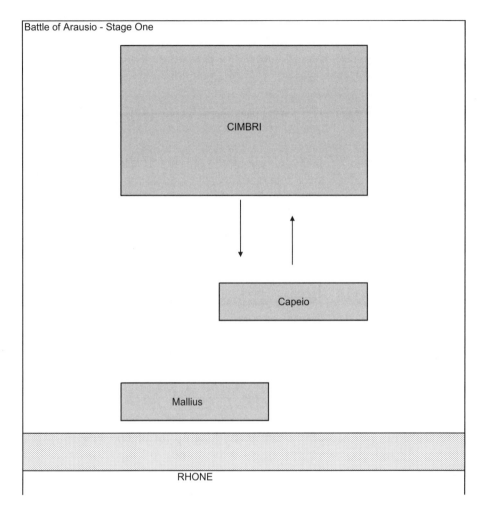

Battle of Arausio - Stage One

After this battle, in spite of losing his horse and being seriously wounded, Sertorius swam across the Rhone in the teeth of a strong current still carrying his shield and his breastplate.[331]

The first aspect to note is the closeness of the fragments of Dio and Licinianus, with Licinianus naming Rutilius Rufus (Marius' deputy) as the source (see Appendix V). Both sources detail the lack of agreement between the two commanders, with both placing the blame squarely on Caepio for his refusal to cooperate. This was crucial to the defeat at Arausio, the two Roman armies operating as two individual forces. Together they numbered up to 80,000 men,

IX. The Battle of Arausio (105 BC), Stage 2

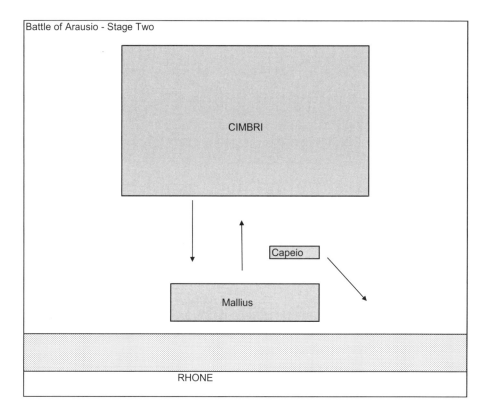

if we are to believe the sources, facing anything up to 300,000 tribesmen (the number Plutarch gives, which he argues is a low one).[332] Thus, despite the fact that even the combined Roman forces would have been outnumbered by the Cimbri, the two armies refused to coordinate their effort or battle-plans and operated as separate armies. Both commanders were so intent on winning the war themselves that they ensured that neither would. Again we see the fatal combination of desire for personal glory and the arrogance of Roman military invincibility, despite facing an enemy that had already defeated two Roman armies in previous years and routed a smaller force more recently.

Again, both Dio and Licinianus note that before the battle the Cimbri sent emissaries to the Romans. Whilst Dio has this being from a dread of the Romans, which after two victories is difficult to believe, Licinianus states that they again requested land for their tribe to settle on, as they had done before the battle of 109 BC. At the time it would have been impossible to expect this from the Romans, given the desire for glory on the part of the commanders, not to mention revenge for the previous defeats. Given that the Cimbri now represented more than just a wandering tribe, their victories had made them a talisman of anti-Roman efforts (whether they sought that mantle or not) and such an acceptance would have been a severe blow to Roman authority in the region.

With battle a certainty, it is not clear how this failure to cooperate worked in the battle itself. Caepio's army was nearer to the Cimbri and would have borne the first attack, but whether he took the offensive or waited for the Cimbri is impossible to tell. Given his desire for glory it is likely that he initiated the first attack, hoping that Mallius would back him up. Clearly, it seems that this attack failed, which would have forced his army back towards the Rhone and possibly even towards Mallius' army. If the two Roman forces did become entangled, with one retreating into the other, then we can understand the slaughter. Furthermore, the Roman retreat was cut off by the river itself, which would now have acted like a barrier. Sertorius may have survived by swimming it, but many would not have and this would have only increased the overall number of dead. These losses were further magnified by the apparent slaughter of all Roman survivors by the tribesmen. In addition, a number of sources focus on the fact that the Cimbri were able to storm both Roman camps and slaughter the camp followers, indicating the speed and surprise of their attack.

In short, the Romans were outnumbered, failed to cooperate and had the river behind them to cut off any retreat. Antias, who is quoted by both Livy and Orosius, puts the Roman and allied losses at 80,000 men with 40,000 ancillaries, whilst Rutilius Rufus, puts the figure at 70,000 troops lost. Diodorus places the total number lost at 60,000.[333] We should take Orosius' figure of only ten survivors with a large pinch of salt, especially given the fact that we can name three of them: the two Roman commanders Mallius and Caepio and the then-obscure soldier Sertorius. Furthermore, Vegetius speaks of survivors of the battle.[334] Nevertheless, the impact of the massacre can be seen by Mallius losing two sons in the battle.

As Roman military disasters go, the defeat at Arausio was indeed on par with the Battle of Cannae, which also resulted in part from a dual command structure. Long accepted as the greatest Roman defeat the Republic suffered, Polybius gave casualty figures of 70,000 Roman and allied troops for Cannae, compared to 60,000 to 80,000 at Arausio.[335] Livy only gave a figure of 45,000 for Cannae and 80,000 for Arausio.[336] Whilst these ancient figures for battle losses have long been treated with suspicion, the scale of the comparison, with Arausio being greater than Cannae in Livy's account (albeit from the *Periochae*), only shows the significance of the Roman losses that day and the terrible effects of the battle. Regardless of whether we have a detailed account of the battle or not, the Battle of Arausio stands as one of Rome's greatest defeats.

The Aftermath of Arausio

Furthermore, both Dio and Licinianus report the news of the defeat reaching Rome, which is on a par with comparable accounts in Livy following Cannae. Dio wrote:

> So great a multitude had perished, some grieved for sons, others for brothers; children left fatherless bewailed the loss of a sire and the desolation of Italy; and large numbers of women, bereft of their husbands were made acquainted with the sad fate of widowhood. The Senate, with courageous fortitude in the face of disaster, sought to restrain the general mourning and the excessive lamentation and bore their heavy load of grief without showing it.[337]

Licinianus has it as follows:

> The consul Rutilius, the colleague of Mallius, remained in sole charge of the government. Therefore, since the whole state was in trepidation and fear of an attack by the Cimbri, Rutilius made the young men take an oath, that none of them would travel anywhere outside Italy. Messengers were sent along all the coasts and ports of Italy, with instructions that no-one under the age of 25 years should be allowed to board a boat . . . [338]

It appears that Rutilius kept his head and assembled a large force from scratch in order to meet any invasion of Italy. Furthermore, Valerius Maximus provides us with an interesting note on the training methods Rutilius used:

> Practice in handling arms was passed on to soldiers by the consul P. Rutilius Rufus, Cn. Mallius' colleague. Following the example of no previous general, he called in gladiator instructors from the school of C. Aurelius Scaurus to provide the legions with a more sophisticated system of avoiding and striking a blow.[339]

Thus it appears that Rufus brought in gladiators to train these inexperienced soldiers and shows that Marius was not the only military reformer at the time.

However, the overall situation at the time must have looked bleak. Sallust sums the situation up nicely:

> About the same time (as Jugurtha's capture) the Gauls (Cimbri) inflicted upon our commanders Q. Caepio and Cn. Manlius (Mallius)

a defeat that made all Italy tremble with terror and inspired in the Romans a belief which existed even to our own day that, while all other peoples could easily be subjected by their (Roman) valour, a war against the Gauls was a struggle for very existence and not just a matter of making a bid for glory.[340]

Whether or not the Cimbri intended to invade Italy is not the issue. In Rome, amongst both the citizenry and the elites, they clearly believed that such an event was imminent. Once again, the spectre of the Gallic sack of Rome would have come to the forefront of their minds. It was now that timing played a hand in Roman politics. Whilst two more 'establishment' commanders had failed and, in Roman minds, had left Italy vulnerable to invasion, it was into this atmosphere of doom and disaster that the news of Marius' capture of Jugurtha and the end of the long-running Jugurthine War arrived.

Even without Arausio it had probably already occurred to Marius that he needed to follow up the Numidian command with another command, especially as the Northern Wars had been rumbling on for as long as the Jugurthine one and with less success. The tactics (both political as well as military) which had worked once may well have worked again. What he got, however, was a situation tailor-made for him. Our surviving sources do not mention any pressure on Marius' part, or that of his supporters, to have him appointed to the command in Gaul, nor do we have a timescale for the news of Arausio, the news of Jugurtha's capture and Marius' re-election as consul. As it is portrayed, Marius was elected in absentia with popular and Senatorial backing.

Such an act was technically against the law, with there being a ban on consulships within ten years of each other, though this had been laid aside for the benefit of Scipio Aemilianus (see Chapter 1). In such an emergency, however, whether the Senate were that enthusiastic about this or not, by ending the Jugurthine War there was only one clear choice for command of the Northern War: Marius. By his return to Rome, with Jugurtha in chains, he had already been elected as consul for 104 BC and, in an unprecedented situation, was to continue to be re-elected consul another four times (103–100 BC), though it is unlikely this was ever discussed at this stage. He entered office spectacularly on 1 January by celebrating his triumph over Jugurtha. Though the Romans did not yet know it, the brief Age of Marius had begun.

The Age of Marius
(104–100 BC)

Chapter 9

The Northern Wars:
The War in Spain and the Battle of Aquae Sextiae (105–102 BC)

The Return of Marius

Having been given this extraordinary position in such a time of national emergency, Marius' return to Rome and entry into his second consulship was stage-managed to perfection. He timed his army's return to Rome to coincide with his first day of office (1 January 104 BC) and entered Rome to both celebrate his triumph over Jugurtha and his assumption of the consulship. To the people of Rome, such a triumph must have been a welcome sight after the news of Arausio. At the head of the triumph was the figure of Jugurtha himself, along with his two sons, visible proof of both Roman and Marian military success. Marius continued this theme by convening the Senate on the Capitol and entering whilst still in triumphal dress. This was the first time this had been done and is detailed by Plutarch thus:

> After the procession was over, Marius called the Senate into session on the Capitol, and made his entry, either through inadvertence or with a vulgar display of his good fortune, in his triumphal robes; but perceiving quickly that the Senators were offended at this, he rose and went out, changed into the usual robe with the purple border, and then came back."[341]

Having been a senator for at least fifteen years and with an array of advisors, it is inconceivable that Marius made this gesture by mistake.[342] There was a clear message, namely that he was the man for the moment and that he was an 'outsider', but a highly successful one, who they needed right now.

Following Arausio, the few surviving sources swiftly move on to the year 102 and the first battle between Marius and the tribes. However, although the sources manage this in a sentence, we are left with the years 104 and 103 BC to understand, as they form a crucial backdrop to the battles that were to come, for a number of reasons. It is clear that Marius left Rome with his army soon after his triumph and headed north for southern Gaul. As it happened, the tribes did not make an attempted invasion of Italy, but dispersed. Again, we have no clear chronology for this, but by early to mid-104 BC, it appears that Marius had established a defensive position on the Rhone, based at Arles, where he awaited the return of the tribes. As it turned out, he would have to wait until 102 BC.[343]

Again, what few sources we have inform us of the Cimbri, but not their allies the Teutones or Ambrones. It is possible that the three tribes separated, with the Teutones or Ambrones going off either together or separately to some other part of Gaul. It is also possible that the other two tribes had not yet become involved in these wars.

The Cimbric Invasion of Spain (105–103 BC)

Following the victory at Arausio in October 105 BC, the Cimbri moved on once more, not invading Italy, as many in Rome expected, but instead turning west and invading Spain. This was an important new development and one that requires some discussion, even though it is little covered in the sources.[344] There are several questions that need discussing. Firstly, why did the Cimbri not invade Italy, something that they later attempted? Secondly, with reference to our earlier discussion of the possible evolution of the Cimbric tactics, why did they not settle in the region of southern Gaul, now that it had been 'freed' from Roman rule?

In both cases, the ultimate answers to these questions lie forever in the discussions of the Cimbric leaders at the time and will never truly be known. Nonetheless, we can briefly afford ourselves some speculation on their possible motives. As to the first question, regarding Italy, the Cimbri would have known that any invasion of Italy would have been met with continued Roman resistance and that it would have resulted in a fight to the finish for one side or the other. At the time, the defeat of the Roman armies at Arausio had given them a valuable breathing space from Roman resistance and there were still other options available. As to the issue of remaining in Gaul, as events showed, yet another Roman army soon turned up in Gaul with revenge in mind and again no settlement would ever be free from Roman interference. Furthermore, they had already marched through central Gaul and been driven out by the native tribes. With the north, east and south (the Mediterranean) all discarded, the west was an attractive and nearby alternative.

Thus, we have the short note from the *Periochae of Livy*:

The Cimbri devastated all the land between the Rhone and the Pyrenees, crossed through a pass into Spain and there after devastating many districts . . . [345]

As Evans has pointed out, we have no other evidence for this devastation, but this may have resulted in the destruction of the Roman colony at Narbo, severing the land link between Italy and Spain.[346] We have little clear idea of the state of Spain at this time, again poorly served by our few remaining sources, with the focus being elsewhere, as we have seen. Nevertheless, it appears that Rome was once again at war with the Lusitanians (see Chapter 1). The Praetor of 109 Q. Servilius Caepio, is recorded as fighting them between 109 and 106, when he returned to Rome to celebrate a triumph.[347] However, it appears that whoever succeeded him in Spain met with disaster, as Obsequens records this for the year 105 BC (based on Livy):

A Roman army was slaughtered by the Lusitanians.[348]

The only surviving narrative history for Spain in the period is Appian, who has one section on the period in question.

After this time [the Numantine War] there were other revolts in Iberia and Calpurnius Piso was chosen general.[349] Servius Galba succeeded him, but as the Cimbri were invading Italy [101 BC], and Sicily was also embroiled in the Second Servile War [see Appendix II], they [the Romans] did not send an army to Iberia, because they were so pre-occupied with these matters, but sent legates to put an end to the war by whatever means possible. Once the Cimbri had been driven away, T. Didius came and killed 20,000 Arevaci, and moved Termessus, a large city, which had always been disinclined to obey the Romans...[350]

Furthermore, around 102 BC, we find an M. Marius, possibly the younger brother of the consul, commanding a Roman force in Spain:

There lived in another city near Colenda a mixed race of Celtiberians, whom M. Marius had settled there five years earlier [c.102 BC], with the agreement of the Senate, after they had fought with him against the Lusitanians.[351]

We can see that at the start of the Cimbric invasion of Gaul, Spain appeared already to be unsettled, and that after the Northern Wars had been concluded a major campaign was required to restore Roman rule. If we are to believe the

Obsequens reference then as well as a defeat in Gaul at Arausio, another Roman army had been destroyed in Spain. We have no other details, but throughout the period of 113–105 BC, Roman military effort was focused primarily on Gaul and Macedon, not Spain, and successive defeats only served to undermine Rome's position in Spain, much as it had done in Gaul. Thus it appears that the Lusitanians at least had taken advantage of Rome's defeats elsewhere to revolt once more. During this period all the evidence points to the Romans after 105 BC being unable to send troops to quell the rebellious peoples of Spain and having to co-opt friendly tribes to their service, as seen with M. Marius using the Celtiberians of Colenda against the Lusitanians.

Added to this mixture of rebellion and inter-tribal fighting came a massive Cimbric invasion. Whilst the Cimbri may have believed that Spain offered them the best location to settle and defend themselves from Rome, once again they underestimated the reaction of the natives to this new threat. Whilst the phrase 'the enemy of my enemy is my friend' has always been a valid one in warfare, this did not extend to 'friends' settling in your homeland and the Cimbri found themselves under attack from the Celtiberian natives, repeating the reception they had received throughout Gaul. Again we have no details of the fighting which occurred, but the *Periochae of Livy* line quoted above, ends thus:

> The Cimbri devastated all the land between the Rhone and the Pyrenees, crossed through a pass into Spain, and there after devastating many districts, were routed by the Celtiberians. They returned to Gaul and in the land of the Vellocasses joined the Teutones.[352]

Given that Plutarch dates their return to Gaul in late 103 BC, we can see that the Cimbri spent nearly two years in Spain, adding to the rebellions in progress and probably stoking up many more, reducing Spain to a wreck of a province with a three-way fight between the Romans and their allies, the rebels and the Cimbri. When the Cimbri were finally defeated and driven out of Spain by the natives, the province must have been in ruins and for all intents and purposes out of Roman hands, along with southern Gaul and Sicily at this time (see Appendix II).[353]

104–103 BC: The Cold War in Gaul and Domestic Unease

Whilst Spain bore the brunt of the Cimbric invasion, it did provide Marius with an invaluable opportunity to prepare. Whilst the Cimbric plan was to settle in Spain, in Roman eyes it was only a matter of time before they returned and attempted what all enemies of Rome attempted: an invasion of Italy. Whilst ultimately the Romans proved to be correct and the Cimbri did return, at the time this was by no means a certainty. Had the Cimbri been successful in their attempts to settle in Spain, then ultimately Marius, or his successor, would have had to lead this northern Roman army into Spain to dislodge them.

One important question concerns the nature of the army that Marius took command of. Given his reforms of the recruitment criteria in 107 BC (see Appendix I), it has been suggested that Marius again raised fresh forces from Italy by this method. Furthermore, there is a reference in Diodorus to him requesting fresh troops from overseas.[354] Regrettably, Plutarch ignores this issue. The clearest evidence comes from a short passage of Frontinus:

> When Caius Marius had the option of choosing a force from two armies, one of which had served under Rutilius, the other under Metellus and later under himself, he preferred the troops of Rutilius, though fewer in number, because he deemed them of trustier discipline.[355]

On the face of it this seems strange, given that Marius had gone to great lengths to assemble a large force for his war in Numidia and that those troops were now battle-hardened veterans, rather than raw recruits thrown together in the panic after Arausio.

Furthermore, he apparently deliberately chose the smaller of the two armies to face the Cimbri (under the expectation that they would soon be attacking Italy). One possible solution to this problem is the fact that Frontinus could be referring to the forces which he inherited from Metellus who had been taken to Numidia in 109 BC. Thus Marius discharged those men who had served the longest and added Rutilius' men to those he raised in 107 BC. Ultimately, however, there is no clear answer to this conundrum.

Regardless of this, the absence of the Cimbri gave Marius vital breathing space. Having been given this time without an immediate opponent, Marius utilized it to maximum benefit in training and modifying his army (the details of which will be discussed in Chapter 11). Nevertheless, despite the few details provided by our remaining sources for these years, they represented a golden opportunity for Marius to integrate his army of fresh recruits and veterans, train them up and hone his tactics for what the Roman saw as the inevitable battles to come with the Cimbri. Inevitably, this would lead to slack periods, with Marius having to find work to keep his men occupied, as noted by Strabo, when he tells us that Marius had his men dig a canal from the Rhone to the Mediterranean to ease his supply route.[356]

On a more positive note, both the absence of the northern tribes and the presence of the Roman army must have helped stabilize Roman influence in the region. Whilst Plutarch, in his biography of Marius, is equally impatient to move onto the battle of 102 BC, in his biography of Sulla he actually offers us some details of the lesser military and diplomatic activities of the Romans during the period 104–103 BC.

Having served as Marius' deputy in the Jugurthine Wars, Sulla continued this role in the Northern Wars, first as a legate then as a military tribune. Plutarch records that as legate in 104 BC, Sulla captured the chieftain of the Tectosages tribe, a man named Copillus. Thus it seems that whilst he was waiting for the return of the northern tribes, Marius had his army subdue the rebellious local tribes and secure the region for Rome once more. Frontinus adds the following story:

> During the war with the Cimbri and Teutones, the consul Caius Marius, wishing to test the loyalty of the Gauls and Ligurians, sent them a letter, commanding them in the first part of the letter not to open the inner part, which was specially sealed, before a certain date. Afterwards, before the appointed time had arrived, he demanded the same letter back, and, finding all seals broken, he knew that acts of hostility were afoot.[357]

This brief story not only confirms that Marius spent this period ensuring the loyalty of the local tribes, but also the extent of the potential rebellion against Rome, for this is the only evidence that the Ligurians (who occupied the Alpine region joining Gaul and Northern Italy, and had only been subdued by Rome less than a century earlier[358]) were also disloyal to Rome. Though we have no evidence that the Ligurian tribes joined the Cimbri, it is important to understand that Northern Italy and Southern Gaul were now potentially hostile territory for the Romans. These two years Marius had would have been invaluable in ensuring that when the tribes did eventually move on Italy the locals had been re-subjugated.

Nevertheless, despite all this, Marius would have faced a political problem as 104 BC passed, concerning his position for 103 BC. He had been elected as consul for 104 in the face of an expected Cimbric invasion of Italy, which then had not materialized. Although it appears that his army was actively pacifying the region, it cannot have been the glorious victories that either he, or the people of Rome, had in mind. Under normal circumstances, Marius' command would have become a proconsular one and two fresh consuls would be elected. Yet this is not what happened; instead, we find Marius being elected to a second consulship in a row (his third overall). Plutarch explains this as being due to the expected arrival of the northern tribes in the spring of 103, though whether this was based on genuine intelligence or rumour, possibly even spread by Marius' own supporters, we will never know. In any event, Marius set another milestone with back-to-back consulships, a far more unprecedented act than two consulships in a decade. His colleague for 103 BC was an L. Aurelius Orestes, about whom little is known.

However, as 103 BC passed, still with no sign of the tribes, Marius' position became more open to criticism, with the defeat at Arausio now two years in the past and still no sign of an invasion of Italy. Again the only military activity we hear of comes from Plutarch's biography of Sulla, who as military tribune this year apparently persuaded the tribe of the Marsi to ally with Rome, though the identity of this tribe is open to question.[359] However essential this work was to Rome, it was not what he had been elected for, at least in the eyes of the people.

The death of his colleague during the year meant that he had to return to Rome to hold the consular elections for 102 BC. This gave him a wonderful opportunity to secure his position further, by reconnecting with the people of Rome first hand. Once in Rome it appears that Marius reverted to his old tactic of finding a popular tribune to agitate on his behalf. On this occasion he chose L. Appuleius Saturninus (see Appendix I). Plutarch reports:

> L. Appuleius Saturninus, who had more influence with the people than any other tribune, was won over by the flattering attentions of Marius, and in his harangues urged the people to elect Marius consul. Marius affected to decline the office and declared that he did not want it, but Saturninus called him a traitor to his country for refusing to command the armies at a time of such great peril. Now it was clear that Saturninus was playing his part at the instigation of Marius, and playing it badly too, but the masses, seeing that the occasion required the ability as well as the good fortune of Marius, voted for his fourth consulship, and made Catulus Lutatius [Q. Lutatius Catulus] his colleague.[360]

Thus Marius was able to secure a fourth consulship in a row, but it was clear that without forthcoming military success his support was diminishing. It was at this point, 102 BC, that the tribes made their return to southern Gaul.

The Tribal Alliance against Rome

With the defeat of the Cimbri in Spain, the bulk of the tribes crossed the Pyrenees once more and returned to Gaul. As always we have no idea of how many of the Cimbri actually crossed into Spain, nor what their losses were.

Upon this return from Spain, however, it is apparent that the Cimbri evolved their strategy in a bold and decisive manner. Having been repulsed from Central Europe, Gaul and now Spain, it is clear that they decided upon the final course of action open to them: the invasion of Italy. Whilst they had suffered setbacks at the hands of the other tribes, they had on three occasions proved to be superior to the Roman military. Italy was fertile and had been the location of previous Gallic migrations, showing it to be a viable and defensible location. To accomplish this, though, required the total defeat of Rome and the dismantling of the Roman system. It is also possible that the Cimbric leaders assumed that once they had defeated Rome and settled there then Rome may have become accustomed to their presence, though ultimately we will never know.

We have no evidence for the decision-making process that the Cimbri went through, only their ultimate actions, but clearly this attack on Italy represented both a change in policy and one which they had shied away from for a number of years. Having taken this decision, however, it is clear that the Cimbric leaders realized that to accomplish the invasion and settlement of Italy they needed even greater manpower, possibly due to their losses in Spain, but certainly in order to deliver a single knock-out blow to Rome. To those ends the Cimbri made contact with a number of other tribes and co-ordinated a strategy for the invasion of Italy.

As stated earlier, the sources are too few and too confused to allow us to construct a timeline for the other tribes' participation with the Cimbri in the years preceding 103/102 BC. It is perfectly possible that the tribes of the Teutones and Ambrones were part of the great Cimbric host all the time, but in the scenario presented here, it makes the most sense that the Cimbri, having finally decided on the great step of invading Italy, called for allies in this enterprise and that now the other, lesser, tribes appear in matters. All we have in our sources for this alliance between the tribes is one line from the *Periochae of Livy*.

> They [the Cimbri] returned to Gaul and in the land of the Vellocasses [Gaul] joined the Teutoni.[361]

Had we Livy's fuller account then no doubt we would have a narrative for the meeting between the tribes, the agreement to this course of action and far greater detail on the planning. As it is we have no such details. All we do have is the ultimate course of action, a two-pronged attack on Italy, with the Teutones and Ambrones attacking Italy from the northwest and the Cimbri and Tigurini attacking from the northeast.[362]

Rome's Tribal Enemies

Before we move onto the attacks of the two armies and the battles that resulted, it would be beneficial to briefly analyse the tribes that made up this grand tribal alliance:

i) The Cimbri

They are the most familiar to us, having fought Rome on three previous occasions (113, 109/108 and 105), each time resulting in a greater Roman defeat. As acknowledged earlier, we have no clear evidence for why the Cimbri fought Rome on three occasions and finally invaded Italy only on the fourth campaign. A theoretical framework was put forward based on an evolution in the Cimbric attitude towards Rome, which began with them being unaware of Rome, requesting the right to settle in Italy, a desire to eliminate Roman influence from mainland Europe and finally the need to dismantle Roman control of Italy. We will never know the fine details of this planned invasion, whether an attack on Rome itself was planned or whether they intended to destroy the Roman military to such an extent that their settlement became an accepted fact. Given the events of 101 BC, when the Cimbri settled in northern Italy and did not advance on Rome, it is possible that the latter is the more likely, though again we will never know.

ii) The Teutones

The Teutones also hailed from the North Sea region and are mentioned by Pytheas in his voyages of that region in the 320s BC. Again the immediate tendency is to take their name, Teutones and derive the Teutonic description from it, but again we have no firm evidence whether they were German or Celtic. Evidence from nomenclature again points towards a Celtic origin. We do not know whether they were forced to migrate due to rising sea levels or some other reason, whether they travelled the same route as the Cimbri or whether they simply answered the Cimbric call for allies in their invasion of Italy.

iii) Ambrones

The Ambrones are even more mysterious, only appearing in our sources in this middle period of the wars. They appear to have been far less in number than either the Cimbri and Teutones and it has been speculated that they were a small allied tribe from the Zuiderzee region of Holland (now a large North Sea inlet). Festus reports that they were a Gallic tribe, displaced by rising sea levels that took up with the larger tribal movements, and seem to have been more closely affiliated with the Teutones.[363]

iv) Tigurini & Toygeni

The Tigurini and Toygeni stand out from the above named three tribes, coming from the region of Helvetia (Switzerland). They were not part of the tribal migration from the North Sea region, but invaded the region of southern Gaul for different, and now unknown, reasons. It is possible that they became swept up by the Cimbric movements through the region or that they initially acted separately from the Cimbri and saw their chance to expand their territory at their neighbours' expense and gain plunder. By 102/101 BC, they had evidently become part of the grand alliance against Rome, though their reluctance to invade Italy perhaps showed a more pragmatic streak; certainly, they were not under the same pressures as the other tribes as they were not looking to settle. Although the Tigurini are mentioned by several sources, Strabo is the only one to mention that a lesser Helvetian tribe, the Toygeni also joined them, on their attacks on Rome.[364]

v) Local Gallic Tribes

We have already seen that a number of Gallic and Spanish tribes had taken the opportunity presented by the reversals suffered by Rome at the hands of the Cimbri to re-assert their independence. Although a number had been subdued in the shadowy campaigns of 104 and 103 BC it is possible that a number of tribes joined this two-pronged attack on Italy, though none appear in our few surviving sources.

Thus the stage was set for a massive attack on Italy by the native tribes of Europe, one far greater than Hannibal was able to mange a century earlier. If it succeeded then Roman power would have been severely diminished if not crushed. Had Rome itself survived then it would have a new and permanent Celtic presence in North Italy, overturning several centuries of subjugation of the region. Certainly, North Italy and Gaul would have been outside of Roman power, in the short term. What the knock on effects for the rest of the Roman Empire would have been, we can only speculate. It is also possible that Rome may have ultimately overcome these disasters and incorporated these new tribes into the Roman military and political system. Such a move would have anticipated the changes that the Roman Empire underwent by 300 to 400 years and forever altered the history of Western Europe, and Western Civilization. That it didn't ultimately rested on the shoulders of one man, Caius Marius, who had been impatiently awaiting the return of these tribal armies for more than three years.

The Battle of Aquae Sextiae – The Prelude

It appears that Marius was still in Italy when he heard of the advancing tribes, but moved swiftly across the Alps and met up with his army and built a forti-fied forward position along the Rhone, though Plutarch does not make it clear where this forward base was. Orosius, however, places Marius' fortified camp further north at the confluence of the Isère and Rhone rivers, thus securing the Rhone valley, there to await the arrival of the tribal forces.[365] Plutarch provides us with a colourful story concerning Marius' intelligence gathering, with a young Sertorius apparently being sent undercover amongst the tribes and reporting on their movements.[366]

Again there is some argument in the sources over exactly who Marius faced in the initial clash. Orosius would have it that the initial encounter was the whole combined might of the Cimbri, Teutones, Ambrones and Tigurini, whereas Plutarch has Marius facing the combined forces of the Teutones and Ambrones, the lesser of the three northern tribes.[367] Of the two, Plutarch's version is the more consistent, with the Cimbri choosing another route into Italy, and being met by another Roman army, led by Marius' consular colleague, Q. Lutatius Catulus.

Both Plutarch and Orosius are consistent in the fact that upon the approach of the tribal force down the Rhone valley, Marius did not move out to engage them, but remained in his fortified position on higher ground.

> Marius, now consul for the fourth time, pitched his camp near the confluence of the Isère and Rhone rivers. The Teutones, Cimbri, Tigurini and Ambrones fought continuously for three days at the Roman camp, trying by every means to dislodge the Romans from their ramparts and drive them out onto level ground.[368]
>
> They covered a large part of the plain and after pitching their camp challenged Marius to battle. Marius, however, paid them no heed but kept his soldiers inside their fortifications . . .
>
> But he [Marius] would station his soldiers on the fortifications by detachments, bidding them to observe the enemy, and in this way accustomed them not to fear their shape or dread their cries which were altogether strange and ferocious; and to make themselves familiar with their equipment and movements, thus in the course of time rendering what was only apparently formidable familiar to their minds from observations.[369]

Despite the obvious desire of the Roman soldiers to get to grips with the enemy, Marius held them firm and remained in his defensive position, thus frustrating the Teutones/Ambrones and denying them an encounter on their terms. Furthermore, he forced them to wear down their forces attempting to dislodge him, being unwilling to leave a large Roman army in their rear.

> But the Teutones, since Marius remained where he was, attempted to take his camp by storm; many missiles however were hurled against them from the fortifications and they lost a number of their men. They therefore decided to march forward, expecting to cross the Alps un-opposed. So they packed up their baggage and began to march past the Roman camp. Then, indeed, the immensity of their numbers were made evident by the length of their line and the time required for their passage; for it is said that they were six days in passing the Roman fortifications.[370]

Whilst we must treat this tale with extreme scepticism, Plutarch does make his point well, for the combined force of the Teutones and Ambrones, together with their women and children apparently passed the 200,000 mark, vastly outnumbering the Romans. Once the tribesmen had marched past the Romans, Marius too broke camp and trailed them along the Rhone valley:

> Once the barbarians had passed by and begun to move forward, Marius also broke camp and followed after them, never losing contact with them and always stopping for the night close beside them, but fortify-ing his camps strongly and keeping difficult ground between himself and the enemy, so as to be able to pass the night in safety. So they went on until they reached a place called Aquae Sextiae.[371] From here it was a short march to the Alps and it was here that Marius prepared to give battle.[372]

Thus we can see that Marius kept his head, in all senses of the phrase, when he first encountered the northern tribes. Rather than rush headlong in battle with them at the time and ground of their choosing, he waited it out. Certainly, it would have been unpopular with his soldiers, but he could see the benefits of both assessing and frustrating the enemy and fighting at his time of choosing on ground that favoured the Romans. Furthermore, having been positioned in the region for nearly two years, he would have had plenty of time to choose ground that favoured him. If that created the impression in the tribes' minds of a Roman reluctance to fight or cowardice then all the better to lull the enemy into a false sense of security.

Certainly, Marius had chosen his ground well; Aquae Sextiae was a wide plain by the river, which sloped steeply upwards, covered in woodland (see diagram). Marius chose to occupy the higher ground, overlooking the tribes, with the river behind them. The only drawback to this position was that it placed the tribesmen between his men and the sources of fresh water, which both Plutarch and Orosius comment on. Both note that upon Marius hearing his men's complaints, he allegedly told them that if they wanted drinking water they would have to fight for it.[373]

As Plutarch records, when the first encounter did take place, it apparently happened by accident. According to his account a group of camp servants made an attempt to get to the river to gain fresh water but stumbled on a party of Ambrones who were enjoying the hot springs at that spot. The group had been drinking and eating and were taken by surprise and not in prime fighting condition. At this point it appears that a force of Ligurians in Marius' army broke from the main force and rushed to engage the Ambrones.[374] Plutarch numbers the Ambrones at 30,000 at this particular stretch of the river.

> The Ambrones became separated by the river. Before they could form up on the other side the Ligurians had quickly rushed down on those who had been the first to cross and engaged them in hand-to-hand fighting. Then the Romans came to the aid of the Ligurians and charged down on the Ambrones from the higher ground, forced them back and routed them. Most of them herded and jostled together in the stream and were cut down on the spot and the river was filled with their blood and with the bodies of the dead. The Romans then crossed the river and finding that the enemy would not stand up to them, continued killing them as they fled right up to their camp and their wagons. Here the women came out against them, armed with swords and axes and making the most horrible shrieking, attacking both the pursuers and the pursued; the former as their enemies and the latter as the men who had betrayed them. They threw themselves into the thick of the fighting, tearing at the Romans shields with their bear hands or clutching at their swords, and though their bodies were gashed and wounded, their spirits remained unvanquished to the end. So then, as we are told, the battle at the river was brought about by accident rather than by the intention of the commander. After destroying many of the Ambrones, the Romans withdrew as night fell.[375]

Thus first blood had been drawn by the Romans. Whatever the merits of the story about the clash being started by the camp servants, it is clear that the Romans had spotted a vulnerable section of the enemy force, isolated from the main body and had utilized the two key strengths they had in this position: attacking downhill and trapping the enemy with the river at their back. Certainly, the initial encounter had gone to Rome, but the Ambrones' losses would not have altered the fact that tribes still massively outnumbered the Romans. Nevertheless, it was a morale boost for the Romans and the first success of any sort against this previously-undefeated enemy.

Orosius also has the same story, but in a much simpler form:

> The camp servants, shouting loudly were the first to rush into the fray; then the army immediately followed. Lines of battle were quickly formed for regular combat. An engagement was fought in which the Romans were victorious.[376]

An interesting variation can be found in Frontinus:

> When Marius was fighting against the Cimbrians and Teutons, his engineers on one occasion had heedlessly chosen such a site for the camp that the barbarians controlled the water supply. In response to his soldiers' demands for water, Marius pointed with his sword towards the enemy and said 'There is where you must get it'. Thus inspired, the Romans straightway drove the barbarians from the place.[377]

The latter variation is interesting; with engineers instead of camp servants and confusion over whether it was a deliberate or accidental location, as although it states that the location was chosen by accident, Marius clearly knew that it would force his men to fight. Thus we must question whether the elaborate story in Plutarch is a more embroidered version of events. Clearly, this initial engagement between the Romans and the Ambrones ended in a Roman victory and control of this stretch of the river.

The Battle of Aquae Sextiae (102 BC)

Nevertheless, Orosius goes on to tell us that the main battle was fought on the fourth day, presumably since the Romans had arrived and camped.[378] This elapse of time was crucial to Marius, who drew up a careful battle plan utilizing the terrain to his advantage, though he had possibly already chosen the ground in the previous few years. The battle that followed was the first one that had been fought on Roman terms and after due consideration, rather than having been rushed into.

As can be seen from the diagram, Marius occupied the higher ground, with

X. The Battle of Aquae Sextiae (102 BC), Stage 1

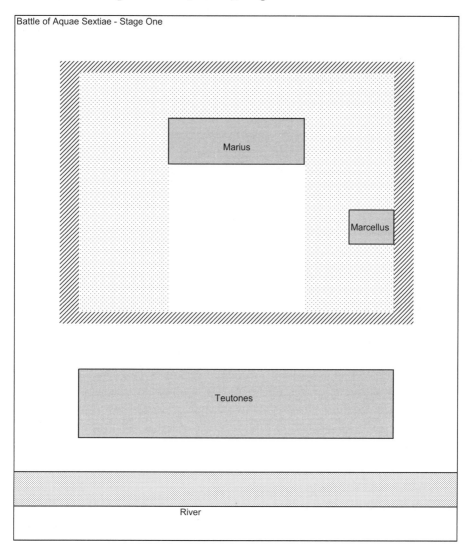

Battle of Aquae Sextiae - Stage One

Marius

Marcellus

Teutones

River

tribesmen in the plain below. To engage the Romans they would have to attack uphill and be funnelled towards them by the nature of the slopes and the woods on them. Thus at a stroke Marius went a great way to negating the vastly superior numbers of the enemy. They could not easily surround or flank him and the funnelling effect meant that when the two sides clashed, far fewer tribesmen would be able to engage the Romans. Marius further used the terrain to his advantage by secretly deploying a force of 3,000 legionaries, under the

XI. The Battle of Aquae Sextiae (102 BC), Stage 2

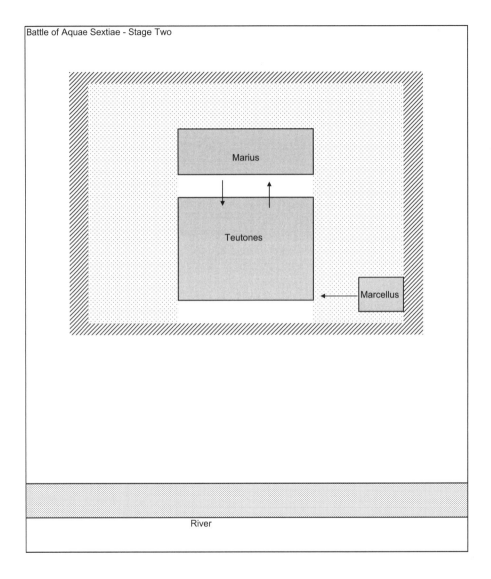

Battle of Aquae Sextiae - Stage Two

command of M. Claudius Marcellus, on the side of the hill under the cover of the wood, with orders not to reveal themselves until battle had commenced and then attack the enemy in the rear, once they had passed.

Marius' plan hinged on the tribesmen taking the bait and attacking his position uphill, rather than waiting until the battlefield was more favourable. If the enemy had refused to fight and moved on to find flatter ground, which favoured their vastly-superior numbers, then he would have been undone.

Plutarch himself notes that the tribesmen rashly attacked the Romans, rather than waiting:

> he [Marius] led out at daybreak and drew up in front of the camp, and sent his cavalry out into the plain. The Teutones seeing this, could not wait for the Romans to come down and fight with them on equal terms, but quickly and angrily armed themselves and charged uphill.[379]

Thus Marius played on the tribes' frustration at his previous unwillingness to fight and at his ambush a few days before to force them into a rash action, using his cavalry as bait. Furthermore, the uphill charge also favoured the Roman method of initial assault with the pilum.

> [Marius] exhorted the soldiers to stand their ground and when the enemy had gotten within reach to hurl their javelins, then take to their swords and crowded the barbarians back with their shield; since the enemy were on precarious ground, their blows would have no force and the locking of their shield no strength, but the unevenness of the ground would prevent them from standing firm in a line.[380]

Thus, the tribesmen rushing up the hill were met with a hail of pila and slowly forced back down the hill into the plain, with heavy casualties. As they were forced down, Marcellus sprung the ambush and attacked the tribesmen from the rear, thus trapping them between the two Romans forces and throwing the whole opposing force into chaos.

> Those in the rear forced along those who were in front of them, and quickly plunged the whole army into confusion, and under this double attack they could not hold out long, but broke ranks and fled. The Romans pursued them and either slew or took alive over 100,000 of them.[381]

Orosius quotes higher figures for the enemy losses:

> Two hundred thousand of the Gallic soldiers, according to reports, were slain in the battle, 8,000 were captured and barely 3,000 fled. Their general [chieftain] Teutobodus was killed.[382]

Whether it was 100,000 or 200,000, the tribal casualties were massive and must have included a large number of civilians, caught up in the fighting or the flight. In one battle the Teutones and Ambrones who had left their homeland had been wiped out. By any measure it was a massive victory for the Roman Republic and for Marius.

The extent of the tribal casualties can be seen by a story reported by Plutarch:

> it is said that the people of Massilia fenced their vineyards round with the bones of the fallen, and that the soil, after the bodies had wasted away in it and the rains had fallen all winter upon them, grew so rich and became so full to its depths of the putrefied matter that sank into it, that it produced an exceedingly great harvest in the years that followed.[383]

Plutarch further reports that the kings, or chieftains, of the Teutones and Ambrones survived the battle and fled, but were captured in the Alps by a Roman allied tribe, the Sequani.[384] This is confirmed by Florus who interestingly names one of them as Teutobodus, despite the fact that Orosius reports him dead in battle.[385] We are not told of how many casualties the Romans sustained, or even what their total force was in the battle. Following the battle, Marius set up a massive pyre of enemy weapons and possessions as an offer to the gods. Plutarch reports that just as he was about to light the pyre messengers arrived confirming his re-election as consul for 101 BC.[386] Whatever the timing, the confirmation that the remaining tribes were moving towards Italy would have meant that Marius would have no longer needed subterfuge and tricks to secure a continuation of his consulships. Nevertheless, he would not have had too much time to savour the victory as the other tribal army of the Cimbri, by far the larger and most dangerous of the northern tribes, was also heading for Italy by a separate route and he would have to support his colleague Catulus in his defence of Italy.

Summary

After a period of over ten years of fighting in the Northern Wars, Rome had finally won a victory in the northwest. Furthermore, this was not just any victory, but had seen one of the two main tribal armies, albeit the smaller of the two, obliterated. We have to ask ourselves what was it that separated Marius from all of his predecessors, who had overseen catastrophic failures. The one factor that strikes any observer of this campaign of 102 BC is the extraordinary patience and level-headedness that Marius showed. On the three previous occasions of 113, 109 and 105, the Roman commanders had apparently attacked the enemy without putting any thought into how they were going to negate the vastly superior numbers they faced. They faced the tribesmen on open ground, with apparently nothing more than a firm belief in the superiority of the Roman legionary. Whilst this was certainly the case in a one-on-one situation, the tribes they faced had sheer weight of numbers of their side, which could translate itself into steamrollering the Romans in a face-to-face charge, or the ability to flank or surround them.

Marius on the other hand showed incredible patience, firstly by not meeting the enemy in the Rhone valley, and then by carefully selecting a battleground that negated the enemy numbers and brought his infantry superiority into play. Whether this counts as tactical genius or simple common sense is for each individual to decide. Furthermore, as was always the case, the Romans benefited from having one sole commander, who had been with his army for a period of time, establishing discipline and a bond of trust between the two. This allowed for greater discipline when Marius' cautious tactics seemed like an unwillingness to fight and for a greater awareness of his tactics and how the soldiers would benefit from them.

On the Teutones/Ambrones side, they made the basic mistake of underestimating their enemy, poor intelligence (not scouting the sides of the battlefield) and the fundamental error of allowing the enemy to choose the ground that played to his strengths and weakened them. If their superiority came from their vast numbers then attacking uphill and on a narrow field played right into Marius' hands. Had they remained in the plain or moved on and forced a battle elsewhere, then we may well have seen a different outcome.

Furthermore, we have to question the two-pronged attack on Italy which divided the tribes' numbers. Although this was designed to split the Roman forces, it also split their numbers and allowed Marius the opportunity to face the two main tribes separately, though we must always be watchful for the benefit of hindsight creeping in. Nevertheless, although the Teutones and Ambrones had been wiped out the Cimbri presented a different matter, being the largest of the three northern tribes and by far the most deadly.

Chapter 10

The Northern Wars: The Battle of Raudian Plain (Vercellae) (101 BC)

Catulus and the Cimbric Invasion of Italy

While the Teutones and Ambrones moved to invade Italy from the west, via the Rhone Valley, the Cimbri planned to invade Italy from the eastern Alps (via modern Austria). To meet this dual thrust, while Marius was to intercept the western attack, his consular colleague of 102 BC, Q. Lutatius Catulus, who was in command of Italy, moved to the eastern Alps to intercept the Cimbri. What little detail we have from our surviving sources is further complicated by the fact that Catulus wrote a history of the conflict, widely available at the time and to later historians (see Appendix V), which naturally inflated his own contribution, as we shall soon see.

Aside from his literary endeavours, we know that Catulus hailed from a consular plebeian family, which we can trace back to the First Punic War.[387] However, it appears that the family had fallen into the political wilderness, with no consuls recorded between 220 and 102 BC. Furthermore, Cicero informs us that he was defeated in the consular elections for three years running (106, 105 and 104) before securing election in 102, possibly (or only) with the assistance of Marius.[388] We hear nothing of any prior military service or the prior offices he must have held. In short we know little of his record prior to his consulship, but we must assume that the Roman electorate had little faith in his abilities. Plutarch sums him up as 'a worthy man, but too sluggish for arduous contests'.[389]

Nevertheless, Catulus' initial strategy appears to have been to guard the eastern Alpine passes and prevent the Cimbri from crossing into Italy. Plutarch's Life of Sulla once again furnishes us with some details of the activities of Catulus' forces in the region, as by 102 BC, Sulla had been transferred to Catulus' command.[390]

He [Sulla] not only subdued in war a large part of the barbarians of the Alps, but when provisions ran low, he undertook the task of furnishing them, and made them so abundant, that the soldiers of Catulus lived in plenty...[391]

As always, we treat Plutarch's Life of Sulla with caution, given that it was partly based on Sulla's own memoirs, but it appears that Catulus' army conducted campaigns to subdue some of the local Alpine tribes, whose loyalty to Rome was always weak at best, not withstanding numerous defeats to the Cimbri. Plutarch tells us that he had an army of 20,000 men (legionaries and allies combined). Yet at some point, most likely during the winter of 102/101 BC,[392] Catulus withdrew from the high Alps and took up a defensive position on the River Adige.

The latter [the Cimbri] drove back from the Alps and put to flight the proconsul Q. Catulus.[393]

For Catulus, who was facing the Cimbri, gave up trying to guard the passes of the Alps, lest he should be weakened by the necessity of dividing his forces into many parts, and at once descended into the plains of Italy. Here he put the River Atiso between himself and the enemy, built strong fortifications on both banks of it to prevent their [the Cimbri] crossing, and threw a bridge across the stream, that he might be able to go on the other side in case the barbarians made their way through the passes and attack the fortresses.[394]

Furthermore, Frontinus provides us with an interesting, and frustrating, fragment involving Catulus' army:

When Quintus Lutatius Catulus had been repulsed by the Cimbrians, and his only hope of safety lay in passing a stream the banks of which were held by the enemy, he displayed his troops on the nearest mountain, as though intending to camp there. Then he commanded his men not to loose their packs, or put down their loads, and not to quit the ranks or standards. In order the more effectively to strengthen the impression made upon the enemy, he ordered a few tents to be erected in open view, and fires to be built, while some built a rampart and others went forth in plain sight to collect wood. The Cimbrians, deeming these performances genuine, themselves also chose a place for a camp, scattering through the nearest fields to gather the supplies necessary for their stay. In this way they afforded Catulus opportunity not merely to cross the stream, but also to attack their camp.[395]

Among modern historians, Lewis argued that this excerpt describes the first battle Catulus fought, as mentioned by the *Periochae of Livy* above, in which Catulus was repulsed from holding the Alps and forced to retreat to a defensive line on the Adige, managing a cunning counterattack on the Cimbri as he retreated.[396] Plutarch's account makes no mention of this first engagement and tries to argue that Catulus suddenly realized that there were a number of passes through the Alps and after marching his men up the hills, turned around and marched them down again.[397]

Given that we know the Romans were keeping a close watch on the army of the Teutones, we must assume that the same was true for the Cimbri and that Catulus had a good idea of the route they would take. This is especially the case given that the Cimbric force was composed of women and children and would have been far slower than any Roman army. Furthermore, Plutarch's account seems to ignore his own evidence of the activities of Sulla in the Alps earlier in the campaign.

Thus, we can combine the various fragments to see the most logical strategy for Catulus. He initially moved into the Alpine region to meet and hopefully check the Cimbric advance through the Alps. Whilst he was waiting for the Cimbri, Catulus (via his legate Sulla) took the opportunity to ensure that the local tribes were reminded where their loyalties lay and did not aid the Cimbri. Nevertheless, when the Cimbri did arrive, it appears that the Romans were driven back and routed from whichever pass they were trying to hold (as stated by Livy, with added detail by Frontinus[398]), probably by sheer weight of numbers. Catulus' ruse enabled him to regroup and gained him time to create a fresh defensive line on the River Adige, in a second attempt to halt the Cimbric advance.

However, it is clear from our few sources that this second defensive position was no more successful than the first. According to Plutarch, rather than an outright assault on the Roman position, the Cimbri apparently used their natural surroundings to their advantage:

> After they [the Cimbri] had encamped near the river and examined the position, they began to dam it up, tearing away the neighbouring hills, like the giants of old, carrying into the river whole trees with their roots, fragments of rock and mounds of earth, and crowding the current out of its course. They also sent heavy objects whirling down the river against the piles of the bridge and made them shake with the impact, until at last the greater part of the Roman soldiers played the coward and abandoned the main camp and began to retreat.[399]

At this point in Plutarch's narrative we have an outrageous pro-Catulan interpretation of the Roman retreat:

And now Catulus, like a consummately good commander, showed that he had less regard for his own reputation than for that of his countrymen. For finding that he could not persuade his soldiers to stand, and seeing them flee in terror, he ordered his standard to be taken up, and run to the foremost of the retiring troops, and put himself at their head, wishing that the disgrace should attach to himself and not to his country and that the soldiers, in making their retreat, should not appear to be running away, but following their general.[400]

According to Plutarch, when faced with a Roman army which broke in the face of the enemy, the Cimbri were allowed free access to Italy. Fortunately for Rome, not all of Catulus' men showed the same sentiments as their commander, and both Plutarch and the *Periochae of Livy* note a valiant stand made by the soldiers garrisoning the fort. Although both Plutarch and the *Periochae of Livy* report the incident, they differ quite markedly. First Plutarch:

The barbarians attacked and captured the fort on the farther side of the Atiso [Adige], and they so admired the Romans there, who showed themselves the bravest of men and fought worthily of their country, that they let them go, making them take an oath upon a bronze bull. This was subsequently captured after the battle and was carried, we are told, to the house of Catulus, as the chief prize of the victory.[401]

Livy, has it thus:

This cohort [at the fort] however, extricated itself by its own unaided gallantry and overtook the fleeing proconsul and his army.[402]

Not only do the two accounts clash, but the *Periochae of Livy* almost seems to be going out of its way to refute the story presented in Plutarch, which must have been in circulation in Livy's day (see Appendix V). There is no way to combine the two accounts, other than to say that the garrison fought well against the Cimbri and managed to escape, whether by treaty or military prowess. There are several other short notes in the sources concerning the retreat. Whilst Pliny records a celebrated act of bravery in the part of a group of retreating soldiers, the more famous story concerned Catulus' cavalry which retreated all the way back to Rome.[403] The group were led by the son of M. Aemilius Scaurus, who refused to acknowledge his son for his cowardice, with the young man committing suicide in shame.

With Cisalpine Gaul lost to the Cimbri, Catulus retreated to yet another defensive position (his third), this time south of the River Po. Nevertheless, no matter how much Plutarch, or his source, may want to dress these events up with noble sacrifices and tales of heroism, once again a Roman army had been routed by the Cimbri. Catulus had failed to stop them on two occasions and took flight with his army, leaving the region (modern Venetia) to be sacked by the Cimbri. The stark facts are that despite everything a 'barbarian' army had successfully invaded Italy for the first time in a century. A century earlier it had been Hannibal, whose victories on Italian soil had been forever etched into the Roman consciousness. Before that it had been the Gauls, who had sacked Rome; now came the Cimbri.

Marius and the Cimbric Invasion of Italy.

During the winter of 102/101 BC, whilst Catulus was engaging the Cimbri and failing to hold them, it appears that Marius made his way back to Rome without his army. According to Plutarch, he was only summoned to Rome when news of Catulus' reverses was received, but it was likely that he had made his way there following his victory at Aquae Sextiae. Plutarch further informs us that he did not celebrate his triumph for the victory as expected, which given the uncertain outcome of Catulus' engagements was understandable.[404] He entered into his fifth consulship (for 101 BC) and had with him a trusted old lieutenant, M. Aquilius, as fellow consul.

That he left his army is interesting; it is possible that he returned to Rome to await the result of Catulus' engagement. If Catulus did manage to keep the Cimbri from crossing the Alps, then he would be able to rejoin his army and fight the decisive battle away from Italy. We are not told where he stationed his army, but he must have been aware of the distinct possibility that Catulus would not be able to stop the Cimbri and thus needed to keep his own forces on the Italian side of the Alps in readiness. Certainly, when called upon, his forces were able to intercept the Cimbri apparently with ease, though again the Cimbri would be far slower than Marius' forces on the march, given the large numbers of women and children, not to mention baggage.

This leads us onto one of the key issues when dealing with the Cimbri in 101 BC, namely their actions, or the lack of them, after defeating Catulus, and their eventual location when they faced Marius in battle. Florus sums the situation up and contains a number of useful flaws:

> If they had immediately marched on Rome with hostile intent, the danger would have been great; but in Veneteia, a district in which the Italian climate is almost at its softest, the very mildness of the country and of the air sapped their vigour. When they had been further de-

moralized by the use of bread and cooked meats and the delights of wine, Marius opportunely approached them.[405]

Thus Florus assumes that the Cimbri became enamoured of the soft life and could have attacked Rome, but did not. Yet Florus, as is quite common in this war, misunderstands the nature of Rome's enemy. The Cimbri were not a foreign army on a set campaign, but comprised whole tribes, including women and children. In the past few years they had been driven out of Spain and marched across the Alps in winter. It is hardly surprising that they chose to make a protracted stay in a warm, safe and plentiful region. Furthermore, although we have no direct evidence for it, the Venetia region offered the Cimbri everything they needed for a new homeland to settle in. That region of Italy, north of the Po, had only been pacified by Rome earlier in the century and had for centuries been inhabited by Gauls.

Plutarch raises a different factor, namely that the Cimbri were awaiting the arrival of the Teutones and Ambrones, in order to combine their might, though he himself questions how they could remain ignorant of the result of Aquae Sextiae, which must have been common knowledge throughout the Alpine region. Plutarch does, however, state that when Marius met with the Cimbric ambassadors prior to battle, they once again demanded land to settle on.[406] Given that they already occupied Cisalpine Gaul, it does add weight to the theory that they intended to settle in Italy, north of the Po, which would have returned Rome to the position of over 100 years earlier. Nevertheless, even if they had not been buoyed up by the victory at Aquae Sextiae, neither the Senate nor the People of Rome, let alone Marius himself, would have countenanced a hostile tribal presence in northern Italy, no matter how much the Cimbri would have professed future friendship. Once again Marius staked everything on a decisive battle.

The location of the battle is an interesting one for a number of reasons. For a start we are not even clear on the location nor the name of the battlesite. Both Velleius (writing less than 100 years after the battle) and Florus state that the battle took place at the Raudian Plain, with neither making any mention of Vercellae (the more commonly known name). The *Periochae of Livy* unhelpfully omits the name altogether. Plutarch, whose account is the clearest surviving one, names it as taking place on the plain of Vercellae, though even as late as the *de viris illustribus* (see Appendix V), it is referred to as the Raudian Plain.[407]

The events leading up to the battle can never be recovered from the few fragmentary, and sometime contradictory, sources we have. With the Cimbri remaining north of the Po, Marius recalled his army into northern Italy and met up with the fleeing/retreating Catulus. Their first thoughts must have been to intercept any Cimbri thrust south, but when none was forthcoming they moved north and crossed the River Po into Cimbric-held territory. As mentioned above, the Cimbri once more attempted negotiation, which proved fruitless. To counter this Plutarch reports that Marius worked on demoralizing the Cimbri by parading the captured Teutones chieftains in front of them.[408]

However, for both sides, negotiation was not an option. The Romans were not going to let the Cimbri settle and were buoyed by the victory at Aquae Sextiae. The Cimbri too would have believed that they had a strong hand. They had found an agreeable region to settle in and although their allies had met defeat, they themselves had defeated Roman armies on three previous occasions. A fourth would give them the peace they required to settle, at least in their eyes.

In the days leading up to the battle both sides were apparently manoeuvring. Plutarch reports that the Cimbri advanced against Marius, who refused to give battle. Frontinus also reports that Marius forced the Cimbri to march to him rather than the other way around.[409] Thus Marius once again got to choose the ground and time of the battle, which he used to good advantage, as detailed below. Having led the Cimbri to his position, a meeting apparently took place between a Cimbric chief, Boiorix, and Marius, to agree when the battle would take place. Thus on the morning of what now equates to 30 July 101 BC, the two armies drew up on the Raudian Plain, for what was to become the final act of a long war.[410]

The Battle of the Raudian Plain (Vercellae)

Of all the battles in the two wars under examination, it is the Raudian Plain for which we have the best descriptions in our sources, giving us both numbers and tactics. The Roman forces comprised of two consular armies: the victorious army of Marius and the defeated army of Catulus. Plutarch, quoting Sulla's memoirs, lists Marius' forces as 32,000 and Catulus' as 20,300.[411] We are not told of the composition of these armies, between foot and cavalry. Opposing them, according to the sources, was at least twice that number, if not three times. Plutarch provides a total of 180,000 for the Cimbri as a whole (including women and children), whilst Orosius gives us a figure of 200,000 in total. Of these, Plutarch states that 15,000 were cavalry, which would far outnumber any Roman cavalry on the field.[412]

The two Roman armies were combined into one formation, with Catulus' 20,000 soldiers in the centre and Marius' army of 32,000 split between the two wings, with himself and Sulla in command of each. Marius was clearly in overall command, though Plutarch reports that Marius placed Catulus in the

XII. The Battle of Raudine Plain / Vercellae (101 BC), Stage 1

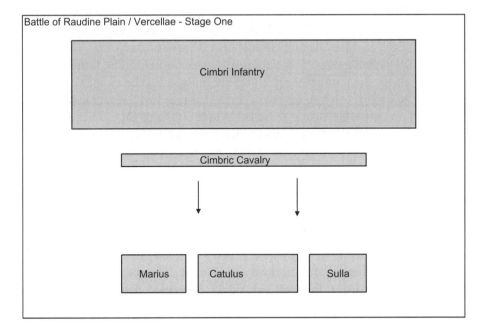

XIII. The Battle of Raudine Plain / Vercellae (101 BC), Stage 2

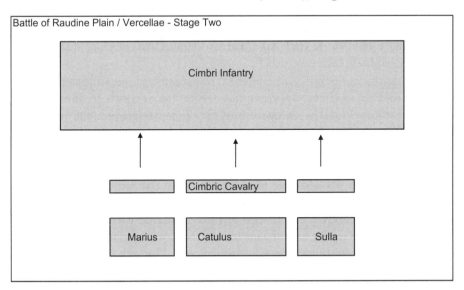

XIV. The Battle of Raudine Plain / Vercellae (101 BC), Stage 3

Battle of Raudine Plain / Vercellae - Stage Three

Cimbri Infantry

Marius   Catulus   Sulla

centre to keep him out of the way, expecting the heaviest fighting on the wings. Plutarch provides us with an excellent description of the Cimbri, based on two eyewitness accounts:

> their foot soldiers advanced slowly from their defences, with a depth equal to their front, for each side of the formation had an extent of thirty furlongs; and their horsemen 15,000 strong, rode out in splendid style, with helmets made to resemble the maws of frightening wild beasts or the head of strange animals, which, with their towering crests of feathers, made their wearers appear taller than they really were: they were equipped with breastplates of iron, and carried gleaming white shields. For hurling, each man had two lances, and at close quarters they used large heavy swords.[413]

As is customary in these cases, we have different versions of the battle in different authors. Plutarch's account is by far the most detailed, but does take a notably different slant than is reported elsewhere. He clearly states that he uses the biographies of Sulla and Catulus for the account, both of whom had became estranged from Marius during their later careers, at the time of writing. This is clearly reflected in the accounts of the battle, with Marius' role being clearly downgraded, along with a rise in the tension between Marius and Catulus.

According to Plutarch, the Cimbri opened the battle with a cavalry charge, which soon turned into a feint meant to lure the Roman infantry into breaking ranks and drawing them onto the Cimbric infantry. Plutarch then states that the Roman soldiers, despite their training, usual levels of discipline and direct orders, broke ranks and charged after the Cimbric cavalry thinking that they had broken. At this point the Cimbric infantry then attacked the ill-disciplined Roman soldiers. Even at this early stage we have to question Plutarch's description, as such a set of circumstances are not only difficult to believe, but nearly always end with the broken side being routed. In response to their soldiers breaking ranks, Plutarch would have us believe that both Marius and Catulus, rather than deal with the situation at the front, then both took time to offer sacrifices to the gods, which should have come before battle commenced.[414]

It seems that Plutarch has welded two accounts into one as he then has the battle commencing, despite this aforementioned initial cavalry charge and infantry clash, which we hear no more about again. We are next treated to some of the clearest bias against Marius as Plutarch then reports that a giant cloud of dust was kicked up by the armies, which meant that Marius' advancing wing missed the enemy altogether and spent a good part of the battle wandering around looking for someone to fight, lost in a cloud of dust. This naturally left Catulus and Sulla to do all the fighting, with their commander left to flounder in a quasi-comic turn on the battlefield.

Plutarch then reports that the Romans had the sun in their favour, as they were positioned with the sun at their backs, shining directly into the faces of the enemy, though Plutarch does not ascribe this to good tactical positioning on Marius' part. Furthermore Plutarch would have us believe that the Cimbri were blinded by bright sunlight whilst Marius was still lost in a dust cloud so dense that he could not locate an army of 200,000 men!

Plutarch goes on to provide the detail that the Cimbri, being used to colder climes, were not used to the bright sunlight and sweated profusely, whilst the Romans were cool and unruffled. Although this is a nice stereotype it overlooks the fact that the Cimbri had spent the over a decade in the centre and south of France, not to mention a few years in Spain and were not fresh from a harsher clime; unless of course he is referring to fresh Cimbric reinforcements.

Despite these colourful details, Plutarch's account is desperately short of tactical analysis or any detail to explain how 50,000 Romans were able to defeat an enemy so superior in both infantry and cavalry. In fact, his only tactical comments are the aforementioned Cimbric feint and Roman breaking of ranks. What we have for the end of the battle is thus:

> The greatest number and the best fighters of the enemy were cut to pieces on the spot; for to prevent their ranks from being broken, those who fought in front were bound together with long chains which were passed through their belts. The fugitives, however, were driven back to their entrenchments; where the Romans beheld a most tragic spectacle. The women, in black garments, stood at the wagons and slew the fugitives; their husbands or brothers or fathers, then strangled their little children and cast them beneath the wheels of the wagons or the feet of the cattle, then cut their own throats. . . . Nevertheless, in spite of such

self destruction, more than 60,000 were taken prisoner and those who fell were said to have been twice that number.[415]

Thus for Plutarch, Roman victory was inevitable; the Cimbri could not take fighting in the heat of the midday sun, or the brave stands of Catulus and Sulla. More lines are devoted to the fascination with the aggression of the Cimbric women and their unwillingness to be taken as slaves, than the battle itself. As for Marius, he seems to have spent the entire battle wandering around in his own personal dust storm.

The *Periochae of Livy* has no detail of the battle, but confirms Plutarch's casualty figures for the Cimbri. The same goes for that of Velleius and Eutropius.[416] Florus has an account that bears many of the same dramatic flourishes as Plutarch's, but adds some additional detail:

> The armies met in a very wide plain which they call the Raudian Plain. On the side of the enemy 65,000 men fell, on our side less than 300; the slaughter of the barbarians continued all day. On this occasion too our general [Marius] had added craft to courage, imitating Hannibal and his stratagem at Cannae. For in the first place, the day he had chosen was misty, so that he could charge the enemy unawares, and it was also windy, so that the dust was driven into the eyes and faces of the enemy; finally he had drawn up his line facing the west, so that, as was learnt afterwards from the prisoners, the sky seemed to be on fire with the glint reflected from the bronze of the Roman helmets. There was quite as severe a struggle with the women folk of the barbarians as with the men; for they had formed a barricade of their wagons and carts and mounting on the tip of it, fought with axes and pikes. Their king Boiorix fell fighting energetically in the forefront of the battle, and not without having inflicted vengeance on his foes.[417]

Thus we have the familiar elements of sun, dust and aggressive tribal women, but we also appear to have a surprise Roman charge, which took the enemy unawares. It is Orosius who adds some important details:

> Following Hannibal's clever plan of selecting not only the day for the battle but also the field, the consuls arranged their battle line under the cover of a mist, but later fought the Gauls in the sun. The first sign of disorder arose on the side of the Gauls [Cimbri], as they realized that the Roman line of battle had already been drawn up ready for action before they came on the field.
>
> In the battle, wounded cavalrymen, driven backward upon their own

men, threw into confusion the entire force that was advancing to the battlefield in irregular formation. The sun too was shining brightly in their faces and at the same time a wind arose. As a result, dust filled their eyes and the brilliant sun dimmed their sight. Under these conditions the casualties suffered were so terrible that only a few survived the disaster, whereas the losses on the Roman side were very slight. A 140,000, according to reports were slain in that battle, whilst 60,000 were captured. ...

Among these many wretched forms of death, it is reported that two chieftains rushed upon each other with drawn swords. The kings Lugius and Boiorix fell on the battlefield; Claodicus and Caesorix were captured.[418]

Finally, it is Orosius who preserves and transmits some idea of the tactics used and the events of the battle itself. Marius and Catulus drew up their armies into formation before the Cimbri realized what was going on or were fully prepared. There is also the faint trace of a surprise Roman attack on the Cimbri whilst they were still forming up. Even if there was no surprise attack, then it is clear that the Romans' actions had forced the Cimbri to advance or alter their plans for the battle.

Orosius supports Plutarch's point on the initial Cimbric tactic being a cavalry assault, though in Orosius it seems that they rushed forward to meet the Roman advance. The clear difference is that in Orosius' account, the Romans held firm and broke the Cimbric assault which turned their cavalry into the path of the onrushing infantry, causing total chaos and a complete rout. Thus, what Plutarch had as a feint and an ambush, in Orosius apparently reflects the true situation, with the Cimbric cavalry broken and the Roman infantry moving forward to press home the attack.

Valerius Maximus preserves a fragment of an account, which is also of use:

In the heat of the battle he gave [Roman] citizenship contrary to treaty to two cohorts of Camertes [an Italian people] who were resisting the assault of the Cimbri with extraordinary valour.[419]

When taken from Orosius' point of view, the tactics of the battle and its result became clearer: an initial surprise Roman assault; the breaking of the Cimbric cavalry, their retreat into their own infantry, which led to total chaos and slaughter amongst the Cimbri. Thus Marius chose his ground well and used his smaller army in a more disciplined manner, and utilized simple but effective tactics, all of which resulted in the annihilation of the Cimbric tribes, including the civilians.[420]

Aftermath – The Tigurini

As discussed earlier, there is some considerable confusion as to what role the Tigurini played in the events of 102–101 BC. Some sources dismiss them altogether from these events, as they were not a migrating tribe in the manner of the Cimbri, Teutones or Ambrones. Orosius clearly has them involved with the grand alliance of tribes that determine to invade Italy, though he, and he alone, places them with the Ambrones at Aquae Sextiae and has the Cimbri and Teutones at Raudian Plain (Vercellae).[421] Florus, however, also has the Tigurini involved in these events. Rather than having them at either Aquae Sextiae or Raudian Plain, he states that they followed the Cimbri, but did not join them in invading Italy and so avoided their fate in battle:

> The third body, consisting of the Tigurini, who had taken up a position as a reserve force among the Norican ranges of the Alps, dispersing in different directions, resorted to ignoble flight and depredation and finally vanished away.[422]

Thus the last of the four tribes of the anti-Roman alliance, slipped away, after discovering the destruction of their allies. It was not until the time of Caesar that Rome faced them again.

Summary – Rome

Whilst we will be dealing with the aftermath of the wars later (Appendix I), it is appropriate to consider the impact of the campaigns of 102 and 101 BC in ending a series of wars that had been plaguing Rome's northwestern border for over a decade. Ultimately, we must assess the central figure of Marius himself, and his contribution.

As we can see, not only is our understanding of the campaign and the battle affected by the few meagre sources we possess, but these very sources are highly susceptible to the prejudices of their own original sources. Of the three key commanders in the final battle, two of them wrote memoirs, and did so at times when one had become estranged from Marius and the other had become his mortal enemy (see Appendix V). Both can be seen to downplay Marius' role and enlarge their own contribution. In the particular case of the Battle of Raudian Plain, there is a constant attempt to downplay Marius' role and increase Catulus'. This can be seen through the above examples and with an additional piece of information given by Eutropius and found nowhere else:

> Another battle [Raudian Plain] was fought with them [the Cimbri], by Caius Marius and Quintus Catulus, though with greater success on the part of Catulus . . .
>
> Thirty-three standards were taken from the Cimbri; of which the army of Marius captured two, that of Catulus thirty-one.[423]

Whilst we can clearly see that the histories took against Marius, both as a reaction to the man himself, and his later actions (see Appendix I) and due to the fact that his two subordinates wrote autobiographies whilst they were political enemies of him, we need to take a step back and analyse the situation. Raudian Plain/Vercellae was the fourth time a Roman army had faced the Cimbri in a set-piece battle, the previous three being heavy defeats, culminating in the Battle of Arausio, widely accepted as being one of the greatest defeats the Romans ever suffered. The key question we are faced with is what the Romans did on this occasion that they had not done before. The Roman army at Raudian was smaller than the one at Arausio and again seemed to suffer from a joint command.

However, there is a clear difference between quality and quantity. The army of Marius had been in the field since 104 BC and had received vigorous training and re-equipping (see Chapter 11), not to mention its having been battle hardened with the victory at Aquae Sextiae. Furthermore, the two Roman forces acted and fought as one, with a clear overall commander (despite the attempts by certain sources to play up the discord between Marius and Catulus).

In terms of Marius himself, the two battles of the Northern Wars he fought are both marked by a careful selection of ground and tactics to suit (unlike the Battles of Cirta in the Jugurthine Wars). The comparison is a useful one, as Jugurtha always sought to fight on his own terms to make up the deficiencies of a weaker army. It is an interesting question as to how much Marius learnt from his near defeat at the Battles of Cirta, and whether this convinced him never to fight unless it was on his own terms. Furthermore, there are elements of the Raudian battle that point to Marius forcing the enemy to fight before they were fully prepared, thus pushing them into mistakes, much as Jugurtha had tried.

In the end, his tactics in both battles (Aquae Sextiae and Raudian Plain) allowed the Romans to avoid being swamped by the enemy's superior numbers, one by utilizing topography and the other by seizing the initiative and turning the enemy's numbers against him. For the earlier Roman losses, we have little information about the tactics used, but both Noreia and Arausio smack of rash command decisions by the Roman generals and no real thought being given on how to negate the enemy's numerical superiority.

Throughout this work the impression one receives, rightly or not, is that Marius was really no innovative tactical genius, but merely a superbly competent general, thoroughly grounded in the basics of Roman warfare, centered on the principal of fighting battles on his terms not the enemy's. This included choosing his ground carefully, identifying his enemy's strengths and negating them and always keeping an element of surprise. At Aquae Sextiae he had a force hidden in the woods which attacked the enemy from the rear, and at Raudian Plain it involved forming up before the enemy was ready and forcing their hand. Thus in short, Marius appears to have been thoroughly accomplished in the basics of warfare, which when applied to a Roman army were highly successful.

Summary – The Tribes

We have far too little information to analyse the Cimbric tactics, even though they are often dismissed as nothing more than a barbarian mass charge. Clearly, the Cimbric chieftains were now used to the Roman manner of fighting, but for all their supposed invincibility they had been defeated on numerous occasions throughout this period, though not by Roman armies; we hear of defeats en-route to Illyria, in Gaul and in Spain. Thus in mass pitched battles they seemed to be bested, yet possess an ability to defeat Roman armies. We must be careful not to dismiss this as merely the traditional Roman weakness against 'barbarian' enemies, as voiced by Polybius himself, as only a decade before their first encounter with the Cimbri, the Romans had defeated the massed armies of the Arverni and Allobroges.[424] Thus, either the Roman commanders that faced the Cimbri in the battles were so much poorer than their earlier counterparts, which is always a possibility, or the Cimbri possessed some form of combat that was especially suited to defeating a more developed infantry army. This may have been something as basic as sheer weight of numbers or some variation which utilized their greater manpower.

Unfortunately, we do not possess enough evidence to judge, but that should never allow us to dismiss them as merely the nameless enemy Rome was fighting, as it takes two sides to fight a battle. One interesting indicator comes from Orosius, who provides the names of four separate Cimbric kings or chieftains. It is all too readily assumed that the Cimbri were a single mass and fought as such. However, with so many chieftains, the more likely situation is that they lived and fought as a number of separate tribes and thus may have been prone to the same problems of separated command as the Romans suffered. Whilst this may have not been a problem when the enemy was on the back foot, when they were under pressure, it may well have resulted in disruption – either at a rushed start of the battle at Raudian Plain or when the cavalry were turned back upon their own lines.

Whilst we know the Cimbri were battle hardened against Rome, we must not assume this for all the tribal groupings, especially if the Teutones and Ambrones were new to the region (prior to 102 BC) and had not fought the Romans before. This would perhaps explain the ill-disciplined stand the Ambrones made at the river of Aquae Sextiae and the rash uphill charge several days later.

Ultimately, we do not have the evidence to tell, but we must exercise caution when viewing the tribal enemies Rome faced, and not view them as being a single and homogenous entity, but a collection of different groups with different leaders and experience. In cases like this, then, their very size may well have worked against them.

Chapter 11

New Roman Army? –
Marius and Military Reform

One of the most noted aspects of Marius' tenure as Rome's leading commander in this period is a number of reforms he made, or is alleged to have made, to the Roman military, both in terms of manpower, equipment and tactics. As a number of these have become quite contentious in historical scholarship, it is necessary to study them separately from the analysis of the warfare to gain a better understanding of them. In fact, there can rarely be a topic in Roman history which has so much written about it based on so little actual evidence. Thus, as always, we must begin by going back to our surviving source to see what they actually say.

Recruitment

i) Reform of qualification criteria for military service (107 BC)

Of all of Marius' reforms, none have provoked more debate than the apparent changes he made to the eligibility criteria for military service. To be eligible for military service in the Roman army, each Roman citizen (as opposed to Italians) was assessed once every five years at the census, to see how much he was worth (in terms of assets). Each citizen was then placed into one of five bands according to their wealth, along with a sixth category for those whose assets fell below the minimum standard. This was the system that had evolved from Rome's earliest days, with the citizenry divided by wealth. This allowed the state to see the total wealth available to the city and was the basis of the political and military system, with each band having more military duties but rewarded by a greater political say. Thus the more money a citizen was worth the more he had to contribute to the city's defence, but this was rewarded by having a more influential vote in the public assemblies. Those that fell below the minimum amount for a citizen were exempted from military service; the underlying ethic being that such men would not be able to afford their own military equipment and that a man who fights for his own land is far more valuable a soldier than a mercenary who fights for money.

Naturally enough, a system that was created before the sixth century BC (it is claimed that it dated back to the early kings) would have evolved a great deal before reaching the period under analysis.[425] The problem we have today is that we have no clear idea of this process of evolution. All we have are the accounts of Cicero,[426] Livy and Dionysius, who ascribe minimum values for each census class, but these accounts were written long after the system's creation. Polybius, who was writing in the mid-second century BC , placed the minimum amount a citizen needed to be eligible for military service at 400 drachmas.[427] This has been calculated to be the equivalent of 4,000 Roman *asses* (the unit of measurement). Citizens above this level were referred to by the Latin term of *assidui*; those who fell below these criteria and were ineligible for military service were labelled as *proletarii* or *capite censi*. Polybius says that they were only fit for service in the navy, as oarsmen.

Naturally enough, from a purely military point of view this meant that there was a large group of men not eligible for military service. This was exacerbated by Rome's increased military commitments. However, we must not make the mistake of assuming that the Romans never recruited the *proletarii* into their armies. In times of national emergency (*tumultus*), as we would expect, such social norms went out of the window. This can be seen in 281 BC when they fought Pyrrhus and in 217 BC against Hannibal.[428]

Nevertheless, this system remained throughout the second century BC, though many have argued that the actual monetary level of the lowest class was lowered to enable more men to be eligible for military service. It has to be stressed that this is speculation only and there is no actual evidence for this (see Appendix III). Thus, the important aspect for us is that when Marius was elected consul in 107 BC this distinction remained, and men below the set level were ineligible for military service. It was this eligibility criterion that Marius challenged:

> He [Marius] himself in the meantime enrolled soldiers, not according to the classes in the manner of our forefathers, but allowing anyone to volunteer, for the most part the *proletarii*. Some say he did this through a lack of good men, others because of a desire to curry favour, since that class had given him honour and rank [by voting for him].[429]

Plutarch has it thus:

> Contrary to law and custom he enlisted many a poor and insignificant man, although former commanders had not accepted such persons, but

bestowed arms, just as they would any other honour, only on those whose property assessment made them worthy to receive these.[430]

Florus tells us:

Finally, Marius with considerably increased forces, for acting as one would expect a low man to act, had forced the lowest class of citizens to enlist.[431]

From Valerius Maximus we have:

Laudable also is the modesty of the people who by briskly offering themselves for the toils and dangers of military service saw to it that commanders did not have to ask *capite censi* to take the military oath, whose excessive poverty made them suspect and on that account they did not trust them with public arms. But this custom, fortified though it was by long observance, was broken by C. Marius when he enlisted *capite censi* into the army.[432]

Julius Exsuperantius has this:

When he conscripted new soldiers, he was the first general to take into war the *capite censi*, who were useless and untrustworthy citizens. But the citizens who had no possessions were recorded in the census by their head, which was all they owned, and in times of war they stayed within the city walls, because they could easily turn into traitors, as poverty often leads to evil. Marius took these men, who should not have been entrusted with public business, to fight in the war.[433]

Gellius quotes Sallust[434] but also throws in some doubt as to the date of this action:

Caius Marius is said to have been the first, according to some in the war with the Cimbri, in a most critical period for our country, or more probably, as Sallust says, in the Jugurthine War, to have enrolled soldiers from the *capite censi*, since such an act was unheard of before that time.[435]

Thus we can see that we actually have little detail to go on, with most merely quoting what was commonly accepted in the historical tradition of this period. As we can see, all of the sources overlook the fact that commanders prior to

Marius had recruited the *capite censi* in times of emergency, and there is absolutely nothing to say that Marius abolished the old system, merely that on this one occasion he ignored it. Furthermore, as we have already seen in this work, Marius hardly stands out as the first man to tackle the issue of recruitment. In the 140s, Marius' former commander and, as we have seen, sometime role model, P. Cornelius Scipio Aemilianus, recruited an army of volunteers to fight at Numantia. Ti. Sempronius Gracchus fought to increase recruitment, and his brother formalized the procedure whereby the state paid for the troops' equipment (Chapter 1). Furthermore, the consuls of 109 BC tried to increase the available manpower (Chapter 6). This move by Marius can thus be seen as a temporary solution to a temporary problem, regardless of any longer-term trends (see Appendix III) caused by the heavy losses in Gaul, Macedon and North Africa. A further interesting point is made by Sallust when he states that: 'Marius set sail for Africa with a considerably larger force than had been authorized'. But authorized by whom? The assembly had given him the command in Numidia, and it is tempting to see the Senate attempting retaliation against this attack on their prerogative by limiting the army he could take to Africa and thus limit his effectiveness.

From a military point of view, this greatly-increased force provided Marius with enough troops to occupy the towns and fortifications of Numidia and still pursue Jugurtha. If Marius was planning a surge then a far greater army was needed than the one currently in Africa. Furthermore, Marius was able to take an army composed of volunteers rather than those who had been drafted, which always makes for a more effective fighting force. Such a campaign offered the riches of Numidia as loot, though there is no evidence to suggest that he offered land as well, as an inducement. Evans, in his excellent article on the evasion of military service in Rome, points out that one of Marius' first acts when in Numidia was to march into a rich Numidian region and allow his men some plunder, thereby giving them an immediate payback.[436]

ii) Military consequences

Thus we come to the issue of long-term and short-term effects of this reform. It is unlikely that Marius was motivated by a desire to overturn the traditional method of recruitment, but that in the short term, with manpower such an issue, the constitutional niceties needed to be dispensed with. In the short term, this reform clearly worked, allowing Rome to tap into greater reserves of manpower than previously they had been able to utilize. An interesting question is whether he repeated this move for the campaigns against the northern tribesmen, as the two sources which mention this appear to be confused between the two wars. One obvious source of this confusion is that Marius did indeed repeat this tactic from 104 onwards, which given the circumstances is understandable. If Rome was suffering from manpower shortages before 105, then the loss of 60,000 soldiers or more at Arausio only made the issue worse. In fact, when you consider these losses, it is hard to argue against Marius repeating this recruitment tactic after 104 BC.

The problem that Marius did raise, was that an army composed primarily of the *capite censi* (though we have no figures for their percentages) was just as competent in the field as those recruited from the traditional Roman classes; in fact many may argue that it was more so. Although this went against tradition, it was only supposed to be an emergency measure. Yet, this emergency measure seemed to hold many advantages over the traditional methods of recruiting and went a long way to solving the manpower issue that had been plaguing Rome, or at least had seemed to be plaguing Rome. The problem with a good idea such as this was that it would have been difficult to turn the clock back and return to the traditional method, especially if another crisis occurred, as they had the habit of doing. Thus, whilst Marius seems not to have deliberately aimed to overturn the system of recruitment on a permanent basis, he may have un-wittingly found that he did so by example.

An issue consistently raised about this 'reform' is that it made soldiers more loyal to their commander than the state, and thus when the two came into conflict they chose their commander. This argument is flawed on a number of levels, beginning with the premise that landless soldiers had a greater desire for plunder than any previous 'landed' Roman soldiers. Whilst a conscripted Roman soldier had little choice in fighting for his country, unless he avoided being called up altogether, the greatest benefit was the booty that a campaign brought. The central basis of a soldier's loyalty to his commander always remained his competency, based on a soldier's calculation of survival and pros-perity. On the battlefield, soldiers fought primarily for survival and the chance of booty rather than loyalty to one's country.

Another argument often used is that Marius' reform meant that Rome changed from having a citizen army raised whenever it was necessary, to having a professional standing army. A consequence of this being that it led to there being a greater bond created between commander and men as they served more time together. If we deal with consequences first, such a view overlooks the actual situation, as Roman armies had been fighting long campaigns for more than a century. Rosenstein's recent work makes a case for it being the third century BC when Rome began fighting longer and more arduous campaigns rather than the second century.[437] The Roman legionaries were hardly amateur in these days, but had been hardened by continuous fighting on multiple campaigns and had been doing so generation after generation.

Furthermore, it is clear that Rome had no real standing army as such until the Principate. Both Civil Wars produced long-standing armies yet this repre-sented merely a lengthy campaign. Commanders such as Sulla, Pompey and Caesar all disbanded their legions once they had finished campaigning. A standing army only really came about with permanent legions under the Emperor Augustus. Thus it is difficult to find any evidence in the period im-mediately after Marius.

It is clear that for many of the landless poor a career in the army was an attractive proposition, but only so far as it provided some reward, which meant that they could enjoy a better life after campaign, with booty, or latterly with land. In many ways this had been the basis of the amateur citizen soldier. Although he had little choice in fighting overseas, he did so primarily hoping that there would be some tangible reward from it. Thus both types of men had the same motivations once they were actually serving, the only difference is whether they volunteered or were drafted.

iii) Political consequences

Two other issues become entangled in this question, based on the veterans of these campaigns, in both their colonial settlement and their political use. Following the war in Africa, Marius did organize colonies in Africa for his veterans and again after the Northern Wars. From a strategic point of view this made perfect sense, merely exporting the policy the Romans had used for centuries in securing Italy to their control, across the Mediterranean. However, most previous colonial settlements had been organized by the Senate in conjunction with the tribunes and the assemblies. C. Gracchus' clash with the Senate and his proposed colonies had set the tone for a more confrontational policy. Thus we have two models to choose from. As we will see when exam-ining Marius' sixth consulship (Appendix I), his African colonies seem to have passed without incident whilst the colonial programme of 100, led by the tribune Saturninus, followed the more confrontational route. The key point here is that the foundation of colonies for veterans was a sound policy for both strategic and social reasons (relieving tension amongst the landless citizens) and did not intrinsically lead to clashes between Senate and general, only in cases where there was existing tension or when a third party (such as a particular tribune) was involved.

Furthermore, it is true that Marius utilized his veterans in Roman politics, but then it would be difficult to say that this was any different from usual Roman custom and practice. Any leading Roman statesmen utilized his clients in Rome for his own political ends and if he had been a general then a number would be veterans of his. What we have to separate is this usual non-violent practice from the events that took place in Rome in 133, 121 and 100, when normal Roman political practice was transformed into bloodshed. Whilst the Gracchan bloodshed was managed without the use of veterans, they certainly made it easier and if Roman politics was becoming bloodier, it was certainly safer to use veterans in Rome.

Attested Military Reforms (104–102 BC)

During the three years that Marius had command of his army in Gaul, awaiting the return of the northern tribes, it is clear that he undertook an intensive programme of training and reform. This crucial period apparently allowed him to mould his army into one capable of reversing a decade of losses and defeat to the vastly-numerically-superior tribal armies. Regrettably for us, this is one of the least-known periods in our surviving sources, who are all too eager to move onto accounts of the battles that followed. Thus, despite all that is said about the Marian reforms of the Roman army we actually possess very little real evidence for these reforms, around half a dozen passages at most.

Furthermore, this situation is further complicated by the poor state of our knowledge concerning the Roman army prior to this period, as so well detailed by Rawson.[438] Added to this is the question of permanency. Each army was moulded by its commander and then disbanded upon the completion of a campaign. Thus there is no certainly that an innovation introduced by Marius would automatically be copied by the commanders and armies that followed. Given that so much is made of these reforms, we need to go back to the evidence and see what we actually know.

i) Mobility

In terms of mobility, Marius is credited with the introduction of the practice whereby each legionary carried his own baggage. Frontinus' *Stratagems* tells us:

> For the purpose of limiting the number of pack animals, by which the march of the army was especially hampered, Caius Marius had his soldiers fasten their utensils and food up in bundles and hang these on forked poles, to make the burden easy and to facilitate rest, whence the expression Marius's mules.[439]

From Plutarch:

> he [Marius] laboured to perfect his army as it went along, practicing the men in all kinds of running and in long marches and compelling

them to carry their own baggage and to prepare their own food. Hence, in later times, men who joined upon them contentedly and without a murmur were called Marian mules.[440]

Thus each legionary carried his own tools and utensils. We are given no details as to what they comprised, but in later times legionary had to carry his bed roll and cloak, cooking pot and three days worth of supplies as well as a number of tools, all supported on a T-shaped pole carried on their backs.

Carrying the bulk of their own supplies greatly increased the army's mobility as a whole (even if it did weigh the individual soldiers down), and reduced the size of the baggage trains. This would have allowed them to move quicker, and thus be more responsive. This would especially have been useful against an army the size of the northern tribes, who, as well as their vast numbers, also had their families with them. It must be pointed out that this did not eliminate the need for baggage trains altogether from the Roman army, and as late as 36 BC, Antony's Parthian campaign was undermined by the loss of his baggage train.[441] In the short term, however, it made the Roman army far more adept at responding to any moves made by the tribes.

ii) Weaponry

Plutarch reports that Marius introduced a new type of javelin (*pilum*) to the legion:

> Marius introduced an innovation in the structure of the javelin. Up to this time its seems that part of the shaft which was let into the iron head was fastened there by two iron nails; but now, leaving one of these as it was, Marius removed the other and put in its place a wooden pin that could easily be broken. His design was that the javelin after striking the enemy's shield should not stand straight out, but that the wooden peg should break, thus allowing the shaft to bend in the iron head and trail along the ground, being held fast by the twist at the point of the weapon.[442]

The point behind this was that it rendered the pilum buckled and useless and thus was not able to be used by the enemy. Archaeology, however, has shown that both types of *pilum* (modified and not) were still in use in the late Republic. Here we again encounter the issue of whether a Marian reform was introduced as standard after these wars.

iii) Standards

Although the legionary eagle is considered to be the archetypal Roman standard, it was not always the case. Pliny reports the following:

> The eagle was assigned to the Roman legions as their special badge by Caius Marius in his second consulship (104 BC). Even previously it had been their first badge, with four others; wolves, minotaurs, horses and boars going in front of the respective ranks; but took a few years before the custom came into action, the rest being left behind in camps.[443]

Thus it seems that Marius made the legionary eagle the sole standard, instead of being just one amongst many.

Possible Military Reforms – The Introduction of the Cohort

Given the noted role Marius is supposed to have played in reforming the Roman military, it is perhaps surprising that we have evidence only for the three reforms attested above. Thus Marius gave his legionaries more mobility, with less reliance on a baggage train, armed them with a modified type of pilum, and made the legionary eagle the sole Roman standard. Yet given the paucity of our evidence, why has so much been made of the so-called Marian military reforms? In short, this is a recent construct, created by modern historians. The argument goes that these few fragments form part of an overarching process of military reform that Marius undertook in this period. Central to this problem is the replacement of the maniple by the cohort as the basic tactical unit in battle. Bell sums up the problem that modern historians face with this issue most succinctly:

> At some point between the time of Polybius and that of Julius Caesar, a major tactical reform of the Roman army took place, which is not explicitly described by any ancient authority. The major component of this reform was the replacement of the legion of thirty maniples by the legion of ten cohorts. In addition, the *velites* or Roman light troops distributed among the maniples were abolished.[444]

Thus the problem is one of modern making, in that Polybius' account of the Roman military centres primarily on the use of the maniple, whereby a hundred years later in the accounts of Caesar we have the cohort. Put simply, many historians, unable to accept that there was a major military reform which is no longer documented, chose Marius as being the most logical source of this reform, given that he is recorded as having introduced some measure of military reform. Parker, in his work on the Roman legions even goes into the details of why Marius would have introduced the measures, being that the maniple was a smaller tactical unit and fought with more gaps between them, thus making them unsuited to meet the challenge of a massed tribal army.[445] This ignores the fact that such an army seemed to present no problems to the Romans in their victories in southern Gaul in the 120s BC (see Chapter 1).

Aside from the inherent problems of ascribing such a sweeping change in the Roman military system to a particular time period without a single shred of actual evidence, it is clear that Polybius' account is far from consistent in his use of the terms maniple and cohort (when translated from the Greek), and that whilst his main account of the Roman army is based on the maniple, cohorts crop up in a number of places in his narrative, from as early as 206 BC onwards.[446] Further uncertainty is added by both Livy and Sallust. In his histories, Livy consistently uses the term cohort from the Second Punic Wars onwards. This is naturally complicated by his works not being contemporaneous. Sallust in his account of the Battle of Muthul, where Metellus fought Jugurtha, uses the term maniple.[447] Thus we have total confusion in our few sources about what the major Roman tactical unit was.

We have to raise the possibility that this 'confusion' was a reflection of the true situation. Even if the sources are completely accurate in their use of the correct terms for the correct period (which is a large debate in itself) there is nothing to say that the Romans rigidly used the same formation on each occasion and that at some fixed point they altered one for the other. This is the conclusion that Bell comes to, detailing the various occasions when a Roman commander would use one rather than the other. Again we must remember that during this period of Roman history, the Republic had no standing armies. Instead, they were raised as necessary for each campaign by each commander and trained and fought in the manner that their commander was most comfortable with.

Thus we have to conclude that there is no evidence whatsoever that Marius was responsible for reorganizing the Roman legion based on the cohort as opposed to the maniple. In fact, the existing evidence suggests that this change had already taken place and that it was not a straight replacement of one with the other, once again being more a case of evolution rather than revolution.

Summary – A New Roman Army?

Thus we come down to the question of whether there was a 'Marian' programme of military reforms based on one man's desire to reshape the Roman military system, or merely a series of ad-hoc innovations with no greater aim than to mould an army capable of defeating the northern tribes. Ultimately, it is up to every reader to decide for themselves, based on the evidence they have analysed.

However, there are several aspects that need to be highlighted in this process. Firstly, there is a fundamental understanding needed of the nature of the Roman Republican army. Each army was raised as was needed for each campaign; Rome had no standing armies either before or immediately after Marius. In fact, so many of the domestic disputes of the first century BC revolved around the need for commanders to dismiss their armies. As such it makes it difficult for one commander's innovations to automatically be copied by the commanders that followed, even if they served under him as junior officers, such as L. Cornelius Sulla and Q. Sertorius. Certainly, word of mouth would have passed them on, but there was no necessity for a new commander to follow what had been done before, if he did not think it was necessary or helpful to him.

Secondly, what were Marius' aims? A wholesale reform of the Roman military system or the need for a well-manned and well-trained army to fight the tribes? Thirdly, even with his multiple consulships, did Marius have the authority to abandon the class-based recruitment system that underpinned Roman society? Lastly, do we believe that the evidence for wider-scale reforms of the Roman military once existed and is now lost to us? No source even mentions that there was a deliberate and consciousness reform of the maniple to the cohort. Or is this a modern invention?

Ultimately, unless our sources for this period drastically improve, we can never know, but in the author's opinion, the balance of evidence favours Marius making small-scale innovations to create the best force possible, one capable of defeating the tribal armies. Far more important than any individual innovations is the fact that the lull in fighting and his continuous command gave him two whole years to train his army for the coming battles. Veterans and raw recruits, whatever their class, were drilled and disciplined in the art of fighting a tribal enemy. Marius trained them to march and fight quickly, matching the speed of the tribal armies, and thus fight them on an equal footing. Therefore, the period 104–103 BC was probably one of the most crucial ones for Marius and Rome. The Cimbric invasion of Spain gave Marius the time he needed to forge his army as well as perfect his tactics and choose his ground. When the tribal forces did attack Italy, they found a Roman army that had been specifically prepared and trained to fight them, the one factor that had been missing from Rome's effort in 113, 109 and 105. It was this careful preparation and meticulous planning that allowed the Roman military dominance to finally tell. Once again, we are left with the question of whether this represents military genius or a man who was clearly the most competent Roman commander of his day.

Appendix I

A Bloody Roman Peace: Marius and Rome in 100 BC

No account of the period can be complete without examining the events of Marius' sixth consulship (100 BC), which saw fighting, not on Rome's borders, but on the streets of Rome itself. This year saw a number of issues come to head that had been brewing during the previous years but suppressed by the more pressing issues of the barbarian threat; with that threat removed they came to the fore. Here we must be especially careful as our sources paint a contradictory and somewhat simplistic picture of events.

Marius the Victor

Whilst we have a fairly clear narrative of the major events of the year 100 BC, understanding them is another matter. There are two clear schools of thought in our surviving sources, with some middle ground. On the one hand we have the version as best espoused by Plutarch, which has Marius as the arch manipulator and populist outsider, determined to cling to power in whatever way necessary.

> At any rate, while in war he had authority and power because his services were needed, yet in civil life, his leadership was more abridged, and he therefore had recourse to the goodwill and favour of the multitude, not caring to be the best man if only he could be the greatest. The consequence was that he came into collision with all the aristocrats.
>
> It was Metellus, however, whom he especially feared, a man who had experienced his ingratitude, and one whose genuine excellence made him into the natural enemy of those who tried to insinuate themselves by devious methods into popular favour and sought to control the masses by pleasing them.[448]

Domestic politics are thus boiled down to the Senatorial (*optimate*) faction as championed by Metellus Numidicus and the populist (*populares*) faction championed by Marius. As we would expect, such a stark dichotomy is simplistic in the extreme. Roman politics in any period were shades of grey, but this is especially the case when looking at C. Marius. A number of points need to be made concerning Marius. Firstly, by birth he was an aristocrat (albeit an Italian not a Roman one), now married into the Iulii family, one of Rome's oldest. Regardless of the methods used, he was widely acknowledged as the leading general of his day and the man responsible for saving Rome (see below), no matter how much Catulus' memoirs attempted to steal the glory. He had been consul six times in total, and five in succession, unheard for centuries in Roman politics. Furthermore, fighting two successful wars had made him one of the richest men in Rome and added to this were the opportunities for patronage that six consulships had given him. It is always difficult to speak of or identify factions in Roman politics, yet by his prestige, patronage and wealth, Marius had considerable following amongst the Roman elite, both established Senatorial and rising stars. Added to this was his popularity amongst the people for his accomplishments and the equestrian order for his championing of their cause. It is clear that in 100 BC Marius was the most dominant figure in Rome. The question was how would he use this dominance?

The most obvious manifestation was the sixth consulship and the celebrations of his victory. Here we can clearly see the two schools amongst our surviving sources. In the one strand we have Plutarch, who gives us the classic image of Marius the great general, but inept politician, scared of a Metellus (probably Numidicus) running for the consulate, and relying on outright bribery and the use of his soldiers in the elections to secure a sixth consulship for 100 BC.[449] Representing the other strand, we have Velleius (far closer in time period to the events described):

A sixth consulship was given him, in the light of a reward for his services.[450]

Furthermore, he managed to secure the election of a friendly co-consul, in the form of L. Valerius Flaccus, who was such an adherent of Marius that Rutilius is reported to have termed him a servant rather than a colleague.[451] Given the time elapse between Velleius and Plutarch and the latter's known use of sources hostile to Marius, we can assume that Marius was offered a sixth consulship, rather than bought one. Furthermore, the military situation cannot have been as clear cut as it looks with hindsight. The war in Sicily was still raging at the time of the consular elections (101 BC), nor can the Senate have been sure that the Tigurini, the remaining tribe of the grand alliance, were not still going to attack also. Thus a sixth consulship could be seen as being both a reward and a sound precaution.

The reward element was also present during the celebration of Marius' victories with a grand triumph, which also demonstrated Marius' tact and diplomacy. The *Periochae of Livy* sums the situation up well:

> Marius was hailed with the unanimous applause of the whole state, but was satisfied with a single triumph instead of the two which were offered him at the time. The leading men of the state, who had for some time held a grudge against him as a man without family background who had been elevated to posts of such importance, now admitted that the state had been preserved by him.[452]

Even Plutarch joins in with the following:

> Above all the people hailed him as the Third Founder of Rome,[453] on the ground that the peril which had been averted from the city was not less than that of the Gallic invasion; and all of them, as they celebrated at home with their wives and children, would bring ceremonial offerings of food and libations of wine to Marius as well as to the gods, and they were insistent that he alone should celebrate both triumphs.[454]

He made a show of celebrating the triumph along with his former colleague Q. Lutatius Catulus, though the latter ascribed this to guilt and fear of his soldiers.[455] However, it is well known that as soon as a triumph is celebrated and a hero lauded, then the gloves are off and the normal cut and thrust of domestic politics resumes, and we can have expected nothing else in this case. This naturally left Marius with a problem. After reaching the pinnacle of his career, there was only one way he could go: downwards. Such a phenomenon has been common throughout the Republic. In an oligarchy based on a system of competing individuals, any one man who so obviously stood above the others was always going to be a target.

For Marius, there were two possible routes open to him: conduct further military campaigns or cement his position as an elder statesman in Rome (not forgetting that Marius was now in his late fifties). With the threat from the northwest successfully dealt with, there were a number of other possible campaigns. Actions were still proceeding against the slaves in Sicily and the pirates in Cilicia (see Appendix II), but neither were wars of comparable standing to the one that Marius had successfully concluded, and by 100, both were in their final stages. As mentioned earlier (Chapter 9) the Cimbric invasion of Spain had left a number of tribes in revolt and loosened Roman control there. Yet again, this would require a long-drawn-out campaign of submission and was hardly a 'grand campaign'. Another possibility has always been raised by commentators on this period, focussed on the figure of Mithridates VI of Pontus. Plutarch gives us details of a meeting between Marius and Mithridates in Asia in 98 BC, which he states was down to Marius' attempts to provoke Mithridates into war with Rome.[456]

For Plutarch, Marius was looking to restore his prominence by another great campaign against a dangerous enemy. The clear problem with this is that Plutarch is clearly looking forward to the threat that Mithradates became, rather than the minor player he was in 98 BC, nothing more than a lowly, minor eastern client king. Therefore, once again, such a campaign would have been beneath him at the time. The Jugurthine and Northern Wars had seen Marius become the greatest commander of his day, a saviour of Rome and made him immensely wealthy. In 100 BC there was little challenge left for him on the battlefield.

The one clear challenge that was in front of him lay in Rome itself and the Senatorial aristocracy. This may seem an odd statement considering he had been consul for five years in a row (104–100 BC), yet he had been away from Rome for the majority of the period from 107 onwards. As pointed out above, Marius had considerable resources to call on in Rome, both from the Senatorial order, the equestrians and the people. Yet, he will forever be associated with the second and third tumultuous tribunates of L. Appuleius Saturninus and his associates.

Marius and Saturninus: Conspiracy or Convenience?

Marius' association with Saturninus went back to 103 BC, when he used him to assist in his re-election as consul (see Chapter 9). Saturninus, however, is far from a one-dimensional figure, as we know a good deal about his own political career. In 104, he had been the quaestor in charge of the grain supply. During the crisis caused by the Second Servile War (see Appendix II), grain supplies naturally began to be tightened with an accompanying price rise. M. Aemilius Scaurus saw this as an opportunity and got the Senate to appoint him as a special commissioner to deal with the problem.[457] This naturally humiliated Saturninus, who used this anger to run as tribune for 103 BC.

During 103 BC we know of actions he took for himself and on behalf of Marius.[458] For Marius there was the aforementioned re-election ploy, whilst there was also a measure to establish colonies in Africa for Marius' veterans. Acting on his own behalf, he was possibly involved in establishing a special court to try treason cases with an equestrian jury and involved in the exile of Cn. Mallius, the commander of Roman forces at Arausio. The following year Metellus Numidicus, one of two Metellan censors that year, attempted to have Saturninus and his ally C. Servilius Glaucia, who had himself been a troublesome tribune, excluded from the Senate. However, a disagreement between the two censors prevented this. Although the attempt failed it merely increased the pairs' enmity with the Metelli. Both Saturninus and Glaucia succeeded in gaining election for the year 100, Saturninus as a tribune once more (his second) and Glaucia as a praetor.

Plutarch sees both these men being elected as a clear case of Marius engineering allies in key magistracies, as the three men conducting some secret arrangement for the year to come.[459] Yet we must stop and ask ourselves why Marius would need to solely rely on these two men, when he must have had huge resources at his call. His patronage would have been able to ensure as many tribunes or praetors as he needed would either be loyal allies before their election or secure their services for their year of office. Indeed, he had secured his own consulship with a compliant colleague. Yet we must also remember Velleius' view on the whole episode takes the opposite position and makes no mention of a connection between the men.[460]

Clearly, Marius has used Saturninus before, and they did have a mutual enemy in the form of Metellus Numidicus. However, even if he did support Saturninus' and Glaucia's election they would probably have been one of many such men he sponsored into useful political positions in this year. Saturninus paid him back by passing more laws establishing veteran colonies, this time in Sicily, Achaea and Macedonia, and more controversially a law confiscating land that had been occupied by the Cimbri in Gaul. Although a controversial land grab in itself, Saturninus added a unique clause to the law, requiring all Senators to swear to uphold it on pain of exile. Although a unique innovation in its own right and one designed to guard against the law's repeal, it also put Saturninus' (and Marius') old enemy, Metellus Numidicus, in a bind. If he swore to it then he would be supporting a man he clearly and publicly opposed, thus undermining him; if he failed to swear then he would be exiled. In Metellus' case he chose a comfortable exile and became a martyr.

Yet we must never make the mistake of assuming that Saturninus was only ever a tool of Marius. Saturninus' previous tribunate had shown him both working for Marius and pursuing his own agenda. He would simply have been one of many agents used by Marius, albeit a prominent one. Both he and Glaucia went further in their legislative programme and here the differences between these men and Marius began to show. Saturninus proposed a law setting a low price for grain for the city's populace, always a sure-fire populist measure, especially given the shortage caused by the Servile War. It was passed using violence in the Forum and the overriding of his colleagues' vetoes. Worse came when both men sought re-election for 99 BC, Saturninus for a second consecutive tribunate (always a provocative issue), while Glaucia sought the consulship (which was illegal given that he was a serving praetor). Saturninus secured his election along with a number of allies, whilst Glaucia's election proved to be more troublesome. With one place filled (by M. Antonius), it apparently came down to Glaucia and a Memmius for the second one. Here our accounts vary slightly, though only with regard to motive rather than outcome, which was that during the election Memmius was attacked and murdered.

Appian states that Saturninus and Glaucia ordered him to be beaten up by an armed gang they had with them, whilst not directly stating that they intended to kill him. Orosius, however, states that Saturninus did order Memmius' death and sent a P. Mettius to club him to death with an 'unshapely bludgeon'. Interestingly, Plutarch omits all mention of Memmius' death and has Marius being forced to take up arms against Saturninus by a coalition of the Senate and Equestrian order who wanted to put an end to Saturninus' sedition (again with no mention of Glaucia either).[461]

We do not know Marius' view of Saturninus and Glaucia' activities during the year that were not focussed on his needs, which seem to have simply been the veteran colonies and the land in Gaul. Certainly, the exile of Metellus was a bonus, but there was enough enmity between Metellus and Saturninus to explain its origins; it certainly did not have to come from Marius himself and was such a crude method that bellies what had been an adept political touch. In the case of the elections, it was a different matter. In fact, Marius would have been far more interested in getting his own adherents into positions for the following year, which was the first in six that he would not be consul himself. It has long been argued that the M. Antonius who was easily elected as consul in 99, ahead of Glaucia, was a Marian client.[462]

War in Rome

What happened after the murder of Memmius is again contested, with both Appian and Orosius providing accounts, again from different standpoints. In Appian, the urban plebs apparently turned on Saturninus for the lawlessness of his activities in Rome and next day gathered together and attacked him, forcing Saturninus to defend himself with a force of rural plebs[463]. Following clashes between the two groups on the streets of Rome, Saturninus and his followers then seized the Capitol, though this could have been out of a need for a defensive position from the urban plebs. It was then that the Senate passed the *senatus consultum ultimum* (which suspended day-to-day rights). It is only at this point that Marius became involved against his former ally and took a force of armed veterans and besieged the Capitol, cutting off its water supply, and arranged for the surrender of Saturninus, Glaucia and their followers, with promises of safe conduct. This point is agreed with by Plutarch. Marius then apparently placed them in protective custody in a building used by the Senate, but they were murdered by a lynch mob, by an angry crowd of urban plebs. In Appian this was achieved by the mob ripping off roof tiles and stoning Saturninus and his colleagues to death in an open court yard. Plutarch does not specify the manner of his death. Thus, for Appian and Plutarch, Marius was reluctant to act against his former allies and tried to save them, failing miserably.[464]

Orosius, however, preserves an interesting alternative to these accounts:

> The consul Marius, adapting his genius to the occasion, allied himself with the cause of the patriots (Senate), and calmed the aroused plebeians by addressing them with soothing words. Saturninus, after daring to commit these infamous deeds, held a meeting at his own house and there was acclaimed king by some and general by others. Marius divided the plebeians into maniples and then stationed the other consul and a garrison on the hill, while he barricaded the gates. The battle took place in the Forum. Marius drove Saturninus from the Forum to refuge on the Capitol. Marius then cut the pipes which furnished that place with water. Thereupon a savage battle took place at the entrance to the Capitol. Many around Saufeius and Saturninus were slain. Saturninus cried out loudly and called to the people to witness Marius was the cause of all their difficulties. Marius next forced Saturninus, Saufeius and Labienus to flee for refuge in the Senate House, where some Roman knights [equestrians] broke down the doors and killed them. C. Glaucia was dragged from the home of Claudius and killed. Furius, the tribune of the plebs, decreed that the property of all these men should be confiscated. Cn. Dolabella, the brother of Saturninus, while fleeing with L. Giganius through the Forum Holitorium was put to death.[465]

Thus Orosius, despite the fact that he is the latest of our sources, provides an account that differs from the ones found in Appian and Plutarch in some important ways. Rather than being forced into acting against Saturninus and almost a passive bystander, here he is the instigator of action against Saturninus. In the hours after the murder of Memmius he swung into action, mobilizing the urban plebs, raising a military force and defending the city. In this account, the timescale is compressed, and the mobilization, garrisoning and defence of the gates could have taken through the day and the night and thus battle commenced next morning, which ties into Appian's timescale. This also ties into Appian's account of the urban plebs attacking Saturninus; what he omits is that Marius was leading them.

This whole account also ties in with Velleius statement (mentioned earlier) about Marius' sixth consulship:

He must not, however, be deprived of the glory of this consulship, for during this term as consul, he restrained by arms the mad acts of Servilius Glaucia and Appuleius Saturninus, who were shattering the constitution by continuing in office, and were breaking up the elections with armed violence and bloodshed, and caused these dangerous men to be put to death in the Curia Hostilia.[466]

Thus the accounts found in Velleius and Orosius present Marius the opportunist, who saw a chance to save Rome once more, this time on its very streets. Saturninus was defeated in one battle, forced to seek refuge then flushed out and hunted down. Once again, Marius' swift action had saved the state, at least that is how he would have seen and likely portrayed it. He also removed a man who had become an obstacle to his own political manoeuvrings and one who could be a severe embarrassment if he were given the chance to detail the two men's past associations. Thus for Marius, Saturninus' death wiped the slate clean.

Marius and the Decade of Shadows

For the decade that follows the deaths of Saturninus and Glaucia, we have almost no sources, with the few surviving sources all eager to pass onto the next tumult in Roman politics, centred on the tribunate of M. Livius Drusus in 91 BC. This makes the 90s BC one of the least documented in the late Republic, truly a decade of shadows. Once again, Plutarch provides us with a stereotypical portrayal of Marius in this decade, a man who's power has been destroyed, increasingly seen as a relic of a previous age, spending his old age (he was now in his sixties), reliving past glories.

In no case is this decline in power better illustrated than in the recall of Metellus Numidicus, which is detailed in Plutarch thus:

When a decree was introduced recalling Metellus from exile, Marius opposed it strongly both by word and deed, but finding his efforts in vain, at last desisted, and after the people had enthusiastically adopted the measure, unable to endure the sight of Metellus returning, he set sail for Cappodocia and Galatia.[467]

Thus we have the image of an increasingly irrelevant man, powerless in Rome and determined to conjure up one last foreign war (against Mithridates). Plutarch's other major note on Marius in this period involves an argument with his former deputy, Sulla, when at some point in the nineties, Bocchus commemorated the capture of Jugurtha with a set of statues on the Capitol depicting the handover to Sulla.[468] Naturally, we are told that this benefited Sulla and angered Marius, as it would. Thus Plutarch builds up a picture of Marius, embittered, desperate for more glory, and a rival of Sulla, all of which tie in nicely to the events of 88 BC that triggered off Rome's First Civil War.

Yet, Appian and Orosius preserve an interesting note on Marius in the nineties. In 99 BC, shortly after Saturninus' death, a move was indeed made to recall Metellus Numidicus from exile, by two tribunes, Q. Pompeius Rufus and M. Porcius Cato.[469]

This was vetoed by one of their colleagues, P. Furius, who we are informed was working with (being sponsored by) Marius, though he already had a grudge against Metellus Numidicus himself.[470] Here we have an interesting problem: Metellus was indeed recalled in 98 BC, with ease, according to Plutarch, yet this recall was easily blocked a year earlier. Clearly, something had changed. If Marius and his supporters were strong enough to prevent this in 99 then why were they not in 98? Two factors spring to mind. Firstly, one of the consuls of 98 was a Metellus Nepos (yet another relative, but interestingly the only Metellan consul of this decade). Secondly, we are informed that Marius was out of Rome, in the east this year.[471] Whilst Plutarch places the decision to recall Metellus' before Marius left, it is entirely possible that it was engineered after he left Rome. It is also possible that Marius negotiated with the Metellans to allow his return as a quid pro quo for his mission to the east. Ultimately, as is usual in these cases, we will never know, but what is clear is that Plutarch's image of a broken Marius can be challenged.

Analysing Marius and the rest of the decade is a difficult task and one that does not need to take place here. Marius himself held no further office in the 90s, but we need draw no clear inference from that, as Marius could easily have been working behind the scenes to place his own supporters in key positions. It is interesting that of the censors of 97 (M. Antonius and L. Valerius Flaccus), one was a colleague, and as Plutarch put it 'servant', of Marius and the other followed him as consul in 99 BC. Furthermore, aside from the consul of 98, there were no other Metellan consuls in this period and the Metelli seem to be a waning power in this period. Interestingly, the late 90s saw two consuls from the Iulii Caesares family (both related to Marius) in 91 and 90 BC. At the end of the day, all what can be argued, though, is that we must avoid taking the Plutarchian image of a broken Marius at face value. The man that had claimed six consulships in eight years and amassed all the money and glory he had would not easily fade from the political scene.

The Other Wars of the Period 104–100 BC

As well as the two wars described in the main body of this work, towards the end of the period in question there were several other campaigns that occurred that merely added to the Roman military burden and increased the level of the crisis. These two other campaigns were the Second Servile War in Sicily and a campaign against the pirates of the eastern Mediterranean.

The Second Servile War (104–101 BC)

In 104 BC, Rome was at one of the lowest ebbs it had been at for over a century. Although the war in Africa had been won, the catastrophic defeat at Arausio in 105 had left Italy vulnerable to the northern tribes and many considered it defenceless. It is perhaps no coincidence then, that this year saw a number of outbreaks of slave revolts in Italy and the outbreak of a Second Servile War, once again in Sicily. Diodorus provides detail of a number of smaller isolated slave revolts in Italy during 104 BC, as well as one more serious. This one was actually led by a Roman landowner, T. Minucius or Ti. Vettius,[472] who armed his slaves, apparently proclaimed himself king and rose up in revolt. He created an army of slaves and established a fortified position around Capua as a base for his revolt. The situation so worried the Senate that they dispatched one of the praetors, L. Licinius Lucullus with a force of 4,000 infantry and 400 cavalry to defeat him. Upon Lucullus' arrival in the region, Minucius/Vettius took a position on top of a hill with a force of 3,500 and was able to beat Lucullus off. In the end, Lucullus only succeeded by arranging for one of Minucius/Vettius' subordinates to betray him on promise of a pardon. The rebellion petered out and Minucius/Vettius and the majority of his followers committed suicide. This bizarre episode perhaps reflects the weakness of the Roman position on the home-front following the defeat at Arausio and the (thought to be) impending Cimbric invasion.

If such weakness in Italy could produce a slave revolt then Sicily was far more susceptible to one, given its recent history and the First Servile War of 135–132 BC (see Chapter 1). The perceived weakness of Rome thanks to the atmosphere created by Arausio was not the only factor that helped create an atmosphere for slave revolts in Sicily. As mentioned earlier (Chapter 7), when C. Marius was recruiting fresh forces from the Roman allies, the issue of foreign slaves was raised. This resulted in a Senatorial decree being issued that banned the enslavement of citizens of allied states. Both Diodorus and Dio inform us that this decree was enforced with some vigour by P. Licinius Nerva, the governor of Sicily, which resulted in at least 800 slaves being freed. It also created a general atmosphere of expectation and hope amongst the slave population in general. However, this in turn created a backlash from the slave-owning landowners, who forced Licinius to end the process of freedom.

Naturally enough, this led to discontent and then rebellion across Sicily. An initial armed revolt soon began, led by a man named Varius and was able to take up a fortified position and hold off the governor's forces. Once again, this fortified slave position was only taken through the treachery of a subordinate commander having been promised a pardon. Although this initial revolt had been crushed, others soon rose up near the city of Heracleia, which grew to a force of over 2,000 men. The governor dispatched one of his officers, M. Titinius, to deal with them, but Titinius soon found himself outnumbered and outmanoeuvred and was defeated and routed. This both acted as a call to arms to other disaffected slaves of the region as well as providing them with a large amount of weaponry. The slave army soon numbered more than 6,000. As occurred in the first war, command of this slave army soon fell to a mystic, a man named Salvius, who was proclaimed as king.

We are told that Salvius' army quickly grew to more than 20,000 infantry and 2,000 cavalry. Against them was the governor and his force of 10,000 allied troops. Battle took place at the city of Murgantia, during which the Roman forces were routed and control of the island's interior fell to Salvius. To make matters worse, at the city of Lilybaeum another rebellion broke out, led by a man named Athenion, who also declared himself king of Sicily, again after claiming some mystical abilities, and raised an army of over 10,000 slaves. Thus by the end of 104, to add to Rome's existing problems in the north, they had effectively lost control of Sicily to a number of slave armies.

With military control of the island, Salvius set about establishing his rule, taking the royal name Tryphon (imitating a usurper king of Syria). He established a royal capital at a place named Triocala, complete with palace, and secured control over the slave army of Athenion, having him imprisoned. To oppose him, the Romans replaced Licinius Nerva as governor with L. Licinius Lucullus, who had successfully defeated the slave rebellion the previous year at Capua. With him came an army of 17,000 men: 14,000 Romans and Italians along with allied contingents from Bithynia and Thessaly, all of which were vital forces needed for the expected conflict with the northern tribes. To face the Romans, Tryphon (Salvius) freed Athenion and faced them in battle at his 'capital'. On this occasion, even though outnumbered, Lucullus was able to rout the slave army, killing more than 20,000 if we are to believe Diodorus. Both Tryphon and Athenion survived and fled back to the rebel capital. Lucullus followed this victory up with a siege of the city but was repulsed.[473]

For this failure, Lucullus was prosecuted in Rome and exiled. His replacement, and possibly prosecutor, was a man named Servilius who served as Governor in Sicily in 102 BC. Lucullus, in retaliation, disbanded his army and burnt his camp to ensure that Servilius was unable to profit by his actions. As a result, Sicily once more was dominated by the slave army, with Servilius ineffective. In the meantime, we are informed that Tryphon had died (through we are not told whether this was natural causes or murder) and was succeeded by Athenion.

By 101 BC, the situation was so serious that Marius' consular colleague of the year, M. Aquilius, was dispatched to Sicily to end the war. This move was made easier by the defeat of the Teutones and Ambrones at Aquae Sextiae the previous year. We are not told the size of the force he took with him to Sicily, but he was immediately effective. Florus tells us that he was able to cut off the rebel army and starve them, before forcing them to give battle. Both Florus and Diodorus record that Aquillius comprehensively won the battle that followed, destroying the slave army and effectively crushing the rebellion. Diodorus even records that Aquillius managed to kill the slave king Athenion in battle, though Florus stated that he was murdered whilst a captive.[474]

The survivors fled to various strong points, which Aquilius then reduced one at a time, until he had re-established control of the island. As a postscript, Diodorus relates a story of the final group of survivors surrendering to Aquillius only to be taken to Rome to die fighting wild animals in the circus, but committed suicide rather than die entertaining the Romans. Whether this happened or not we will never know but it certainly made for a dramatic end to Diodorus' evidence and gave the last of the rebel slaves a final dignity.[475]

Thus, we can see that as the early Roman military defeats in Gaul led to rebellions in both Gaul and Spain, the defeat at Arausio inspired a number of slaves to rebel against Rome, believing that the time was right and that Rome was weak and might not survive. This was exacerbated by the Senate's decree on foreign slaves, a price extricated by Rome's eastern allies in return for military help. The war that followed lasted for four years and tied up vital Roman military resources and effectively saw Rome lose control of Sicily and its grain supplies, at a time when they most needed them. Thus we see that for Rome in this crucial period of 104–101 BC, the crisis only deepened.

The Pirate War (102–100 BC)

Throughout this period, it can be seen that Rome, not a natural naval power (at least in this period), suffered to a great degree from Mediterranean piracy. As we have already seen, in the 120s BC, Rome invaded and annexed the Balearic Islands in the western Mediterranean, removing the pirates' main bases and apparently ending the threat. The eastern Mediterranean, however, was another matter, being less under Roman control. Here it has often been said that Rome herself was indirectly responsible for the rise of piracy in the eastern Mediterranean. The great Hellenistic powers had been humbled and had limitations on where their navies could roam. The lesser powers such as Rhodes and Cyprus had, too, been cowed by Rome, via diplomatic rather than direct military means and saw a decline in power also. This meant that there were fewer navies patrolling the region policing it from pirates. Furthermore, with the removal of Seleukid power from Asia Minor following the defeat of Antiochus III in 189 BC, the region of Cilicia, with its mountainous and coastal terrain, became a haven for pirates outside of any state's control.

We have no clear evidence for what caused Rome to act, but in 102 BC, with the northern tribes pressing on Gaul, rebellions in Spain and a massive slave revolt in Sicily, the Senate commissioned one of the praetors, M. Antonius, to deal with the pirate menace in the eastern Mediterranean. We have no clear narrative for the events of this war, merely a handful of scattered references in the sources. Our best sources of information come from several inscriptions, which record the transportation of a fleet across the Isthmus of Corinth, and a wintering in Athens during 102/101 BC. We also possess several versions of an anti-piracy decree that had been erected on stone markers across the eastern Mediterranean, notably Delphi and Knidos.[476]

Preceding Pompey's more famous pirate command by thirty-plus years, Antonius also apparently campaigned in the Cilicia region to rid it of pirate strongholds. He returned to Rome in 100 BC and celebrated a triumph for his activities, also being elected consul for 99 BC, possibly due to his Marian connections (see Chapter 7). Despite the triumph for his endeavours, it is unlikely that Antonius achieved anything more than a temporary lull in pirate activity given the grave threat it posed by the 70s BC. It was not until the more famous command of Pompey in 68/67 that this issue was resolved. Nevertheless, given the grave threats that Rome faced elsewhere in this period, it is interesting to note that they were beginning to take this growing threat seriously and act in military terms rather than regarding it as a local issue. Once again, we can detect the emergence of a more strategic view of the Mediterranean emerging in Roman thinking.

Appendix III

The Roman Manpower Question

Throughout this work, the issue of the shortage of Roman manpower for military service has been a fundamental one. Yet despite all the evidence, the issue of available manpower and the reasons behind it have been a bone of contention amongst historians throughout the twentieth and twenty-first centuries. As it is such a fundamental issue, it is worth reviewing the principal problems that confront us.

The Ancient Evidence

The widely-held assumption that underlined the ancient accounts of the manpower issue that affected Rome in the second century BC, was one of a recruitment crisis caused by military overstretch. In short, the ever-increasing length and complexity of the wars in the second century BC, especially in Spain, meant that the soldiers were away from their farms for ever-increasing amounts of time, and that this neglect led to them falling into ruin and being bought up by the rich landowners who created great estates run by masses of slaves. This, they believed to lie behind the proposed reforms of Ti. Sempronius Gracchus in 133 BC, and was only solved by Marius' supposed abandonment of the property qualification, which allegedly cut the ties between the landed farmer and military service.

As we have already seen, not only were Gracchus' proposals more complicated than that, but Marius' actions did not mean a permanent abandonment of the property qualification needed to serve in the Roman military. As well as the narrative sources attributing these reasons to Gracchus' actions and the underlying problems at the time, there are two other contentious areas of ancient evidence: the Roman census figures and whether the level of the property qualification for military service was lowered during the second century.

Roughly every five years, the Roman Senate elected two senior members from their ranks, distinguished ex-consuls, to serve as censors. These two men served for up to an eighteen-month period and their primary duty was to conduct the census of Roman citizens.[477] For the latter part of the second century BC, the given figures are as follows:[478]

169/168 BC	312,805
164/163	337,022 or 337,452
159/158	328,316
154/153	324,000
147/146	322,000
142/141	328,442
136/135	317,933
131/130	318,823
125/124	394,736
120/119	Unknown
115/114	394,336
109/108	Unknown
102/101	Unknown

There are immediately two problems with these figures. Firstly, we have no clear idea of the criteria used to register the citizens on this list, whether it was all male citizens or simply those of the first five property classes (those eligible for military service). Nor do we know how accurately the census recorded all the Roman citizens in Italy. The ancient sources record the penalties for failing to make oneself available to register, but it has been questioned how enforceable these were in a region the size of Italy.[479]

The second problem is that we have no direct surviving source for these figures, merely the surviving narrative works, primarily Livy's histories and its epitomes. This immediately leaves them open to mis-transmission throughout the 1,500 years between when they were written and the early modern period when the surviving manuscripts were analysed and standardized. Thus, despite the fact that the figures we have show a declining citizen population until 131 and then a massive jump, which is most widely ascribed to the Ti. Sempronius Gracchus' land reforms, there have been enough reasons to argue against them.

The other area of ancient evidence is centred on discussions over what the figure was for the lowest of the five census classes and thus what level of wealth a man needed to be eligible for military service. Here we have three different figures: 11,000, 4,000 and 1,500 *asses*. The figure of 11,000 *asses* comes from Livy and dates back to the supposed origins of this system, back in the sixth century BC (thus some 500-plus years before he wrote about it). The figure of 4,000 *asses* comes from Polybius. Several late Republican sources, including Cicero, give us the figure of 1,500 *asses*, and seem to backdate it to the period under discussion, the second century BC.[480]

The most common arguments presented by modern historians of Rome are that at some point, most likely around the Second Punic War or soon after, the figure needed for military service was dropped from 11,000 to 4,000 and then again to 1,500 after Polybius, but predating Marius. The central problem with these theories is that there is no tangible shred of evidence to support them in the ancient sources. Again, as with Marius' army reforms, much of the modern argument is built from an assumed event that took place in our sources. However, of the three figures, only Polybius' can be treated as contemporary, and even that has the problem that the figure was given in drachmas (as he wrote for a Greek audience, in Greek) and has to be calculated back into *asses* by modern historians of Rome. We do not know how accurate Livy's figure was for the sixth century, or even if the system dated back to the sixth century. Cicero's figure may have been accurate for his day but we have no actual evidence that it was in force prior to Marius.

There is one other possible reference to changes in recruitment practices and that comes from a fragment of Cato, which has been interpreted as advocating the recruitment of the *proletarii* (those who fell below the minimum qualification) into the military, but the source is too fragmentary to allow any clear meaning.[481] Thus many of the arguments over this issue are built on houses of sand, and there is no actual evidence that the Romans did lower the minimum property qualification needed for service in this period.

The Modern Theories

With all these problems with the ancient evidence on this issue, many modern historians of Rome have searched for alternative fields of evidence to validate or invalidate the ancient evidence, notably archaeology and demography. For those who look to archaeology to shed light on this issue, the central argument is whether we can determine evidence of these large-scale slave estates that Gracchus talked of.[482] In short, the answer appears to be a negative one, but that does not automatically mean that they did not occur, due to the vagaries of finding sites that would both give us the detail and the scale needed for such an exercise.

Recent years have seen a growth in the use of demographic models of population growth and decline to see if they can shed light on this situation.[483] Whilst such theoretical constructs do provide us with a new approach to studying the limited evidence we have, we must always be aware of their limitations, namely that they are indeed simply theoretical models, and should exercise extreme caution if they clash with our ancient testimony. Such an example can be found in one of the latest works in this field, by Keaveney, who criticizes an earlier work by Morley:

> There have, however, been attempts to discredit Tiberius on the part of scholars who share Rosenstein's view that there actually was a population increase. Morley (2001) is one of those. Approaching it from the standpoint of the demographer, he comes to the conclusion, based on his own calculations, that Tiberius has got it wrong. I believe we may have a fundamental difference of approach. Morley's calculations can sometimes seem complex, but this is because essentially they are mathematical exercises and cannot have anything more than a hypothetical value. Recognising this I believe, unlike Morley, that when offered a choice between clear-cut unequivocal ancient source and a fragile modern construct, we must surely choose our sources.[484]

Amongst the many factors that may have been involved in this manpower issue in the period under review, two stand out. Evans pointed out the fundamental difference between the manpower theoretically available to Rome for military service, as seen in the census figures and the numbers who actually made themselves available to serve. In short, he focused on the problem of draft dodging.[485] Throughout history, it is a given that there will always be a large percentage of men who will avoid compulsory military service, made all the easier by the vastness of a pre-industrial Italy, no matter the harsh penalties for those caught.

Rosenstein in a recent work has also done much to dispel the simplicities of the ancient model of extended military service resulting in the loss of farms and thus eligibility, from at least two areas. Firstly, he argues that extended military service was not unique to the second century BC and had in fact been a long-standing issue as Rome fought more complicated wars in Italy in third century BC. Secondly, he theorizes that Rome's system of inheritance, whereby a father divides his property up equally between his children, meant that whereas the father might have enough wealth to be eligible for military service, by dividing it, his sons would all be ineligible. This in itself is an excellent theory, though he does then go on to postulate that despite the census figures the Roman citizen population actually rose in the second century BC, rather than falling.[486]

These few examples are merely presented to illustrate what is one of the most complicated and historically fertile issues in Roman history. Two clear conclusions can be drawn. Firstly, it is clear that the picture presented in our few surviving ancient sources can present too much of a simplistic representation of what must have been an extremely complicated socio-economic phenomenon, one that the Roman recognized was having implications for their military system. The second conclusion is that modern commentators on the ancient world must always watch themselves for constructing false arguments where there is no ancient evidence or dismissing the testimony we already have.

Ultimately, we can rely on the basic ancient premise that Rome indeed did suffer a problem in finding enough quality soldiers for her ever-increasing wars. Yet we must be careful not to assume that this was the sole reason for any presumed decline in her military efforts. As the Gallic Wars of the 120s showed, Rome in this period was more than capable of conducting a successful war against a tribal enemy. That they failed against the Cimbri for so long had more to do with more immediate factors, such as Roman commanders and Cimbric numbers rather than any deep-seated flaw in the Roman system. If there was no such flaw then there was no need for such a radical cure, such as the assumed abolition of the property qualification. Rome in this period did face a crisis on a number of issues, but these were temporary ones with temporary solutions; crisis did not mean inevitable collapse.

Appendix IV

The Dominance of the Metelli (123–98 BC)

Throughout this period of Roman history one family stands out: the Caecilii Metelli. Even in a dynastic system such as Rome's, the success of the Metelli in the period was unique. Even families such as the Scipiones had never achieved so much success by so many family members in such a short period of time, achieving seven consulships, four censorships and five triumphs within twenty-five years. Unfortunately for them, these successes occurred during a period for which our sources have now almost disappeared, leaving the majority of them in obscurity. The most well-known of this period is Metellus Numidicus and then mostly for his part in the rise of Marius, rather than on his own merit (though hopefully the preceding chapters have gone some way to correct this balance). There exists an excellent analysis of the Metelli by Van Ootegheim, which is rather inaccessible to the standard reader, being in French and long out of print.[487] The following is a brief résumé of the Metellan family's success:

The Metelli were an old and established plebeian family, first reaching the consulate in the third century BC, serving as consuls in both Punic Wars. Following the Second Punic War, however, the family's fortunes appear to have dipped and no Metellan reached the consulate for over fifty years. The family's fortunes were reversed by Metellus 'Macedonicus', who not only won great military and political glory, but re-founded a dynasty with his brother, with five of their sons becoming consul (123, 119, 117, 115, 113 and 109 BC).

The Third Century BC

| 284 | L. Caecilius Metellus Denter | Consul |

The first of the family to reach the consulship and the first to bear the cognomen Metellus.

283   L. Caecilius Metellus Denter   Praetor

There is much debate over the accuracy of this praetorship, coming so soon after his consulship. Polybius states that he was killed in the Battle of Arretium.[488]

251   L. Caecilius Metellus   Consul

Served in Sicily during the First Punic War, and won a notable victory over the Carthaginian general Hasdrubal at the Battle of Panormus, capturing over 100 elephants, which he paraded in his triumph.

247   L. Caecilius Metellus (2)   Consul

Elected consul for a second time, he again served in Sicily, laying siege to the city of Lilybaeum.

c.243   L. Caecilius Metellus (2)   Pontifex Maximus

Became Pontifex Maximus around this period and served until his death in 221 BC.[489]

206   Q. Caecilius Metellus   Consul
          M. Caecilius Metellus   Praetor

The first recorded case of two Metelli holding office at the same time, consul and Praetor. Quintus and his consular colleague shadowed Hannibal's movements about Italy.

Second Century BC

148   Q. Caecilius Metellus 'Macedonicus'   Praetor

Perhaps the most famous of all the Metlli, he defeated and captured the Macedonian Pretender Andriscus, ending the Fourth Macedonian War, leading to the annexation of Macedon. He remained in Greece, winning victories at Scarpheia and Chaeronaea.

| 146 | Q. Caecilius Metellus 'Macedonicus' | Triumph |

Celebrated a triumph for his defeat of Andriscus.

| 143 | Q. Caecilius Metellus 'Macedonicus' | Consul |

Thanks to his actions in the Macedonian War, became the first Metellan consul for several generations. Defeated a slave uprising at Miturnae in Italy and then served in the Celtiberian War in Spain.

| 142 | L. Caecilius Metellus Calvus | Consul |

Brother of Macedonicus; the first example of two Metelli following each other in the consulship, but nothing else is known of his activities during the year.

| 131 | Q. Caecilius Metellus 'Macedonicus' | Censor |

First Metellan to become censor; clashed with the Tribune Atinius Labeo, who threatened to throw Metellus from the Tarpeian Rock, after his omission from the Senate. Also of note is the fact that this pair of censors was the first ever all-plebeian pairing (traditionally, it had been a patrician and a plebeian).

The Metellan Period of Dominance

| 123 | Q. Caecilius Metellus 'Baliaricus' | Consul |

Son of Metellus Macedonicus, invaded and annexed the Balearic islands (see Chapter 1).

| 121 | Q. Caecilius Metellus 'Baliaricus' | Triumph |

Celebrated a triumph for the conquest of the Balearic Islands.

| 120 | Q. Caecilius Metellus 'Baliaricus' | Censor |

| 119 | L. Caecilius Metellus 'Dalmaticus' | Consul |

Son of Metellus Calvus; in Rome he clashed with the tribune C.

Marius, who threatened him with imprisonment, whilst in his province he fought the Dalmatians, earning the cognomen 'Dalmaticus'.

| 117 | L. Caecilius Metellus Diadematus | Consul |

A son of Metellus Macedonicus; no clear detail on his activities as consul.

| | L. Caecilius Metellus 'Dalmaticus' | Triumph |

Celebrated his triumph for fighting the Dalmatians.

| 115 | M. Caecilius Metellus | Consul |

Another son of Metellus Macedonicus received Sardinia and Corsica as his province, possibly to fight increased banditry.

| | L. Caecilius Metellus 'Dalmaticus'/Diadematus | Censor |

It is unclear which of the two L. Caecilii Metelli became censor this year.

| c.114 | L. Caecilius Metellus 'Dalmaticus' | Pontifex Maximus |

We are not told for certain when he took office but he was certainly in post this year.

| 113 | C. Caecilius Metellus Caprarius | Consul |

Another son of Metellus Macedonicus campaigned in Thrace against the Scordisci (see Chapter 3).

| 111 | M. Caecilius Metellus | Triumph |
| | C. Caecilius Metellus Caprarius | Triumph |

In an unprecedented move, both brothers celebrated their triumphs on the same day; Marcus for his activities in Sardinia and Caius for those in Thrace.

| 109 | Q. Caecilius Metellus 'Numidicus' | Consul |

| 106 | Q. Caecilius Metellus 'Numidicus' | Triumph |
| 102 | Q. Caecilius Metellus 'Numidicus'
C. Caecilius Metellus Caprarius | Censors |

Again, in another unprecedented move, both censors came from the same family. Their censorship also saw the attempt to remove Saturninus and Glaucia from the Senate.

| 98 | Q. Caecilius Metellus Nepos | Consul |

Thus this period saw seven different brothers and cousins become consul, with four of them going on to reach the censorship, including the extraordinary double censorship of 102 BC, at a time when Marius was consul for the fourth time. One of their number even became *Pontifex Maximus* (Rome's chief priest). Furthermore, they celebrated five triumphs, including the extraordinary feat of two triumphs on the same day in 111 BC. It is easy enough to understand why this dominance petered out, given that all available Metelli of that generation had been advanced through the *cursus honorum* (the sequence of offices a senator aspired to gain). Following this period, the children and grandchildren of these men achieved consulships in 80, 69, 68, 60, 57 and 52 BC, with a second period of consulships, the last of which being the noted Q. Caecilius Metellus Pius Scipio Nasica, a Scipio by birth, but a Metellan by adoption, who was the father-in-law of Pompey and fought Caesar at the Battle of Thapsus in 46 BC. Like his colleague Cato, he too committed suicide rather than come to terms with Caesar.[490]

The key issue that has not yet been accounted for is how these two branches of the family came to exercise such dominance in this period. Certainly, Metellus Macedonicus raised the profile of the family once more and made the elections of his sons much more likely, as well as his own brother. Yet to have all the available sons of both brothers reach the consulship was unprecedented. Regrettably, like much in this period, without a good surviving narrative source we have little clear information to go on. Nevertheless, it does hint at a degree of co-ordination and resources that no other family was able to muster.

Although this period of dominance was always going to come to an end, the rise of Marius too has often been overstated in its impact on the Metelli, especially in the light of the double Metellan censorship of 102 BC. The family did survive the disruptions and mass murder of the First Civil War and was able to gain a number of consulships in the late Republic, albeit without the same level of dominance that they saw in this period.

Appendix V

Sources for the Period

As has been mentioned throughout this work, the fundamental problem we have when analysing the wars of this period, is the lack of surviving sources. As we have seen, wars were raging throughout Spain, Gaul, Sicily, Africa, Illyria, Macedon and Thrace, not to mention an invasion of Italy itself. Yet in most cases all we have are a few lines or at most a few paragraphs of detail. Had we fuller sources then this period would have a far higher profile than it currently does, especially given fuller accounts of the key battles of Arausio, Aquae Sextiae and Raudian Plain. The following is a brief overview of the surviving and lost sources for the period.

Surviving Roman Sources

Sallust – *The Jugurthine Wars* (First Century BC)

Sallust's narrative of the Jugurthine Wars is an invaluable piece of evidence and the only in-depth narrative of the period to survive. Furthermore, it was written just sixty years after the war itself and benefited greatly from Sallust's use of the works of men such as Cornelius Sulla, Rutilius Rufus and Aemilius Scaurus, who had taken part in the events described. It also benefited from Sallust' governorship of Africa Nova, the name given to the new province created from eastern Numidia when it was annexed in 46 BC. The position gave him access to the library of the Numidian kings (itself composed of a number of volumes taken from the sack of Carthage in 146 BC). Sallust refers to *The Libri Punici* in his work.[491] The major danger in using the *Jugurthine Wars* is Sallust's stated intent to show how corrupt and degenerate the Romans had become, which had led to the civil wars of his day and explains the constant barrage of accusations of corruption against key figures of this period. Furthermore, as has been detailed, he was not writing a military history, and misses or condenses vital information for our understanding of the war.

Plutarch – *Lives of Marius, Sulla & Sertorius* (First Century AD)

Plutarch's 'lives' are today indispensable biographies of a number of the Republic's most famous figures. His life of Marius gives us our best source for the final clashes with the Cimbri and Teutones. Furthermore, he also made use of the biographies of both Sulla and Catulus, key figures involved in these wars. This latter point is his key weakness as he uses material written by men who became enemies of Marius in latter life and wanted to thoroughly darken his name and downplay his abilities.

Orosius – *Seven Books against the Pagans* (Fifth Century AD)

Orosius was a Christian writer of the fifth century AD, whose work on pagan history preserves a number of interesting accounts of Roman history. In particular, his details on the Jugurthine War, though brief in places, gives us a good source to compare to the account of Sallust.

(Unknown) *Periochae of Livy*

Despite the loss of Livy's grand narrative history of the Republic, for events after 167 BC, we do have a surviving collection of summaries of his lost books. We have little idea when they were summarized or by whom, but they condense Livy's narrative into a series of headlines for events that took place each year. Even reduced to such a format they still provide us with valuable information for the period.

Florus – *Epitome of Roman History* (Second Century AD)

Florus wrote a short abridgement (epitome) of Roman Republican history. Despite its brevity he preserves accounts for a number of the wars of the period and gives us an insight into the narrative histories that are now lost.

Velleius Paterculus – *Roman History* (First Century AD)

Paterculus also wrote a short history of the Republican period, but preserves less military material than Florus for the period in question.

Diodorus – *Library of History* (First Century BC)

Diodorus' work took the form of a universal history of the ancient world from its earliest day down to his time. Although much of it has been lost, his later chapters on Roman history provide a wealth of previously unknown details, including a full account of the Servile wars.

Appian – Histories of the Civil, Gallic, Illyrian, Numidian & Spanish Wars (Second Century AD)

Appian was a second-century AD Greek scholar, who wrote a series of works charting the various wars the Romans fought, separated geographically, along with his *Civil Wars*, Unfortunately, aside from his work on the Civil Wars, the other wars survive in varying degrees of completeness. Nevertheless, they prove a number of useful narratives.

Granius Licinianus – *Roman History* (Second Century AD?)

We only have a handful of fragments of Licinianus' work, but it is believed to have been an epitome of Roman history. The few fragments we have cover the period
163–78 BC and provide some interesting insights into the events under discussion.

Unknown – *De viris illustribus* (Late Empire)

The *de viris illustribus*, or lives of famous men, is a compilation of short biographies of famous Romans and non-Romans, mostly from the Republican period. Despite its brevity and unknown sources, we have biographies of Marius, Metellus Numidicus, Sulla, Aemilius Scaurus and Saturninus, as well as Scipio Aemilianus, the Gracchi, Metellus Macedonicus and even Viriathus.

Strabo – *Geography* (First Century AD)

Strabo's work on geography contains the most detailed accounts of the tribes that were at war with Rome in this period, notably the Cimbri and the Scordisci. He made extensive use of Poseidonius and allows us a glimpse at the origins and culture of Rome's enemies.

Lost Roman Sources for the Period

Detailing all the sources that have been lost to us but which would have covered the events of this period would be another book in itself. Nevertheless, there are a few which have been mentioned in the preceding text.

Livy – *History of Rome from the Foundation of the City* (First Century BC)

Of all the lost Roman works, it is perhaps Livy's that stand out the most. His history of Rome from Romulus to Augustus was composed of 142 separate books. Today all that survive are books 1–10 (753 to 293 BC) and 21–45 (218–167 BC). Thus books 46 to 142 covered the last 100-plus years of the Republic and would provide us with such a wealth of information that it would transform the study of Roman history. We know from the summaries that books 62–69 covered the period 120–100 and would have provided us with details on all the wars that Rome fought in this period.

L. Cornelius Sulla – **Autobiography** (Second / First Century BC)

Sulla famously wrote an autobiography of his life, giving later historians a first-hand account of the events he took part in, although as such it was prone to increasing his own role at the expense of others, notably Marius, who became his sworn enemy during the First Civil War.

Q. Lutatius Catulus – **Autobiography** and **history of the Cimbric War** (Second/First Century BC)

Catulus, consul 102 BC, was another contemporary Roman who wrote on the events of his life. As well as an account of his won consulship, used by Plutarch, which clearly disguised his military shortcomings, he also wrote a history of the Cimbric War. He too clearly suffered from the desire to inflate his own achievements and also became a sworn enemy of Marius, an act that cost him his life; a victim of the bloodbath that accompanied Marius' capture of Rome in 87 BC, though by his own hand.

P. Rutilius Rufus – **Autobiography and** *History of Rome* (Second / First Century BC)

Rutilius Rufus was another of the men involved in these events to write an autobiography. He was a legate to both Scipio Aemilianus in Numantia and Metellus Numidicus in Numidia, serving with Marius on both occasions, and was elected to the consulship in 105 BC. Following the disaster at Arausio it was Rutilius who had charge of Italy. He was exiled from Rome in 92 BC, a victim of an equestrian rigged jury, due to his campaign against corruption in the provinces. Nevertheless, this exile allowed him to avoid the bloodshed of the First Civil War and live out a comfortable exile in the Greek islands, writing his accounts of the events in which he had taken part.[492]

Poseidonius – *Histories* and *Geography* (First Century BC)

Poseidonius was a Greek scholar of the first century BC who wrote extensively on matters of science and nature. He also wrote historical works continuing Polybius' histories from 146 to 88 BC. From the references in Strabo it appears that his works contained detailed accounts of the various tribal enemies which faced Rome, especially the Cimbri.

Lost Sources – Non Roman

As always we must remember that many of the other races of the ancient world had a corpus of literature as well. As already noted (Chapter 2) the Numidian court of Micipsa was famous for its patronage of scholars. Sallust refers to a number of now-lost native works detailing the Numidian peoples. Further-more, the royal court received many of the works salvaged from the sacking of Carthage. It must be noted, however, that any Numidian writing a history of the Jugurthine Wars would be taking a grave risk if it took anything other than a pro-Roman bias, as a loyal client of Rome.

Perhaps the greatest problem for the historian is the lack of any material from the tribal nations involved in these wars. For the Cimbri and Scordisci there were no such chroniclers, though there may have been a flourishing bardic tradition which maintained elements of their histories in an oral tradition. Without such counter-balancing evidence we always risk the danger of only seeing these wars from the Roman point of view.

African King Lists

Numidia (Unified Kingdom)

Syphax	206 – 202 BC
Masinissa	202 – 148 BC
Micipsa	148–118 BC
Gulassa	148 - unknown
Mastanabal	148 – pre–134
Jugurtha	118 – 105 BC
Adherbal	118 – 112 BC
Hiempsal	118 BC
Gauda	105 – pre 88 BC

After Gauda, we have no clear dates for the monarchs that followed, only their names and the period they came into contact with Rome.

Mastanabal II	Unknown
Hiempsal II	c.80s–60s
Juba I	c.60s–46

46 BC	Massinissan Dynasty removed from the throne, eastern Numidia annexed and becomes the Roman province of Africa Nova.
29 BC	Massinissan Dynasty restored to Western Numidia by Augustus.

Juba II   29 – 25 BC

25 BC Augustus removes Juba from the throne of Numidia to that of Mauretania and annexes the remainder of Numidia to Roman Africa.

Mauri Kingdom

Bocchus   Late second – early first century BC

On Bocchus' death the Mauri kingdom was split between his two sons Bocchus II and Bogud, on a geographic basis. When Bogud backed Antony in the Second Civil War, his kingdom was annexed to that of Bocchus'.

Bocchus II   Early First Century - 33 BC

33 BC   Bocchus II wills his kingdom to Rome.

25 BC   Augustus installs Juba II, king of Numidia, as king of the Mauri.

Juba II   25 BC – AD 23

Ptolemy I   AD 23 - AD 40

AD 40   Ptolemy murdered by Emperor Caius (Caligula).

AD 44   Mauri kingdom annexed by Emperor Claudius, becomes the provinces of Mauretania Caesariensis and Mauretania Tingitana.

Notes and References

All translations are taken from the Loeb unless otherwise specified, and amended by the author where necessary.

Below are a list of the full titles of the ancient works referenced and their modern short codes.

Amm. Marc	Ammianus Marcellinus – *History of Rome*
Ampel.	Ampelius – *Epitome of History*
App. *BC*	Appian – *Civil Wars*
App. *Gall.*	Appian – *Gallic Wars*
App. *Iber*	Appian – *Spanish Wars*
App. *Illyr*	Appian – *Illyria Wars*
App. *Lib*	Appian – *Libyan Wars*
App. *Pun*	Appian – *Punic Wars*
Ascon	Asconius – *Commentaries on Cicero*
Athen.	Athenaeus – *Authorities on Banquets*
Aug. *Res Gest*	Augustus – *Deeds of the Divine Augustus*
Caes. *BA*	Caesar – *African War*
Caes. *BG*	Caesar – *Gallic War*
De vir ill	*De Viris Illustribus* (*Lives of Famous Men*)
Dio	Dio Cassius – *History of Rome*
Diod.	Diodorus – *Library of History*
Eutrop	Eutropius – *Epitome of Roman History*
Exsuper	Julius Exsuperantius – *Epitome of Roman History*
Fest	Festus – *Lexicon*
Fest. *Brev*	Festus – *Epitome of Roman History*
Flor	Florus – *Epitome of Roman History*

Frontin. *Str.*	Frontinus – *Stratagems*
Gell.	Gellius – *The Attic Nights*
Gran.Lic	Granius Licinianus – *Epitome of Roman History*
Herodot.	Herodotus – *Histories*
Homer.	Homer – *Odyssey*
Iord. *Rom*	Jordanes – *History of Rome*
Iustin	Justin – *Epitome of Pompeius Trogus' History of the World*
Liv.	Livy – *History of Rome*
Liv. *Oxy*	*Oxyrhynchus Fragments of Livy*
Liv. *Per*	*The Periochae of Livy*
Lydus. *de. mag.*	Lydus – *On Magistrates*
Obseq	Julius Obsequens – *Summary of Livy*
Oros.	Orosius – *Seven Books against the Pagans*
Polyb.	Polybius – *Histories*
Plin. *NH*	Pliny – *Natural History*
Plut. *Ant.*	Plutarch – *Life of Marcus Antonius*
Plut. *CG*	Plutarch – *Life of Caius Gracchus*
Plut. *Luc*	Plutarch – *Life of Lucullus*
Plut. *Mar*	Plutarch – *Life of Caius Marius*
Plut. *Mor*	Plutarch – *Moralia*
Plut. *Sert*	Plutarch – *Life of Sertorius*
Plut. *Sull*	Plutarch – *Life of Sulla*
Plut. *TG*	Plutarch – *Life of Tiberius Gracchus*
Sall. *Iug*	Sallust – *Jugurthine Wars*
Strabo	Strabo – *Geography*
Varr. *RR*	Varro – *On Agriculture*
Val Max.	Valerius Maximus – *Memorable Doings and Sayings*
Vell.	Velleius Paterculus – *History of Rome*
Vegit. *RM*	Vegetius – *Epitome of Military Science*
Zon	Zonaras – *Extracts of History*

Cicero – Works

Cic. *Brut.*	Cicero – *Brutus*
Cic. *Fin*	Cicero – *About the Ends of Goods and Evils* (*De Finibus Bonorum et Malorum*)
Cic. *Inv*	Cicero – *On Invention* (*De Inventione*)
Cic. *Leg*	Cicero – *On Laws* (*De Legibus*)
Cic. *ND*	Cicero – *On the Nature of the Gods* (*De Natura Deorum*)
Cic. *Rep*	Cicero – *On the Republic* (*De Republica*)

Cicero – Speeches

Cic. *Flacc*	Cicero – *In Defence of Flaccus*
Cic. *Har Resp*	Cicero – *On the Reply of the Soothsayers*
Cic. *Leg Agr*	Cicero – *On the Agrarian Law of Rullus*
Cic. *Mil*	Cicero – *In Defence of Milo*
Cic. *Off.*	Cicero – *On Duties* (*De Officiis*)
Cic. *Phil*	Cicero – *Philippics*
Cic. *Pis*	Cicero – *Against Piso*
Cic. *Planc*	Cicero – *In Defence of Plancius*
Cic. *Prov.Con*	Cicero – *On the consular Provinces*
Cic. *Sest*	Cicero – *In Defence of Sestius*

Latin Inscriptions

CIL	Corpus Inscriptionum Latinarum
ILLRP	Inscriptiones Latinae Liberae Rei Publicae
ILS	Inscriptiones Latinae Selectae

Greek Inscriptions

IG	Inscriptiones Graecae
IGRR	Inscriptiones Graecae ad Res Romanas pertinentes
SIG	Sylloge Inscriptionum Graecarum

Chapter One

1   Book 45 is the last one we have intact, taking events up to the defeat of Macedon in 167 BC.

2   Sall. *Iug.* 10.

3   Polyb. 35.1.1–2

4   C. Calpurnius Piso and L. Quinctius Crispinus; Liv. 39.42.2–4

5   Appian. *Iber.* 56

6   The Third Punic War in Africa, the Fourth Macedonian War in Greece (followed by the Achaean War) and the Lusitanian and Celtiberian Wars in Spain.

7   App. *Iber.* 67

8   In 140 BC. App. *Iber.* 69

9   They have different names due to Servilianus being adopted into the family of the Fabii.

10   Diod. 33.21a

11   App. *Iber.* 76–78

12   App. *Iber.* 83. The Numantines refused to accept him.

13   Cicero states that this was in absentia (Cic. *Lael.* 11).

14   App. *Iber.* 84

15   App. *Iber.* 89, twelve elephants along with archers and slingers.

16   App. *Iber.* 84–98

17   Eutrop. 4.15, Liv. *Per.* 53, Varr. RR. 2.4.1–2

18   Obseq. 16 is the only source that names the Scordisci. Other references to the war can be found in Liv. *Per* 47, Flor.2.25 and App. *Illyr* 11. There is much debate over the role the Scordisci played in the war; main protagonists or minor allies of other Pannonian tribes? See Papazoglu, F, *The Central Balkan Tribes in pre-Roman Times* (Amsterdam, 1978), pp.284–285

19   Liv. *Per.* 54

20   App. *Illyr.* 14

21   Gwyn-Morgan., M, 'Cornelius and the Pannonians': Appian, Illyrica 14, 41 and Roman History, 143–138 B.C.', *Historia* 23, 1974, pp.183–216.

22   App. *Illyr.* 10, Liv. Per. 56.

23   App. *Illyr.* 10. Liv. Per. 59

24   For a fuller account, see Bradley, K, *Slavery and Rebellion in the Roman World 140 BC- 70BC* (Indiana, 1989), pp.46–65.

25   Diod. 34/35.2.5

26   Diod. 34/35.2.15–16

27   Diod. 34/35.2.18

28   Liv. *Per.* 56, Oros. 5.9.6

29 Oros. 5.9.6, Val. Max.2.7.9 & 4.3.10, Frontin. *Str.* 4.1.26.

30 Oros. 5.9.7

31 Diod. 34/35.2.23

32 Q. Caecilius Metellus and Cn. Servilius Caepio crushed 4,000 slaves at Sinuessa, whilst a Heraclitus had to deal with that in the Athenian mines (Oros. 5.9.2, Diod. 34/35.2.18).

33 Oros. 5.9.2, Diod. 34/35.2.19

34 IGRR IV. 289, see Sherk, R., (ed.), *Rome and the Greek East to the Death of Augustus* (Cambridge, 1984), pp.39–40.

35 Ibid.

36 Strabo.14.1.38

37 CIL 1².2.2502, Plut. *TG.* 21.2, Cic. *Flacc.* 75, & *Rep.* 1.6, Val. Max. 3.2.17 & 5.3.2, Plin. *NH.* 7.120 *de vir ill.* 64.9

38 The son of King Eumenes II of Pergamum (197–159 BC) and a concubine.

39 Vell. 2.4.1

40 Vell. 2.4.1 & 2.38.5, Flor. 1.35.6, Iustin. 1.35.6, Eutrop. 4.20, Oros. 5.10.4–5, Liv. *Per.* 59, Strabo. 14.1.38, Val. Max. 3.4.5

41 Matyszak, P, *Mithridates the Great* (Barnsley, 2008).

42 Appian (*BC.* 1.34) claims that he was only dispatched by the Senate to prevent him from continuing his campaign on the issue of Italians receiving Roman citizenship.

43 Liv. *Per.* 60. See Benedict, C. 'The Romans in Southern Gaul', *American Journal of Philology* 63, 1942, pp.38–50 and Stevens, C. 'North West Europe and Roman Politics (125–118)', *Studies in Latin Literature and Roman History II* (Brussels, 1980), pp.71–97.

44 Diod. 34/35.23, Eutrop. 4.22

45 Polyb. 33.8

46 Liv. *Per.* 61

47 Liv. *Per.* 61, the figure for the Roman forces can be found in Strabo 4.1.11. The battle is also referred to by Caesar (*BG.* 1.45.2).

48 There is a brief account in Florus 1.37

49 See Stevens (1980), pp.88–92 for a discussion on the size of the Arvernian Empire at the time.

50 Vell. 1.15.5, Eutrop. 4.23, Cic. *Brut.* 160

51 Named after the consul of 122, Cn. Domitius Ahenobarbus.

52 Flor. 1.44

53 Vell. 2.6.4, Liv. *Per.* 60, Val Max. 2.8 4, Cic. *Fin.* 5.62, *Inv.* 2.105, *Phil.* 3.17, *Pis.* 95 & *Planc.* 78

54 Taylor, L, 'Forerunners of the Gracchi', *Journal of Roman Studies* 52, 1962, pp.19–27.

55   Just exactly what type of man held the tribunate is a much argued question. Old assumptions that all tribunes were members of the Senatorial oligarchy have been challenged by recent research on the holders of the office. See Sampson, G. *A Re-examination of the Office of the Tribunate of the Plebs in the Roman Republic* (494–23 B.C.), (Manchester, 2005, unpublished).

56   Anonymous tribunes in 151 BC (Liv. *Per*.48, App. *Iber*. 49). Tribunes C. Curiatius and S. Licninius in 138 BC (Cic. *Leg*. 3.20, Liv. *Per*.55 & Liv. *Oxy*.55).

57   Plut. *TG*. 8. It is not known which office Laelius was holding when he proposed it, but the tribunate is the most likely. Given that he was Praetor in 145 BC, it would have been prior to this.

58   See Astin, A, *Scipio Aemilianus* (Oxford, 1967), pp.307–310

59   Cic. *Leg*. 3.35, *Lael*. 41, *Leg. Agr*. 2.4, Liv. *Oxy. Per*. 54

60   Cic. *Brut*. 97 & 106, *Lael*. 41, *Leg*. 3.35–37, *Sest*. 103, Ascon 78C

61   Liv. *Per*.50. App. *Lib*.112.

62   Liv. *Per*.51, App. *Iber*. 84

63   He was consul in 177 and 163, and censor in 169/168 BC.

64   The first man of the Senate; the elder statesman of the house.

65   Appian choose to start his work on Rome's civil wars in 133, reflecting the widespread belief of those Romans who viewed this period. See Nagle, D, 'The Failure of the Roman Political Process in 133 B.C.', *Athenaeum* 48, 1970, pp.372–394.

66   The principal sources for this reform are; Plut. *TG*. 8–20 and App. *BC*. 1–17, Liv. *Per*. 58, Cic. *Leg Agr*. 2.10 & 2.31, *Sest*. 103, *Off*. 2.80, Diod. 34/35.6.1–2, Val. Max.7.2.6, Vell. 2.2.3, Flor. 2.2.3 & *de vir ill*. 64. There is an extensive number of modern works on the subject, see bibliography.

67   Notably the Lex Licinia of 367 BC. This in itself is a contentious point as it has recently been argued that the Licinian law was not restricted to *ager publicus*. See Rich. J, 'Lex Licinia, Lex Sempronia: B.G Niebuhr and the Limitation of Landholding in eth Roman Republic', in L. de Ligt & S. Northwood (eds.) *People, Land and Politics, Demographic Developments and the Transformation of Roman Italy 300 BC-AD 14* (Leiden, 2008), 519–572 and Sampson. G, 'The Rise and Fall of the Roman Historian: The Eighteenth Century in the Roman Historical Tradition', in J. Moore, I. Macgregor-Morris & A. Bayliss (eds.) *Reinventing History. The Enlightenment Origins of Ancient History* (London, 2009), pp.206–208.

68   App. *BC*. 1.13, C. Sempronius Gracchus and Ap. Claudius Pulcher.

69   See Briscoe, J, 'Supporters and Opponents of Tiberius Gracchus', *Journal of Roman Studies* 64, 1974, pp.125–135.

70 The implications of a tribunician veto (*intercessio*) and just how final it was is a matter of some debate. See Sampson (2005), pp.292–296.

71 Plut. *TG*. 10–12 & 14–15, Diod. 34/35.7.1, Flor. 2.2.5, Vell. 2.2.3, Oros. 5.8.3, Cic. *Brut*. 95, *Leg*. 3.24, *Mil*. 72, *ND*. 1.106

72 C. Licinius Stolo & L. Sextius Sextinius. They were elected tribunes each year between 376 and 367 BC. The caveats must be that we only have the names of just under 13% of all known tribunes, so we cannot say this for certain. There is evidence that second tribunates were held, though not consecutively. See Sampson (2005), pp.199–201.

73 Linderski, J, 'The Pontiff and the Tribune: The Death of Tiberius Gracchus', *Athenaeum* 90, 2002, pp.339–366

74 Plut. *TG*. 21.5

75 See Astin (1967), pp.227–241.

76 Liv. *Per*. 59, Oros. 5.10.9, Vell. 2.4.5, App. *BC*. 1.20, Plut. *CG*. 10.5, *de vir ill*. 58, Cic. *Mil*. 16, Val Max. 5.3.2

77 The actual law for the foundation of the colony of Iunonia was passed by a colleague of Caius', Rubrius.

78 Diod. 34/35.25.1, Ascon. 68C

79 Plut. *CG*. 5.2, App. *BC*.1.21, Flor. 2.1.7, Vell. 2.6.3. Such a practice was to become a common feature of the late Republic and a fundamental right under the emperors; the so-called bread of the 'bread and circuses' fame.

80 Roman citizenship would be given to those of Latin status, and Latin status to those of Italian status. Inhabitants of Italy fell into one of a three citizenship classes, Roman, Latin or Italian, with fewer legal and electoral rights with each lesser category.

81 Many were related to the Senatorial class, including younger sons.

82 *App. BC*. 1.23, Plut. *CG*. 9.2

83 A fundamental aspect of the tribunate was that the holders of the office were not allowed to spend a night outside of the city of Rome. Several exceptions to this rule can be found in the surviving sources (in 310 and 204 BC, Liv.9.36.14 & 29.20.4 respectively). Apparently this dispensation could be granted by the assemblies. See Sampson (2005), pp.343–347.

84 Plut. *CG*. 13.1–2, App. *BC*. 1.24, Flor. 2.3.4 Oros. 5.12.5, *de vir ill*. 65.5

85 Plut. *CG*. 13–17, App. *BC*. 1.24–26, Diod. 34/35.29–30, Liv. Per. 61, Flor. 2.3, Oros. 5.12.5–8, Val. Max. 2.8.7, *de vir ill*. 65.5–6

Chapter Two

86 The name initially comes to use from Sallust's work on the war.

87 Flor.1.36.1–2 *'Quis speraret post Carthaginem aliquod in Africa bellum'*.

88 Daly, G, *Cannae; The Experience of Battle in the Second Punic War* (London, 2002), pp.81–112.
89 App. *Iber.* 15. Liv. 24.48–49.6
90 Liv.24.48
91 Liv. 24.49.4. We must always treat the casualties given in ancient sources with caution, given their tendency to exaggerate both the size of the armies and the total losses.
92 App. *Iber.*16
93 Polyb. 6.16.
94 Liv. 27.4.5–9
95 Liv. 28.17.1–18.12, 29.23.3–9 & 30.13.3–6, App. *Iber.* 29–30
96 App. *Iber.* 37
97 Liv. 29.29.4–33.10
98 Liv. 29.31.8–11
99 Carey, B, *Hannibal's Last Battle* (Barnsley, 2007).
100 Liv. 30.12.2–3
101 Saumagne, C, *La Numidie et Rome, Masinissa et Jugurtha* (Paris, 1966) & Walsh, P, 'Massinissa', *Journal of Roman Studies* 55, 1965, pp.149–160.
102 Badian has an excellent summary and analysis of these events; Badian, E, *Foreign Clientelae (264- 70 B.C.)* (Oxford, 1958), pp.125–137.
103 App. *Pun.* 67
104 Liv. 31.19.4, 32.27.2, 36.4.8 & 43.6.13
105 IG XI.4.1115–16
106 IG II.2.968
107 C. Little, 'The Authenticity and Form of Cato's Saying "Carthago Delenda Est', *Classical Journal* 29, 1934, pp. 429–435.
108 App. *Pun.* 68.
109 App. *Pun.* 71
110 App. *Pun.* 73
111 Kahrstedt argued that Rome attacked Carthage precisely to stop Numidia annexing the remaining Carthaginian state and thus create a buffer zone in North Africa; Kahrstedt, U, *Geschichte Der Karthager, von O. Meltzer III* (Berlin, 1913), p.615.
112 Ridley, R, 'To be Taken with a Pinch of Salt: The Destruction of Carthage', *Classical Philology* 81, 1986, pp.140–146.
113 Polyb. 36.16.1–10
114 Walsh (1965), pp.152–154
115 Sall. *Iug.* 5.4–6. Trans. S. Handford (1963).
116 App. *Pun.* 106. Trans. H. White (1982).
117 Liv. *Per.* 50
118 App. *Pun.* 106. Zon 9.27. The fragments of Polybius' book 36 detail

Masinissa's death and mentions Scipio's arrangements but with no detail (Polyb. 36.16).

119   Zonaras (9.27) has Micipsa placed in charge just of the Numidian finances.

120   App. *Pun.* 111.

121   App. *Iber.* 67

122   Sall. *Iug.* 7.1–7, App. *Iber.* 89

123   Diod. 34/35.35 (Trans. F. Walton. 1984).

124   Flor. 1–1.36.2

125   Sall. *Iug.* 6.1

126   Ibid. 7.1

127   Sall. *Iugv.* 7.5–7

128   Ibid. 9.2

129   Sall. *Iug* . 11.6

130   Ibid. 11.5

131   Sall *Iug.* 14–15.1

132   Ibid. 16.4–5

133   Sall. *Iug.* 21.1–3

134   For more on Scaurus, see Bates, L, "Rex in Senatu": A Political Biography of M. Aemilius Scaurus', *Proceedings of the American Philological Society* 130, 1986, pp.251–88.

135   This point is much debated; see Badian (1958), p.139.

136   Sall. *Iug.* 25.11

137   Sall. *Iug.* 26.1–3

138   The scope and severity of this 'massacre' have long been questioned. See Morstein-Marx, R., 'The Alleged "Massacre" at Cirta and Its Consequences (Sallust Bellum Iugurthinum 26–27)', *Classical Philology* 95, 2000, pp.468–476.

139   Sall. *Iug.*25.3

140   Sall. *Iug.*27.2

141   See Oost, S, 'The Fetial Law and the Outbreak of the Jugurthine War', *American Journal of Philology* 75, 1954, pp.147–159.

142   Rich argues that this assigning of provinces is evidence that the Senate had already decided to send a consul to Numidia before the siege of Cirta ended, but we have no clear chronology of the events and given the Senate's previous reluctance to involve themselves directly, this does seem an unusual change of policy, derived from the benefits of hindsight; Rich, J, *Declaring War in the Roman republic in the period of transmarine expansion* (Brussels, 1976), pp.50–55.

Chapter Three

143 Liv. *Per.* 62.
144 Eutrop. 4.23.2
145 App. *Illyr.* 11
146 Morgan, M, 'Lucius Cotta and Metellus. Roman Campaigns in Illyria during the Late Second Century', *Athenaeum* 49, 1971, pp.271–301.
147 For a fuller discussion of this, see Syme, R, *Rome and the Balkans 80BC-AD14* (Exeter, 1999) and Papazoglu, F, *The Central Balkan Tribes in Pre-Roman Times* (Amsterdam, 1979).
148 Strabo. 7.5.12, Iust. 32.3, Liv. *Per.* 63, Athen. 6.25,App. *Illyr.* 2, Flor. 1.39
149 Polyb. 1.6.5, 2.20.6 & 4.46.1, Paus. 1.4.4, 10.3.4, 10.8.3, 23.1–10; Iustin. 24.7.8–8.10 & 32.3.6, Ampel.32.2, Liv.40.58.3, Diod.22.9.1, Cic. *Div.*1.81
150 The traditional date for the Gallic Sack of Rome is 390 BC, based on consular years. However, given that there are four years without consuls or military tribunes in office, the so-called 'Dictator Years', the dating of all events in this period has a four-year margin of error. See Drummond, A, 'The Dictator Years', *Historia* 27, 1978, pp.550–572.
151 Strabo. 7.5.12 See Alföldy, G, 'Des Territories Occupés par les Scordisques', *Acta Antiqua Academiae Scientiarum Hungaricae* 12, 1964, pp.107–127.
152 Gwyn-Morgan., M, 'Cornelius and the Pannonians': Appian, Illyrica 14, 41 and Roman History, 143–138 B.C.' *Historia* 23, 1974, pp.183–216.
153 Diod. 34/35.30. The attestation of these two events is still somewhat speculative, though given the events of 114 BC, the Scordisci do remain the prime candidates for this invasion.
154 SIG³ 700, Sherk, R., (ed.), *Rome and the Greek East to the Death of Augustus* (Cambridge, 1984) pp.51–53.
155 Papazoglu (1979), pp.295–296
156 *The Periochae of Livy* (63) states Thrace, whereas Florus (1.39) implies Macedon.
157 Flor. 1.39.4 and App. *Illyr.* 5 respectively.
158 Plut. *Mor.* 284, See Eckstein, A, 'Human Sacrifice and Fear of Military Disaster in Republican Rome', *American Journal of Ancient History* 7, 1982, pp.69–95.
159 Flor. 1.39, Fest. It has been argued that both sources mistake this Didius for a late commander in Macedon and that there was no commander between Cato and Metellus. However, given that we have two clear sources stating this and that there was no need for this Didius to be a

consul or governor, merely an ad-hoc commander, the evidence favours his inclusion here.

160   Vell. 2.8.2; Eutrop. 4.25.1

161   See Papazoglu (1979), pp.288–291.

162   The tribune who had opposed C. Gracchus, in 122 BC.

163   Flor. 1.39

164   Amm. Marc. 27.4.10. This can also be found in Festus *Brev*.9.2 and Iord. *Rom*. 219

165   C. Scribonius Curio between 76 and 73 BC, see Syme (1999), pp.134–136.

166   Levick, B, 'Cicero, Brutus 43. 159 ff., and the Foundation of Narbo Martius', *Classical Quarterly* 21,1971, pp. 170–179

167   Frontin. *Str*. 4.3.13, *de vir ill*. 72.7

168   Strabo. 5.214, App. *Gall*. 13, Vell.9.1

169   Plin. *NH*. 37.35–36. See Cunliffe, B, *The Extraordinary Voyage of Pytheas the Greek* (New York, 2001).

170   Plut. *Mar*. 11

171   Faux, D, (2007) 'The Cimbri Tribe of Northern Jutland, Denmark, During the La Tene Period: 400 BC to 15 AD', (2008a) 'The Cimbri Tribe of Jutland, Denmark: Their Origins and Descendants as Indicated by the Archaeological, Historical and Genetic Data', & (2008b) 'The Cimbri of Denmark, the Norse and Danish Vikings and Y-DNA Haplogroup R–U152 '. All can be found on the internet.

172   Plut, *Mar*. 11. Homer. *Odyssey*. 9.14.19, Herodotus. 4.11–14

173   Plut. *Mar*. 11.5, Strabo. 7.2.1–2

174   Plut. *Mar*. 11.2

175   Aug. *Res Gest*. 5.26, Strabo. 7.2.1

176   Liv.5.34

177   Strabo. 7.2.2, based on Poseidonius. Strabo (4.43) and Caesar *BG*. 5.4 also preserve an encounter between the Belgae and the Cimbri and Teutones, with the Belgae winning the encounter.

178   Faux (2008b), p.42.

179   Appian (*Gall*.13) merely states that he took up position where the pass was the narrowest without giving us a specific location.

180   Ibid

181   Ibid

182   Plut. *Mar*. 16.5

183   The seemingly erratic reports of the Cimbri throughout this period may be the result of there being more than one tribal group.

Chapter Four

184 Given the fragmentary records for office-holding (except the consulship), we can only say that he is the first recorded one.
185 Cic. *Brut.* 128. The date of his tribunate is uncertain, though Broughton argued for 121 BC; Broughton, T, *Magistrates of the Roman Republic 1* (New York, 1952), p.524.
186 Oros. 5.15.6
187 Sall. *Iug.* 28.4
188 Ibid. 28.6–7
189 Sall. *Iug.* 29.1–2
190 Ibid. 31.1–29
191 Sall. *Iug.* 32.2–4
192 Ibid. 35.1–6
193 Sall. *Iug.*35.2
194 Ibid. 36.1–4.
195 From the consul Q. Fabius Maximus Verrucosus in the Second Punic War.
196 Sall. *Iug.*37.1–3
197 Orosius (5.15.6) names the city as Calama, which may be the Roman name for the city of Suthul.
198 Sall. *Iug.*38.4–10
199 Oros. 5.15.4
200 Oros. 5.15.5
201 Sall. *Iug.*39.4
202 See Hayne, L, 'The Condemnation of Sp. Postumius Albinus', *Acta Classica* 24, 1981, pp. 61–70.
203 Ibid. 40.1–5

Chapter Five

204 It was custom for the choice to be made by the drawing of lots.
205 Sall. *Iug.* 65.1
206 Ibid. 46.4
207 Possible the modern river Wäd Mellag.
208 Sall. *Iug.* 48.3–49.2.
209 Ibid. 49.6.
210 Sall. *Iug.* 50.4–5.
211 Ibid. 52.2
212 Sall. *Iug.*51.4

213   Ibid. 53.4
214   Sall. *Iug.*54.4
215   Ibid. 54.6
216   Sall. *Iug.* 54.10
217   Ibid. 56.3–6
218   Sall. *Iug.* 58.4–7
219   Ibid. 61.5
220   Sall. *Iug.* 66.3
221   Ibid. 69.3
222   Sall. *Iug.* 69.4
223   Plut. *Mar.* 8
224   Sall. *Iug.*73.1
225   Ibid. 74.2–3
226   Pliny (*NH.* 5.17) names three separate tribes: the Autoteles, the Baniurae and the Nesimi.
227   Sall. *Iug.* 80.1
228   Liv. 23.18.1
229   Bocchus was Jugurtha's son in law; Sall. *Iug.* 80.6, Plut. *Mar.* 10
230   Sall. *Iug.* 80.4
231   See Paul, G, *A Historical Commentary on Sallust's Bellum Jugurthinum* (Liverpool, 1984), pp.192–194. Also see Pelham, H, 'The Chronology of the Jugurthine War', *American Journal of Philology* 7, 1877, pp.91–94, Canter, H, 'The Chronology of Sallust's Jugurtha', *Classical Journal* 6, 1911, pp.290–295 & Holroyd, M, 'The Jugurthine War: Was Marius or Metellus the Real Victor?', *Journal of Roman Studies* 18, 1928, pp.1–20.
232   Sall. *Iug.* 74
233   Sall. *Iug.* 83.1
234   Ibid. 88.3–5
235   Flor.1.36.2

Chapter Six

236   Flor.1.38.1–4
237   Liv. *Per.* 65
238   Vell. 2.12.2, Eutrop.4.27.5
239   Cic. *Corn* 2, Ascon.80C
240   Evans, R, 'Rome's Cimbric Wars (114–101 BC) and their Impact in the Iberia Peninsula', *Acta Classica* 48, 2005, p41.
241   Ibid.
242   Oros. 5.15.23–24

243 Caes. *BG.* 1.7.4 7 & 1.12.5, though he is the only source who mentions this.
244 Ascon. 68C (Trans. S. Squires, 1990).
245 Which forms part of the border between Greece/Turkey and Bulgaria.
246 Flor. 1.39
247 Amm. Marc. 27.4.10
248 Fest. *Brev.* 9.2
249 Frontin. *Str.* 2.4.3
250 Vell. 2.8.3
251 Liv. *Per.* 65
252 Eutrop. 4.27
253 CIL. I² 692, ILS 8887, SIG³, ILLRP 337, though the Greek and Latin versions differ slightly in the wording.

Chapter Seven

254 Evans, R, *Gaius Marius, A Political Biography* (Pretoria,1994), pp.18–51.
255 This was an important distinction during this period of Roman history, as it was not until 89 BC that all Italians received Roman citizenship. Marius, however, was born a Roman citizen.
256 Evans (1994), p. 23.
257 Wiseman, T, *New Men in the Roman Senate 139 B.C.-A.D.14* (London, 1971).
258 Plut. *Mar.* 3.2
259 Evans (1994), pp.28–32.
260 Sall. *Iug.* 63.5
261 Val Max. 6.9.14
262 Ibid, also see CIL.I²1.195
263 Val Max. 6.9.14
264 Plut. *Mar.* 4.1
265 Cic. *Leg.* 3.38–39
266 Plut. *Mar.* 4.2. See Bicknell, P, 'Marius, the Metelli and the Lex Maria Tabellaria', *Latomus* 28, 1969, pp.327–348.
267 L. Caecilius Metellus 'Delmaticus' was consul this year.
268 Plut. *Mar.* 4.3
269 Plut. *Mar.* 4.4. There is no direct evidence that it was tribunician, but that is the most likely source.
270 Two places each. Plutarch states that he lost both elections on the same day. This has been widely dismissed on account of it being considered

both impractical to hold both elections on the same day and that this was not the custom. See Evans (1994), pp.44–45.

271 Plut. *Mar.* 5.2–5

272 Plut. *Mar.* 6.1

273 See Carney, T, *A Political Biography of C. Marius* (Assen, 1961), p.23.

274 The exact length of his command in Spain is unknown and the source of some debate, again see Evans, 1994, pp.54–57.

275 Plut. *Mar.* 6.2.

276 Evans (1994), pp.57–62.

277 Sall. *Iug.* 40.1–5.

278 Farney, G, 'The Fall of the Priest C. Sulpicius Galba and the First consulship of Marius', *Memoirs of the American Academy of Rome* 42, 1997, pp.23–37.

279 See Sall. *Iug.* 63–65 & Plut. *Mar.* 7.2–8.3

280 Sall. *Iug.* 63–65

281 App. *Pun.* 112

282 Plut. *Mar.* 8.1–2

283 Sall. *Iug.* 73.5

284 Ibid. 85.1–50. See Skard, E, 'Marius' speech in Sallust, Jug. chap.85', *Symbolae Osloenses* 21, 1941, pp. 98–102 & Carney, T, 'Once again Marius' speech after election in 108 B.C.', *Symbolae Osloenses* 35, 1959, pp.63–70.

285 Cic. *Prov. Con.* 19

286 Sall. *Iug.* 84.2, Plut. *Mar.*9.1, Diod. 36.3.1. Diodorus does date this to the Cimbric War, c.105 BC, but Sallust places it in 107 BC.

287 Sall. *Iug.* 84.2, Plut. *Mar.* 9.1

288 Evans (1994), pp. 75–76.

289 Sall. *Iug.* 91.6–7, not that it was particularly uncommon for the era.

290 The modern Moulouya, the western border of Algeria.

291 Sall. *Iug.* 92.5–94.6

292 Plut. *Mar.* 10.2–3

293 Oros. 5.15.9

294 See Canter (1911) & Holroyd (1928).

295 We are told the time of year, with the siege near Muluccha being the apparent last act of the campaigning season before Marius retired to winter quarters. From the timescale that this process must have taken, the year is assumed to be 106 BC, though this is never explicitly stated in Sallust.

296 Sall. *Iug.* 87.4

297 Ibid. 88.3–4

298 Again, the date is implied rather than explicitly stated.

299 Sall. *Iug*.97.2
300 Ibid. 88.1 the triumph is detailed on the inscribed list of triumphs as well as Vell. 2.11.2, Gell. 12.9.4, Eutrop. 4.27.6, *de vir ill*. 62.1
301 Sall. *Iug*. 97.4–99.3
302 Oros. 5.15.9–18
303 This story is also repeated by Frontinus (*Str*. 2.4.10) most likely taken from Sallust's' own account.
304 Sall. *Iug*. 101.8–11
305 Oros. 5.15.18
306 Sall. *Iug*. 104.5
307 Ibid. 106.2–3
308 Sall. *Iug*. 108.3
309 Ibid.
310 Though if all were murdered it is not clear how the Romans got hold of Jugurtha's sons at the same time. The handover was captured in both a signet ring which Sulla had commissioned, as well as a statue in Rome commissioned by Bocchus in the 90s (Plut. *Sull*. 3.44 & 6.1–2 respectively).
311 Plut. *Mar*. 12.3–4
312 Oros. 5.15.19. Jugurtha's sons were spared and lived in exile in Italy (App. *BC*. 1.42).
313 Caes. *BA*. 56.3
314 See note 305.
315 See Holroyd, M, 'The Jugurthine War: Was Marius or Metellus the Real Victor?', *Journal of Roman Studies* 18, 1928, 1–20 and Parker, V, 'Sallust and the Victor of the Jugurthine War', *Tyche* 16, 2001, 111–125.

Chapter Eight

316 Oros. 5.15.25, Strabo. 4.1.13, Gell. 3.9.7, Iustin. 32.3.9–11
317 Justin's epitome of Pompeius Trogus gives a figure of 110,000 talents of silver and 1,500,000 talents of gold. Orosius puts it as 100,000 talents of gold and 110,000 talents of silver. Strabo, quoting Poseidonius, stated it as 15,000 talents in total.
318 Dio. 27, fr.90.
319 Brunt, P, *Italian Manpower 225 BC–AD 14* (Oxford, 1971), pp.430 & 685.
320 Dio. 27, fr.91.
321 Liv. *Per*. 67 Gran.Lic 17.
322 Plut. *Mar*. 25.2
323 Oros. 5.16.2

324   The date comes from Plutarch (*Luc.27*), when the anniversary of the battle was mentioned as a bad omen.

325   Gran. Lic. 17

326   Dio.27.fr.91.1–4

327   Oros.5.16.1–7

328   Liv. 67

329   Eutrop.5.1.1

330   Vegit. *RM*.3.10

331   Plut. *Sert*. 3.1

332   Plut. *Mar*. 11.1 & 11.8

333   Liv. *Per*.67, Oros. 5.16.7, Gran. Lic. 17, Diod. 36.1

334   See note 325.

335   Polyb. 3.11, though this figure has been disputed as is in itself inconsistent in Polybius' own works, see Daly. (2002), pp.201–202.

336   Liv. 22.49.15, Liv. *Per*. 67, albeit the latter figure is taken from the epitome of Livy's history, not the history itself.

337   Diod. 34/35.37

338   Gran Lic.21

339   Val. Max.2.3.2

340   Sall. *Iug*. 114.1–2

Chapter Nine

341   Plut. *Mar*. 12.5

342   He would have been made a senator at the next census after his quaestorship, the office giving him the right to be enrolled in the Senate.

343   Strabo 4.1.8

344   The notable exception to this is Evans' recent article; Evans, R, 'Rome's Cimbric Wars (114–101 BC) and their Impact in the Iberia Peninsula', *Acta Classica* 48, 2005, pp.37–56.

345   Liv. *Per*. 67

346   Evans (2005), p.52.

347   Eutrop. 4.27.5, Val. Max. 6.19.3

348   Obseq. 42

349   This is most usually dated as c. 113/112, see Broughton.

350   App. *Iber*. 99

351   Ibid. 100

352   Liv. *Per*.67

353   The tone of the *Epitome of Livy* evidence leads us to the conclusion that the Cimbri were not defeated by loyalist tribes under Roman command.

354 Diod. 36.3.2, though this seems to replicate a request made in 107 BC (see chapter seven). Diodorus clearly states that it was for the war against the Cimbri though he could have been mistaken himself.

355 Frontin. *Str.* 4.2.2

356 Strabo. 4.1.8

357 Frontin. *Str.* 1.2.6

358 In the 190s and 180s BC.

359 Plut. *Sull.* 4. Also see Keaveney, A. (1981). 'Sulla, the Marsi, and the Hirpini', *Classical Philology* 76, pp.292–296.

360 Plut. *Mar.*14.7

361 Liv. *Per.* 67

362 This is the division of the tribes as stated by Livy (*Per.*68) and Plutarch (*Mar.*15.4–5). Orosius (5.16.9), however, has the Tigurini and the Ambrones and the Cimbri and Teutones. Given the uncertain role played by the Tigurini, in the latter stages of the war and the certainty of the other, earlier, sources, we must assume that Orosius has made an error in his understanding of the tribal dispositions.

363 Fest. 15L

364 Strabo. 7.2.2

365 Oros.5.16. 9

366 Plut. *Sert.*3.2–4. Plutarch states that Sertorius infiltrated their camp in Gallic dress and using the Gallic tongue, more evidence for Gallic origin of the Cimbri.

367 See note 352.

368 Oros.5.16.10

369 Plut. *Mar.* 16.1–2

370 Ibid. 18.1

371 18 miles north of Massilia

372 Plut. *Mar.* 18.2–3

373 Ibid. 18.4

374 The presence of the Ligurians is interesting, especially given Marius' suspicions of them earlier in this campaign (Frontin. *Str.* 1.2.6).

375 Plut. *Mar.*19.4–5

376 Oros.5.16.11

377 Frontin. *Str.* 2.7.12

378 Oros. 5.16.11

379 Plut. *Mar.* 20.5

380 Ibid.

381 Plut. *Mar.*21.2

382 Oros.5.16.12

383 Plut. *Mar.* 21.3

384   Ibid. 24.4
385   Flor. 1.38.10
386   Plut. *Mar.*22.3

Chapter Ten

387   Q. Lutatius Catulus, a Roman commander in 241BC.
388   Cic. *Planc.* 5.12
389   Plut. *Sull.* 2.
390   This has been interpreted both as Marius trying to get rid of Sulla from his own staff due to the supposed enmity caused over the capture of Jugurtha or Marius wanting to make up for Catulus' inexperience. See Cagniart, P, 'L. Cornelius Sulla's Quarrel with C. Marius at the time of the Germanic Invasions (104–101 B.C.)', *Athenaeum* 67, 1989, pp.139–149.
391   Plut. *Sull.*4.3
392   Lewis, R, 'Catulus and the Cimbri, 102 B.C.', *Hermes* 102, 1974, pp.91–92
393   Liv. *Per.*68
394   Plut. *Mar.* 23.2
395   Frontin. *Str.* 1.5.3
396   Lewis (1974), pp.99–101.
397   Plut. *Mar.* 23.2
398   Liv. *Per.* 68, Frontin. *Str.* 1.5.3
399   Plut. *Mar.* 23.4
400   Ibid. 23.5
401   Plut. *Mar.* 23.6
402   Liv. *Per.* 68
403   Plin. *NH.* 22.11, Frontin. *Str.* 4.1.13, Val. Max. 5.8.4, Ampel. 19.10, *de vir ill.* 72.10
404   Plut. *Mar.* 24.1
405   Flor. 1.38.14
406   Plut. *Mar.*24.3
407   Vell. 2.12.5, Flor. 1.38. 14, Liv. *Per.* 68, Plut. *Mar.*25.3 *de vir. Ill.* 67
408   Plut. *Mar.* 24.4
409   Plut. *Mar.* 25.6, Frontin. *Str.*2.2.8
410   Carney, T, 'Marius Choice of Battle-field in the Campaign of 101', *Athenaeum* 36, 1958, pp.229–237.
411   Plut. *Mar.* 25.4
412   Plut. *Mar.* 25.4, Oros. 5.16.14

413 Plut. *Mar*.25.7
414 Ibid. 26.1–2
415 Plut. *Mar*. 27.1–2
416 Liv. *Per*. 68, Vell. 2.12.5, Eutrop. 5.2.2
417 Flor. 1.38.18
418 Oros. 5.16.22
419 Val. Max.8.15.7
420 Orosius actually comments upon the Roman mistreatment of the civilians, which involved some method of scalping.
421 Oros.5.16.9
422 Flor.1.38.19
423 Eutrop.5.2.2
424 Polyb. 35.1.1–2

Chapter Eleven

425 Especially given that Romans only developed their own coinage in the third century BC.
426 Cicero states that the level is 1,500 *asses* (Rep. 2.40). It has long been argued that this limit predated Marius' time. See Gabba, E, *Republican Rome; The Army and the Allies* (Oxford, 1976), p.6.
427 Polybius giving this value in drachmas not asses is merely an added complication to this question.
428 Liv. 22.11.8
429 Sall. *Iug*. 86.2–3
430 Plut. *Mar*. 9
431 Flor. 1.36.13
432 Val. Max.2.3.1
433 Exsuper. 2. It can also be found in Lydus. (*de mag*. 1.48).
434 This is repeated in the work of the Pseudo-Quintilian (3.5)
435 Gell. 16.10.14
436 Sall. *Iug*. 87.1–2, Evans, R, 'Resistance at Home: The Evasion of Military Service in Italy during the Second Century B.C.', in D.Yuge & M. Doi (eds.) *Forms of Control and Subordination in Antiquity* (Leiden, 1988), p. 132.
437 Rosenstein, N, *Rome at War* (Chapel Hill, 2004), pp.26–56.
438 Rawson, E, 'The Literary Sources for the Pre-Marian Army', *Papers of the British School of Rome* 39, 1971, pp.13–31.
439 Frontin. *Str*. 4.1.7. This can also be found in Festus (267L)
440 Plut. *Mar*. 13.1

441   Plut. *Ant.* 38

442   Plut. *Mar.* 25.1–2

443   Plin. *NH.* 10.5.16

444   Bell, M, 'Tactical Reform in the Roman Republican Army', *Historia* 14, 1965, p.404.

445   Parker, H, *The Roman Legions* (Cambridge, 1928), p.27.

446   Polyb. 11.23.1 & 11.33.1. An added complication is that the text is Greek not Latin.

447   Liv.25.39.1, 27.18.10, 28.13.8, 28.14.17, 28.23.8, 28.25.15, 28.33.12, 34.12.6, 34.14.1, 34.14.7, 34.14.10, 34.15.1, 34.19.9, 34.19.10, 34.20.3 & 34.20.5. Sall. *Iug.* 49.2. See Bell (1965), pp.404–409

Appendix One

448   Plut. *Mar.*28.3–4

449   If it was indeed Numidicus, it would technically have been illegal for him to hold a second consulship so soon after his first, unless he too received special exemption from the assembly.

450   Vell. 2.12.6

451   Plut. *Mar.* 28.5

452   Liv. *Per.* 69

453   After Romulus, and M. Furius Camillus, who defeated the Gauls that had sacked Rome in c.390/386 BC (see Plutarch's Life of Camillus).

454   Plut. *Mar.* 27.4–5

455   Ibid.27.6

456   Plut. *Mar.* 31

457   Diod. 36.12, Cic. *Sest.* 39, *Har Resp.* 43.

458   Though there is no clear chronology of the measures he undertook during his first two tribunates and many are interchangeable depending upon ones' own preferences.

459   Plut. *Mar.*28.4

460   Vell. 2.12.6

461   Plut. *Mar.* 30.2. The murder of Memmius can also be found in Liv. *Per.* 69 and *de vir ill.* 73.5

462   Evans (1994), pp.158–159.

463   See Beness, J, 'The Urban Unpopularity of Lucius Appuleius Saturninus', *Antichton* 25, 1991, pp.33–61.

464   App. *BC.* 1.32, Plut. *Mar.* 30.3. See also Seager, R, 'The Date of Saturninus' Murder', *Classical Review* 17, 1967, pp.9–10, Badian, E, 'The Death of Saturninus, Studies in Chronology and Prosopography', *Chiron*

14, 1984, pp.101–147 and Evans, R, 'Saturninus and Glaucia: a quest for power', *Questioning Reputations* (Pretoria, 2004), pp.99–131.

465 Oros. 5. 17.6–10
466 Vell. 2.12.6
467 Plut. *Mar.* 31.1
468 Ibid. 32.2
469 App. *BC.* 1.33; Oros.5.17.11
470 Dio. fr.28. He had been a former follower of Saturninus and Glaucia, who had been stripped of his equestrian status by Metellus as censor.
471 For other reasons as to why Marius was out in the east see Broughton, T. (1953), pp.210–211.

Appendix Two

472 Different versions of the fragments of Diodorus preserve different names. Diod. 36.8.4
473 Diod. 36.8.
474 Diod. 36.10.1, Flor. 2.711
475 Diod. 36.10.2–3
476 See Sherk (1984), pp.58–66.

Appendix Three

477 Those with Roman citizenship not Latin or Italian status, see Sherwin White, A, *The Roman Citizenship* (Oxford, 2nd Edition, 1973).
478 Brunt, P, *Italian Manpower* 225 BC–AD 14 (Oxford, 1971), pp.13–14.
479 See Evans (1988), pp.121–140.
480 Liv. 1.43, Dion. Hal. 4.16–21, Polyb. 6.19.3, Cic. *Rep.* 2.40, Gell. 16.10.10. See Rathbone, D, 'The census qualifications of the assidui and the prima classis', in H. Sancisci-Weerdenburg (ed.) *De Agricultura: In Memoriam Pieter Willem de Neeve* (Amsterdam, 1993), pp.121–152.
481 Gell. 6.13.My thanks to Professor Tim Cornell for his thoughts on this fragment.
482 Frederiksen, M, 'The contribution of archaeology to the agrarian problem in the Gracchan period', *Dialoghi di archeologia* 4–5, 1970/71, pp.330–357.
483 See Morley, N, 'The Transformation of Italy, 225–28 B.C.', *Journal of Roman Studies* 91, 2001, pp.50–62 and de Ligt, L, 'Poverty and

demography. The case of the Gracchan land reforms", *Mnemosyne* 57, 2004, 725–757.

484   Keaveney, A, *The Army in the Roman Revolution* (London, 2007), p.20.

485   Evans (1988), pp.121–140.

486   See note 426.

Appendix Four

487   Van Ooteghem, J, *Les Caecilii Metelli de la République* (Brussels, 1967).

488   Polyb. 2.19.8. Also see Gwyn Morgan, M, 'The Defeat of L. Metellus Denter at Arretium', *Classical Quarterly* 22, 1972, pp. 309–325 and Salmon, E, 'Rome's Battles with Etruscans and Gauls in 284–282 B.C.', *Classical Philology* 30, 1935, pp. 23–31.

489   Valerius Maximus (8.13.2) states that he served for 22 years and was elected four years after his consulship.

490   See Wiseman, T, 'The Last of the Metelli', *Latomus* 24, 1965, pp.52–61.

Appendix Five

491   Matthews, V, 'The Libri Punici of King Hiempsal', *American Journal of Philology* 93, 1972, pp.330–335.

492   Hendrickson, G, 'The Memoirs of Rutilius Rufus', *Classical Philology* 28, 1933, pp.153–175.

Bibliography

Roman Background

Astin, A, *Scipio Aemilianus* (Oxford, 1967)

Badian, E, *Foreign Clientelae* (264–70 BC) (Oxford, 1958)

_____, 'From the Gracchi to Sulla', *Historia* 11, 1962, 197–245

_____, 'Tiberius Gracchus and the Beginning of the Roman Revolution', *Aufstieg und Niedergang der römischen Welt 1.1*, 1972, 668–731

Balsdon, J, *Romans and Aliens* (London, 1979)

Benedict, C, 'The Romans in Southern Gaul', *American Journal of Philology* 63, 1942, 38–50

Bernstein, A, *Tiberius Sempronius Gracchus, Tradition and Apostasy* (Ithaca, 1978)

Bispham, E, *From Asculum to Actium* (Oxford, 2007)

Boren, H, *The Gracchi* (New York, 1968)

Bradley, K, *Slavery and Rebellion in the Roman World 140 BC – 70 BC* (Indiana, 1989)

Braund, D, *Rome and the Friendly King; the Character of Client Kingship* (London, 1984)

Broughton, T, *Magistrates of the Roman Republic Volumes I and II* (New York, 1952)

Daly, G, *Cannae; The Experience of Battle in the Second Punic War* (London, 2002)

de Ligt, L, 'Studies in Legal and Agrarian History IV: Roman Africa in 111 B.C.', *Mnemosyne* 54, 2001, 182–217

Dyson, S, *The Creation of the Roman Frontier* (Princeton, 1985)

Earl, D, *Tiberius Gracchus. A Study in Politics* (Brussels, 1963)

Evans, R, *Questioning Reputations* (Pretoria, 2004)

Gargola, D, *Lands, Laws & Gods; Magistrates & Ceremony in the Regulation of Public Lands in Republican Rome* (Chapel Hill, 1995)

_____, 'The Gracchan Reform and Appian's Representation of an Agrarian Crisis', in L. de Ligt & S. Northwood (eds.) *People, Land and Politics,*

Demographic Developments and the Transformation of Roman Italy 300 BC-AD 14 (Leiden, 2008), 487–518

Harris, W, *War and Imperialism in Republican Rome 327 – 70 B.C.* (Oxford, 1979)

Nagle, D, 'The Failure of the Roman Political Process on 133 B.C.', *Athenaeum* 48, 1970, 372–394.

Rich, J, *Declaring War in the Roman republic in the period of transmarine expansion* (Brussels, 1976)

———, 'Lex Licinia, Lex Sempronia: B.G Niebuhr and the Limitation of Landholding in the Roman Republic', in L. de Ligt & S. Northwood (eds.) *People, Land and Politics, Demographic Developments and the Transformation of Roman Italy 300 BC-AD 14* (Leiden, 2008), 519–572

Rich, J. & Shipley, G (eds.), *War and Society in the Roman World* (London, 1993)

Richardson, J, *Hispaniae; Spain and the Development of Roman Imperialism, 218–82 BC* (Cambridge, 1986)

Rosenstein, N, *Imperatores Victi; Military Defeat and Aristocratic Competition in the Middle and Late Republic* (Berkeley, 1990)

Sampson G, *A Re-examination of the Office of the Tribunate of the Plebs in the Roman Republic (494–23 B.C.* (Manchester, 2005, unpublished)

———, 'The Rise and Fall of the Roman Historian: The Eighteenth Century in the Roman Historical Tradition', in J. Moore, I. Macgregor-Morris & A. Bayliss (eds.) *Reinventing History. The Enlightenment Origins of Ancient History* (London, 2009), 187–218

Sands, P, *The Client Princes of the Roman Empire Under the Republic* (Cambridge, 1908)

Scochat, Y, *Recruitment and the Programme of Tiberius Gracchus* (Brussels, 1980)

Seager, R, (ed.), *The Crisis of the Roman Republic* (Cambridge, 1969)

Sherk, R, (ed.), *Rome and the Greek East to the Death of Augustus* (Cambridge, 1984)

Stevens, C, 'North West Europe and Roman Politics (125–118)', *Studies in Latin Literature and Roman History II* (Brussels, 1980), 71–97

Stockton, D, *The Gracchi* (Oxford, 1979)

Syme, R, *Rome and the Balkans 80BC-AD14* (Exeter, 1999)

Taylor, L, 'Forerunners of the Gracchi', *Journal of Roman Studies* 52, 1962, 19–27

Van Ooteghem, J, *Les Caecilii Metelli de la République* (Brussels, 1967)

Williams, J, *Beyond the Rubicon, Romans and Gauls in Republican Italy* (Oxford, 2001)

Wiseman, T, *New Men in the Roman Senate* (Oxford, 1971)

———, *Remembering the Roman People* (Oxford, 2009)

Numidia and the Jugurthine Wars

Allen, W, 'The Source of Jugurtha's Influence in the Roman Senate', *Classical Philology* 33, 1938, 90–92

Berthier, A, Charlier, R, & Juliet, J, 'Le Bellum Jugurthinum de Sallusts et le Problème de Cirta', *Recueil des Notices et Memoires de la Société Archéologique Historique et Géographique* 67, 1950, 1–144.

Canter, H, 'The Chronology of Sallust's Jugurtha', *Classical Journal* 6, 1911, 290–295.

Cameron, H., & Parker, V, 'A Mobile People? Sallust's Presentation of the Numidians and their Manner of Fighting', *Parola del Passato* 15, 1960, 33–57

Classen, J-M, 'Sallust's Jugurtha: Revel or Freedom Fighter? On Crossing Crocodile Infested Waters', *Classical World* 86, 1993, 273–297

Dijkstra, T., & Parker, V, 'Through many glasses darkly, Sulla and the End of the Jugurthine War', *Wiener Studien* 120, 2007, 137–160

Earl, D, 'Sallust and the Senate's Numidian Policy', *Latomus* 24, 1965, 532–536

Fentress, E, *Numidia and the Roman Army* (Oxford, 1979)

———, 'Romanizing the Berbers', *Past & Present* 190, 2006, 3 –33

Fiedler, P, 'Die beiden überfallschlachten auf Metellus und Marius im Bellum Iugurthinum des Sallust', *Wiener Studien* 78, 1965, 108–127

Gilbert, C, 'Five Passages in Sallust's "Bellum Jugurthinum"', *Mnemosyne* 28, 1975, 67–69

Green, C, 'De Africa et eius incolis: The Function of Geography and Ethnography in Sallust's History of the Jugurthine War (BJ 17–19)', *Ancient World* 24, 1993, 185–197

Hawthorn, J, *Sallust: Rome and Jugurtha* (Bristol, 1979)

Hayne, L, 'The Condemnation of Sp. Postumius Albinus', *Acta Classica* 24, 1981, 61–70

Holroyd, M, 'The Jugurthine War: Was Marius or Metellus the Real Victor?', *Journal of Roman Studies* 18, 1928, 1–20

Kahrstedt, U, *Geschichte der Karthager, von O. Meltzer III* (Berlin, 1913)

Kraus, C, 'Jugurthine Disorder', *The Limits of Historiography* (Leiden, 1999), 217–247

Kurita, N, 'Who Supported Jugurtha?, The Jugurthine War as a Social Revolution', in T. Yuge & M. Doi (eds.) *Forms of Control and Subordination in Antiquity* (Leiden, 1988), 164–168

Lafaye, G, 'L'adoption de Jugurtha dans Salluste', in *Mélenages Boissier. Recueil de Mémoires concernant La Littérature et les Antiquités Romaines dédié a Gaston Boissier* (Paris, 1903), 315–317

Levene, D, 'Sallust's Jugurtha: An 'Historical Fragment'' *Journal of Roman Studies* 82, 1992, 53–70

Matthews, V, 'The Libri Punici of King Hiempsal', *American Journal of Philology* 93, 1972, 330–335

Morstein-Marx, R, 'The Alleged "Massacre" at Cirta and Its Consequences (Sallust Bellum Iugurthinum 26–27)', *Classical Philology* 95, 2000, 468–476

_____, The Myth of Numidian Origins in Sallust's African Excursus (Iugurtha 17.7–18.12), *American Journal of Philology* 122, 2001, 179–200

Oost, S, 'The Fetial Law and the Outbreak of the Jugurthine War', *American Journal of Philology* 75, 1954, 147–159

Parker, V, 'Sallust and the Victor of the Jugurthine War', *Tyche* 16, 2001, 111–125

Paul, G, *A Historical Commentary on Sallust's Bellum Jugurthinum* (Liverpool, 1984)

Pelham, H, 'The Chronology of the Jugurthine War', *American Journal of Philology* 7, 1877, 91–94

Radnorthy-Alfoldi, M, 'Die Geschichte des Numidischen Konigreches und seiner Nachfolger', in H. Horn & C. Ruger (eds.) *Die Numider* (Bonn, 1979), 43–74

Rossetti, S, 'La Numidia e Cartagine fre la II e la III Guerra Punica', *Parola del Passato* 15, 1960, 337–353

Saumagne, C, *La Numidie et Rome, Masinissa et Jugurtha* (Paris, 1966)

Scanlon, T, 'Textual Geography in Sallust's The War with Jugurtha', *Ramus* 17, 1988, 138–175

Sumner, G, 'Scaurus and the Mamilian Inquisition', Phoenix *1, 1976, 73–75*

Shaw, B, 'Fear and Loathing: The Nomad Menace and Roman Africa', in C. Wells (ed.), *Roman Africa: The Vanier Lectures 1980* (Ottawa, 1982), 29–50

Suerbaum, W, 'Rex Ficta Locutus est: Zur Beurteilung der Adherbal- und der Micipsa-Rede in Sallusts "Bellum Iugurthimum"', *Hermes* 92, 1964, 85–106

Summers, W, 'A Note on Sallust's Jugurtha', *Classical Review* 17, 1903, 32–34

Thompson, L, 'Carthage and the Massylian "Coup d'Etat" of 206 B.C.', *Historia* 30, 1981, 120–126

Von Fritz, K, 'Sallust and the Attitude of the Roman Nobility at the Time of the Wars against Jugurtha (112–105 B.C.)', *Transactions and Proceedings of the American Philological Association* 74, 1943, 134–168

Vretska, K, *Studien zu Sallusts Bellum Jugurthinum* (Wien, 1955)

Walsh, P, 'Massinissa', *Journal of Roman Studies* 55, 1965, 149–160

Wiedemann, T, 'Sallust's *Jugurtha*: Concord, Discord and the Digressions', *Greece & Rome* 40, 1993, 48–57

The Northern Wars

Alföldy, G, 'Des Territories Occupés par les Scordisques', *Acta Antiqua Academiae Scientiarum Hungaricae* 12, 1964, 107–127

Beckers, W, 'Die Völkerschaften der Teutonen und Kimbern in der Neueren Forshung', *Rheinisches Museum für Philologie* 88, 1939, 52–122

Cagniart, P, 'L. Cornelius Sulla's Quarrel with C. Marius at the time of the Germanic Invasions (104–101 B.C.), *Athenaeum* 67, 1989, 139–149

Carney, T, 'Marius Choice of Battle-field in the Campaign of 101', *Athenaeum* 36, 1958, 229–237

Demougeot, E, 'L'invasion des Cimbres-Teutones-Ambrones et le Romains', *Latomus* 37, 1978, 910–938

Donnadieu, A, 'Campagne de Marius dans la Gaule Narbonnaise (104–102 av. J.-C.)', *Revue des Études Anciennes* 56, 1954, 281–296

Ellis, P, *Celt and Roman, The Celts in Italy* (London, 1998)

Elston, S, *The Earliest Relations between Celts and Germans* (London, 1934)

Evans, R, 'Rome's Cimbric Wars (114–101 BC) and their Impact in the Iberia Peninsula', *Acta Classica* 48, 2005, 37–56

———, 'Gaius and Marus in Iberia and Gaul: Family Affairs and Provincial Clients', *Acta Classica* 50, 2008, 77–90

Hansen, G, 'Das Datum des Schlact bei Vercellae', *Klio* 67, 1985, 588

Keaveney, A, 'Sulla, the Marsi, and the Hirpini', *Classical Philology* 76, 1981, 292–296

Lewis, R, 'Catulus and the Cimbri, 102 B.C.', *Hermes* 102, 1974, 90–109

Morgan, M, 'Lucius Cotta and Metellus. Roman Campaigns in Illyria during the Late Second Century', *Athenaeum* 49, 1971, 271–301

———, '"Cornelius and the Pannonians": Appian, Illyrica 14, 41 and Roman History, 143–138 B.C.', *Historia* 23, 1974, 183–216

Miltner, F, 'Der Germanenangriff auf Italien in den Jahren 102/101 v. Chr.', *Klio* 33, 1940, 289–307

Papazoglu, F, *The Central Balkan Tribes in Pre-Roman Times* (Amsterdam, 1979)

Rawlinson, C, 'On the Ethnography of the Cimbri', *Journal of the Anthropological Institute of Great Britain and Ireland*, 1877, 150–158

Sadée, E, 'Sulla im Kimbernkrieg', *Rheinisches Museum für Philologie* 88, 1939, 43–52

Zennari, J, 'La battaglia dei Vercelli o dei Campi Raudi (101 aC)', *Athenaeum* 11, 1958, 3–32

Marius

There have been a number of biographies of C. Marius, none of which are in print:
Carney, T. *A Biography of C. Marius* (Chicago, 1961)
Evans, R, *Gaius Marius, A Political Biography* (Pretoria, 1994)
Kildahl, P, *Caius Marius* (New York, 1968)
Van Ooteghem, J, *Caius Marius* (Brussels, 1964)

Below is a list of articles on Marius that cover the period in question.
Avery, H, 'Marius Felix', *Hermes* 95, 1967, 324–330
Badian, E, 'Caepio and Norbanus. Notes on the Decade 100–90 B.C.', *Historia* 6, 1957, 318–346
_____, 'Marius and the Nobles', *Durham University Journal* 25, 1963/64, 141–154
Bicknell, P, 'Marius, the Metelli and the Lex Maria Tabellaria', *Latomus* 28, 1969, 327–348
Broughton, T, 'Notes on Roman Magistrates', *Historia* 2, 1953, 209–213
Carney, T, 'Notes on Plutarch's Life of Marius', *Classical Quarterly* 5, 1955, 201–205
_____, 'Once again Marius' speech after election in 108 B.C.', *Symbolae Osloenses* 35, 1959, 63–70
_____, 'Plutarch's Style in the Marius', *Journal of Hellenic Studies* 80, 1960a, 24–31
_____, 'Cicero's Picture of Marius', *Wiener Studien* 73, 1969b, 83–122
_____, 'The Picture of Marius in Valerius Maximus', *Rheinisches Museum für Philologie* 105, 1962, 308–337
Evans, R, 'Missing consuls 104–100 B.C.: a study in prosopography', *Liverpool Classical Monthly* 10, 1985, 76–77
_____, 'Metellus Numidicus and the Elections for 100 B.C.', *Acta Classica* 30, 1987, 65–68
_____, 'The military reputation of Gaius Marius', *Questioning Reputations* (Pretoria), 2004, 11–35
Farney, G, 'The Fall of the Priest C. Sulpicius Galba and the First consulship of Marius', *Memoirs of the American Academy of Rome* 42, 1997, 23–37

Frank, E, 'Marius and the Roman Nobility', *Classical Journal* 50, 1955, 149–152

Gilbert, C, 'Marius and Fortuna', *Classical Quarterly* 23, 1973, 104–107

Hine, H, 'Livy's judgement on Marius', *Liverpool Classical Monthly* 3, 1978, 83–87

Passerini, A, 'Caio Mario come uomo politico', *Athenaeum* 12, 1934, 10–44, 109–143, 257–297 & 348–380

Santangelo, F, 'Cicero and Marius', *Athenaeum*, 2008, 597–607.

Schur, W, 'Das sechste consulat des Marius', *Klio* 31, 1938, 313–322

Shatzman, I, 'Scaurus, Marius and the Metelli: A Prosopographical-Factional Case', *Ancient Society* 5, 1974, 197–222

Skard, E, 'Marius' speech in Sallust, Jug. chap.85', *Symbolae Osloenses* 21, 1941, 98–102

Yakobson, A, 'The Election of Marius to his first consulship', *Elections and Electioneering in Rome; a study of the political system of the late Republic* (Stuttgart, 1999), 13–19

Manpower and the Military Reforms

Bell, M, 'Tactical Reform in the Roman Republican Army', *Historia* 14, 1965, 404–422

Brunt, P, 'The Army and the Land in the Roman Revolution', *Journal of Roman Studies* 52, 1962, 69–86

_____, *Italian Manpower* 225 BC-AD 14 (Oxford, 1971)

Cagniart, P, 'The Late Republican Army (146–30 BC)' in P. Erdkamp (ed.) *A Companion to the Roman Army* (Oxford, 2007), 80–95

Carney, T, 'Roman Manpower Resources and the Proletarianization of the Roman Army in the Second Century B.C.', *The Impact of the Roman Army* (200 BC – AD 476) (Leiden, 2007), 3–20

_____, 'Some Thoughts on the Nature of the Demographic "Crisis" of the Second Century B.C.', in O. Hekster, G de Kleijn & D. Slootjes (eds). *Crises and the Roman Empire* (Leiden, 2007), 167–181

de Ligt, L, 'Poverty and demography. The case of the Gracchan land reforms', *Mnemosyne* 57, 2004, 725–757

_____, 'Roman Manpower Resources and the Proletarianization of the Roman Army in the Second Century B.C.', *The Impact of the Roman Army* (200 BC – AD 476) (Leiden, 2007), 3–20

_____, 'Some Thoughts on the Nature of the Demographic 'Crisis' of the Second Century B.C.', in O. Hekster, G de Kleijn & D. Slootjes (eds). *Crises and the Roman Empire* (Leiden, 2007a), 167–181

_____, 'Roman Manpower and Recruitment during the Middle Republic', in P. Erdkamp (ed.) *A Companion to the Roman Army* (Oxford, 2007b), 114–131

Erdkamp, P, 'The transformation of the Roman army in the Second century BC', in T. Naco del Hoyo (ed.) *War and Territory in the Roman World* (Oxford, 2006), 41–57

Evans, R, 'Resistance at Home: The Evasion of Military Service in Italy during the Second Century B.C.', in D.Yuge & M. Doi (eds.) *Forms of Control and Subordination in Antiquity* (Leiden, 1988), 121–140

Frederiksen, M, 'The contribution of archaeology to the agrarian problem in the Gracchan period', *Dialoghi di archeologia* 4–5, 1970/71, 330–357

Gabba, E, 'Le origini dell'esercito professionale in Roma: i proletari e la riforma di mario', *Athenaeum* 27, 1949, 173–209

_____, Republican Rome; *The Army and the Allies* (Oxford, 1976)

Harmand, J, 'La Réforme Marienne du Recrutmement', in *L'Armee et le soldat à Rome, de 107 à 50 avant notre ère* (Paris, 1967), 11–20

Jongman, W, 'Slavery and the Growth of Rome., The transformation of Italy in the first and second centuries BC', in C. Edwards & G. Woolf (eds.) Rome *the Cosmopolis* (Cambridge, 2003), 100–122

Keaveney, A, *The Army in the Roman Revolution* (London, 2007)

Keppie, L, *The Making of the Roman Army; From Republic to Empire* (London, 1984)

Lo Cascio, E, 'Recruitment and the size of the Roman population from the third to the first century BC', in W. Schiedel (ed.) *Debating Roman Demography* (Leiden, 2001), 111–137

_____, 'Roman Census Figures in the Second Century BC and the Property Qualification of the Fifth Class', in L. de Ligt & S. Northwood (eds.) *People, Land and Politics, Demographic Developments and the Transformation of Roman Italy 300 BC-AD 14* (Leiden, 2008), 239–256

Morley, N, 'The Transformation of Italy, 225–28 B.C.', *Journal of Roman Studies* 91, 2001, 50–62

Parker, H, *The Roman Legions* (Cambridge, 1928)

Rathbone, D, 'The *census* qualifications of the assidui and the prima classis', in H. Sancisci-Weerdenburg (ed.) *De Agricultura: In Memoriam Pieter Willem de Neeve* (Amsterdam, 1993), 121–152

Rawson, E, 'The Literary Sources for the Pre-Marian Army', *Papers of the British School of Rome* 39, 1971, 13–31

Rich, J, 'The Supposed manpower shortage of the later second century BC ',*Historia* 32, 1983, 287–331

_____, 'Tiberius Gracchus, Land and Manpower', in O. Hekster, G de Kleijn & D. Slootjes (eds). *Crises and the Roman Empire* (Leiden, 2007), 155–166

Rosenstein, N, *Rome at War* (Chapel Hill, 2004)

Smith, R, *Service in the Post-Marian Army* (Manchester, 1958)

Votsch, W, *C. Marius als Reformator des röm* (Heerwesens, 1886)

Zhmodikov, A, 'Roman Republican Heavy Infantrymen in Battle (IV-II Centuries BC)', *Historia* 49, 2000, 67–78

Index

Pompeius, Sextus, 47.

Pompeius 'Magnus', Cn. (consul 70, 55 & 52 BC), xx, 105, 126, 185, 204, 214.

Pompeius Rufus, Q. (tribune 99 BC), 200.

Popillius Laenas, M (consul 139 BC), 6.

Porcius Cato, C. (consul 114 BC), 56.

Porcius Cato, M. (consul 195 BC), 48.

Porcius Cato, M. (tribune 99 BC), 200.

Poseidonius, 51, 131, 217, 219.

Postumius Albinus, Sp. (consul 110 BC), 59, 65–67, 70–71.

Postumius Albinus, A, 67–69, 71–72.

Proletarii, 181, 207.

Ptolemy I (Mauri), 125, 221

Publius, C, 96.

Punic Wars, 3, 21, 22–26, 32, 62, 164, 189, 207, 210, 211, 215.

Pytheas, 51, 153.

Raudian Plain (Vercellae), Battle of (101 BC), xx, 164–179, 215.

Rhodes, 27, 204.

Rupilius, P. (consul 132 BC), 9.

Rutilius Rufus, P. (consul 105 BC), 73, 77–79, 89, 107, 135, 137, 139, 140, 149, 193, 215, 218.

Sallust, xx, xxi, 3, 13, 33–40, 43, 55, 59, 61–65, 67, 68, 70, 72, 74, 75, 77–82, 84–88, 101, 103–107, 109–113, 115, 117–119, 122–124, 127, 128, 140, 182, 183, 189, 215, 216, 219.

Salluvii, 11, 12.

Salvius (Tryphon), 202–203.

Saufeius, 198.

Scordisci, 7–8, 46–49, 53–55, 57, 93, 98–99, 213, 217, 219.

Sempronius Gracchus, Ti. (tribune 133 BC), 6, 9, 10, 14, 15–18, 183, 205, 206.

Sempronius Gracchus, C. (tribune 123 & 122 BC), 18–20.

Sempronius Tuditanus, C. (consul 129 BC), 8.

Sequani, 162.

Sertorius, Q, 136, 137, 139, 155, 190, 216.

Servile War, First, 8–9, 16, 201.

Servile War, Second, 147, 195, 196, 201–203.

Servilius Caepio, Q. (consul 140 BC), 5.

Servilius Caepio, Q. (consul 106 BC), 130–140, 147.

Servilius Glaucia, C. (praetor 100 BC), 195–199, 214.

Sextius Calvinus, C. (consul 124 BC), 12.

Sextius Sextinius, L. (tribune 376–367 BC), 17.

Statorius, Q, 22.

Sthembanus, 30, 33.

Strabo, 46, 47, 50–53, 131, 149, 154, 217, 219.

Sulpicius Galba, Ser. (consul 108 BC), 147.

Suthul, Battle of (110 BC), 68–69, 74, 75, 82, 91, 103.

Syphax, 22–26, 31, 41, 220.

Taurisci, 48, 50, 53.

Termessus, 147.

Teuristae, 53.

Teutobodus (Teutones), 161–162.

Teutoburg Forest, Battle of (AD 9), xxi, 55, 96, 133.

Teutones, xxii, 44, 50, 51, 94, 132, 133, 136, 146, 148, 150, 152–166, 169, 170, 176, 179, 203, 216.

Thala, 86, 88, 90, 91.

Thermopylae, Battle of (480 BC), 117.

Thermopylae, Battle of (279 BC), 51.

Tigurini, xxii, 44, 94, 96, 105, 130–132, 136, 152, 154, 155, 176, 193.

Timagenes, 131.

Tipas (Maedi), 47.

Titinius, M, 202.

Tolossa (Toulouse), 130–131.

Toutomotulus (Salluvi), 12.

Tremellius Scrofa, L, 7.

Tribunate of the Plebs, 6, 9, 12, 14–20, 41, 42, 59, 61, 63, 64, 67, 69, 72, 92,